EXPLORING WORLD HISTORY

Annotated Teacher's Edition

Sol Holt and John R. O'Connor

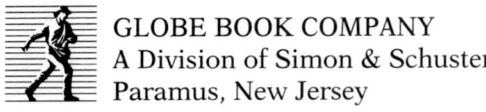

GLOBE BOOK COMPANY
A Division of Simon & Schuster
Paramus, New Jersey

Printed in the United States of America
  3 4 5 6 7 8 9 10   99
ISBN: 835-90645-0

Student involvement means active learning.

Right from the start, engaging, colorful introductions grab your students' interest, focus their attention, and draw them into each Unit and Chapter. A consistent, readable format, with plenty of special features, keeps them involved and interested.

Actual size: 8 × 10″

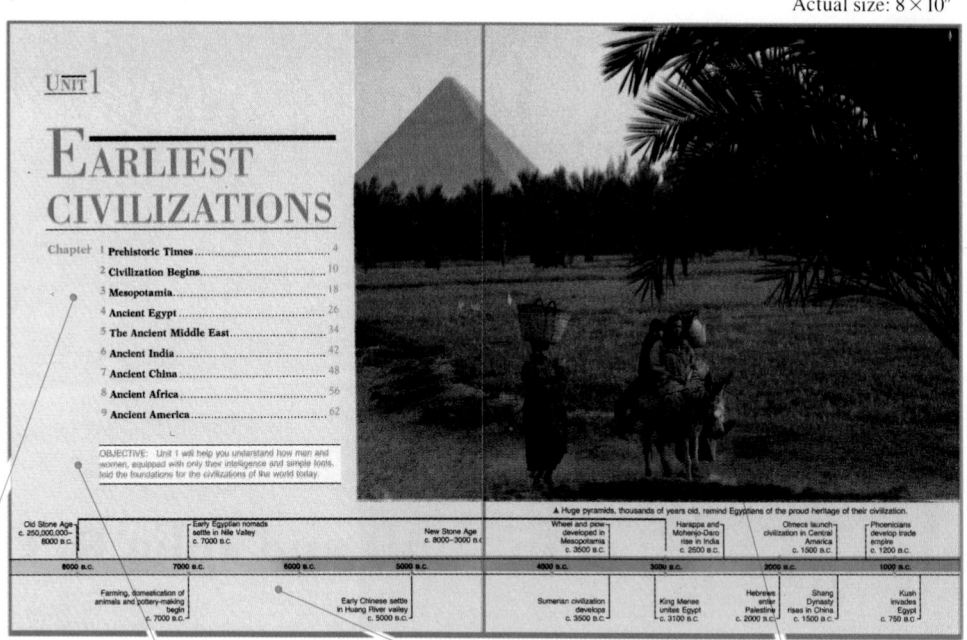

▲ Huge pyramids, thousands of years old, remind Egyptians of the proud heritage of their civilization.

Chapter titles give students a quick outline of the times, places, and events they'll study.

Unit Objectives prepare students for understanding the scope of the material presented in the Unit.

Unit Time Lines show key events and dates from the Unit.

Functional art at the start of every Unit motivates students and stimulates their curiosity about that period in world history.

Student Edition

And because it's from Globe, EX-PLORING WORLD HISTORY delivers a complete in-text skills package that's second to none.

Chapter Objectives direct students' reading and provide a purpose for reading the Chapter.

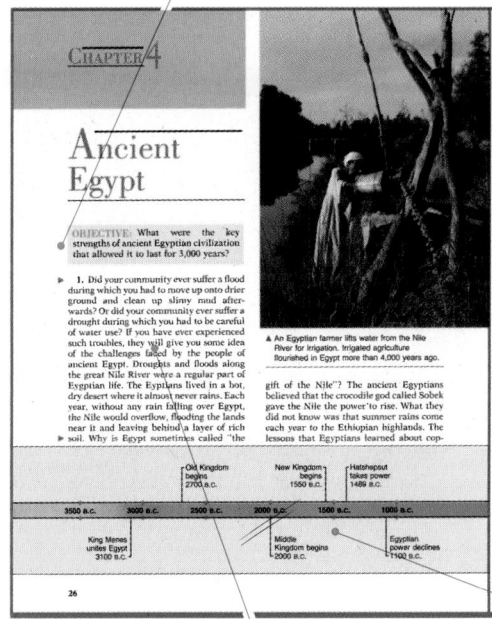

Chapter Introductions help students relate history to their own experience.

Chapter Time Lines highlight chronology. They're also a helpful study aid for remembering key events and dates.

R eadability, controlled chapter length, and section headings improve comprehension.

EXPLORING WORLD HISTORY features an informal narrative style that makes reading about world history interesting, appealing, and accessible to all students. A chronological approach provides comprehensive coverage of all periods in world history with significant coverage of Africa, Asia, the Middle

the gods told about the dead person's good qualities. Here is part of one of these messages:

Hail to Thee, Great God, Lord of Truth and Justice! . . . I bring unto you Truth . . . . I have not oppressed the poor . . . I have not laid labor upon any free man beyond that which he wrought [did] for himself . . . . I have not caused the slave to be ill-treated of his master. I have not starved any man, I have not made any to weep. I have not assassinated [killed] any man . . . . I have not committed treason against any. I have not [reduced in any way] the supplies of the temple . . . . I have not taken away milk from the mouths of sucklings [babies] . . . . I am pure. I am pure. I am pure.
From *Our Oriental Heritage*, by Will Durant

▷ What do you think a modern version of this message might say?
10. Wall paintings in the tomb told about the lives of the pharaoh's and their courts. Much of what is now known about Egypt comes from these tombs. Some tombs were carved out of hillsides in the desert. Other tombs were built in secret hiding places in the **pyramids** of ancient Egypt. A pyramid has a square ground plan with outside walls that form four triangles that meet in a point ▷ at the top. Why do you think the pyramids are still standing today?

EGYPT'S GOVERNMENT: What were the powers of the pharaohs and how did these rulers govern Egypt?

11. The Egyptians believed that each ● pharaoh was a god on earth. The pharaohs had complete power over their people and government. As gods, they owned all the land and the crops that grew on it. Each pharaoh made all the laws and was the chief judge. The pharaoh was the high priest who was able to gain the favor of the sun god and other gods for the people.
12. The pharaohs' duty was to care for the people and to protect them by using

▲ The pyramid of Khafre, the second largest of the great pyramids, has towered over the Egyptian desert for nearly 5,000 years.

great power wisely. Priests and high officials helped the pharaohs to govern Egypt. Some of these officials served the pharaohs at court. Others governed different parts of the kingdom. The Egyptian people gave a large amount of their crops to the pharaohs as taxes. They also had a duty to work for the pharaohs by helping to build religious temples and tombs.

EGYPTIAN CIVILIZATION: What were some of the greatest achievements of the Egyptians?

13. The Egyptians were among the first people to work out a system of writing. This writing, called **hieroglyphics** (hy-roh-GLIF-iks), used about 500 pictures and signs to stand for words and sounds. Egyptians used reed brushes and ink to write these hieroglyphics on scrolls, or rolls, of **papyrus** (puh\PY-rus). Papyrus was thick paper

28

made from plants that grew along the Nile River. Like the Sumerians, Egyptian priests set up schools in the temples to train the scribes.
14. The Egyptians were the greatest builders in the ancient world. Today the 80 pyramids that still stand along the Nile are known throughout the world. The huge pyramid of Pharaoh Khufu at Giza is still the

SKILL BUILDER/MAPS
Understanding Rivers

The Nile River brings lifegiving waters to the deserts of Egypt from the mountains of Central Africa.

1. Into what sea does the Nile River empty?
2. Does the Nile River flow northwards or southwards? How can you tell?
3. What two headwaters join to form the Nile in Nubia?
4. Which of the two Nile headwaters contributes a steadier flow of water throughout the year? Why?

Ancient Egypt
Deserts   Land made fertile by Nile floods
Mountains
Swampland   Pyramids

largest structure ever built. This pyramid is nearly 500 feet (152 meters) high, or about as high as a 50-story building. It covers as much land as 12 football fields. This great pyramid at Giza took 100,000 workers nearly 20 years to finish. About 2.3 million huge blocks of limestone were used to build it. Each of these limestone blocks weighed about 2.5 tons. The workers who built the pyramid had to push and pull these huge, heavy blocks of stone by using their muscle power. Most of the workers who built the pyramids were ordinary Egyptian farmers. They performed this labor as a religious duty for the pharaoh.
15. The Egyptians were skilled at measuring time. They developed one of the most accurate calendars in the ancient world. The year was divided into 12 months of 30 days each. The extra 5 days were used as holidays and religious feasts. The Egyptians used this calendar to tell them when the Nile would flood, when to plant crops, and when to harvest them. Egypt's calendar is the basis of the calendar used today.
16. The Egyptians also invented ways to measure land. Each year the Nile floods washed away many of the markers used to show the land boundaries. To remedy this situation, Egyptians developed skillful ways to **survey** (sur–VAY), or to measure, the land. How do people survey land today?
17. Some of the earliest discoveries in medicine were made by the Egyptians. They studied the human body and learned how to mend broken bones. They also discovered how to treat certain illnesses by using herbs. The Egyptians were one of the first people to perform surgery.

EGYPT'S KINGDOMS: What were the three major periods of Egypt's history, and what changes took place in Egypt in these years?

18. Historians divide Egypt's history into three major periods: the Old Kingdom, the Middle Kingdom, and the New Kingdom. The Old Kingdom in Egypt lasted from about 2700 B.C. to 2200 B.C. In this great period of Egyptian civilization, the largest

29

Short chapters and numbered paragraphs create manageable learning blocks that maintain interest and facilitate study.

Section Headings identify topics and pose a question to direct students' reading.

Topic sentences present the main idea of the paragraph in the first or second sentence.

Student Edition

T4

East, and South America. Your students will learn about political and economic history as well as the historical contributions of many different groups of people.

Key History Words, defined in the text, appear in boldface for easy recognition.

The embedded student edition page contains:

Activity: Ask the students to list the modern African states situated at the approximate sites of the ancient civilizations discussed in the chapter. Have students use an Atlas map of Africa to aid them.

THE KINGDOM OF AKSUM: How was the culture of Aksum different from that of the Cush?

10. Ethopia has its roots in a civilization that arose along the southwest coast of the Red Sea. The civilization began as an area of small settlements. Several groups of people, including southern Arabians, Cushites, and the Habashat, settled here and developed what became the Kingdom of Aksum (AHK-soom). The kingdom was named after its capital city, Aksum.

11. The kingdom of Aksum developed into an important power. Aksum grew to be powerful because it had important trading ports along the Red Sea and was a large supplier of ivory. Besides ivory, Aksum traders traded tortoise shells and rhinoceros horns. Later they traded gold with Greek, Persian, and Indian merchants. Aksum traders were also known for their strong and fast ships. The wealth from trade was seen in the gold and pearl decorated cloth of Aksum kings. The wealth was also seen in the military power that Aksum displayed and in the tall stone needles that decorated the capital city.

12. The people of Aksum brought change to their part of Africa in several ways. Aksum adopted the Greek language and Greek education. Under the leadership of King Ezana and later leaders, Aksum became the African center for the Christian religion. Even after the Arabs and the religion of Islam developed a powerful stronghold in many areas of Africa, Christianity survived in Aksum.

13. In the early 700s A.D. Aksum was weakened by invaders. The Aksumites joined with other groups, including Semites, who crossed to Africa from the Arabian peninsula, in the Ethiopian highlands. Modern Ethiopians are a blend of these groups. When the Portuguese first discovered the kingdom of Ethiopia in the 1400s, it was Christian. Ethiopia was also ruled much like Europe of that time. The

▼ Civilization began in Africa along the Nile river valley and spread out into other parts of the continent. What powerful ancient kingdoms arose south of the ancient Egyptians?

Ancient Africa (map)

▲ This figure is an example of Nok terra cotta sculpture. Why do you think the Nok believed that the head was the source of life's power?

Portuguese admired the Ethiopians' strong moral sense of duty to serve the group. What do you think are the advantages of having such an attitude?

THE PEOPLE OF NOK: What were the chief contributions of the Nok people to African cultures?

14. In West Africa, another early civilization developed in what is now Nigeria. The civilization takes its name from the village of Nok (NAHK), where the first sculptures from that period were found. Look at the map on page 58 to locate Nok. People first settled here about 1000 B.C. The Nok people were farmers who lived in villages. Their dwellings were huts made with frames of reeds covered with mud and straw.

15. Little is known about the Nok culture, which lasted until about A.D. 200. Archaeologists have found that sometime around 300 B.C. iron-making was introduced into the Nok culture. People traveling from either Meroë or Carthage probably were the source of this knowledge. Iron-making changed the Nok culture. With stronger tools, they were able to cut down trees and settle nearby forests. Their crops included yams, palm nuts, peas, okra, and cereal grasses. With stronger iron weapons, the Nok also became better hunters.

16. One of the lasting achievements of the Nok people was their art. Skilled Nok artisans made beautiful sculptures of **terra cotta** (TEH-ruh KAH-tuh), a red and brown baked clay. They also were able to cast sculptures in iron and bronze. The sculptures were mostly of people, although some were of animals. A figure's head on Nok sculpture was always much larger than the body, because the Nok believed the head was the source of life's power. The art of the Nok culture probably influenced the beautiful art of later West African peoples of Yoruba and Benin.

OUTLOOK

17. When the knowledge of iron-making spread from Meroë to other African tribes, many far-reaching changes took place in Africa. Iron tools helped farmers and hunters increase the food supply. More food allowed the population to increase. The expanding population caused the **Bantu** people to begin one of the greatest **migrations**, or movements of population, around A.D. 1. The Bantu spread out through central, southern, and eastern Africa for more than 1,000 years. As the Bantu moved, they spread their knowledge of iron and crops. Bananas, yams, and taro became the main source of food in the newly settled areas of Africa. The great Bantu migration is responsible for the fact that about one third of Africa today is populated by Bantu. How does knowledge of ancient African societies help you to better understand Africa today?

59

Captions add meaning to the many, colorful visuals and connect them to the content of the Chapter and Unit.

Outlook concludes each Chapter with a summary that helps students see the historical relevance of what they've read by relating it to today's world.

Student Edition

T5

A closer look at history keeps interest and involvement high.

Special Features in every Chapter offer appealing, close-up looks at people, places, events, and ideas that have affected the course of history. Students learn how the past has shaped the world they live in today.

The Arts and Artifacts enhances students' appreciation for the culture of different societies with brief articles about the arts of other peoples and lands.

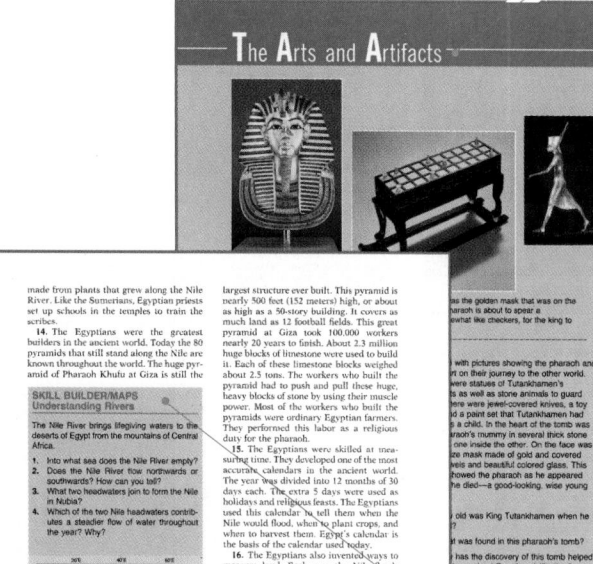

People in History introduces important thinkers and leaders who have influenced history.

Skill Builder/Maps emphasizes the importance of maps to the study of history and encourages students to use historical maps while reinforcing their map skills.

Student Edition

Spotlight on Sources gives
students an opportunity
to read passages
from important original
historical documents.

A Geographic View of
History shows how geography
and location can
play a major role in the
development of historical
events.

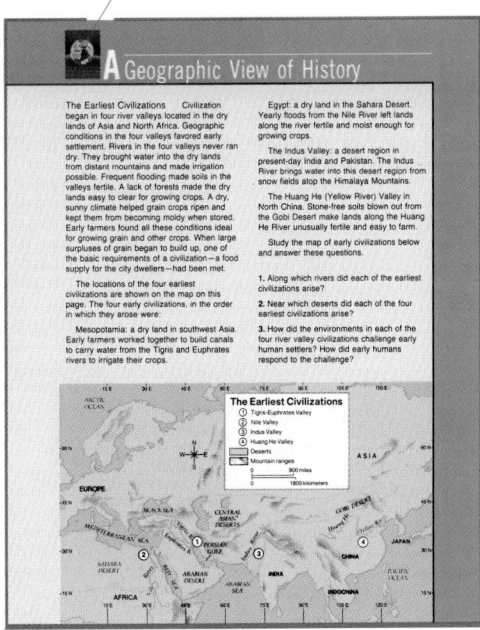

Daily life in…
presents a picture of the
day-to-day lives
of people from historical
periods and places
discussed in the Chapter.

Extensive review ensures comprehension and skills development.

EXPLORING WORLD HISTORY provides the most frequent and complete system of review in any world history text today. Two-page Chapter Reviews reinforce comprehension with skills practice and application, and two-page Unit Reviews summarize the Unit's content.

Study Hints give important tips on improving study skills.

The Vocabulary Review goes over every Key History Word.

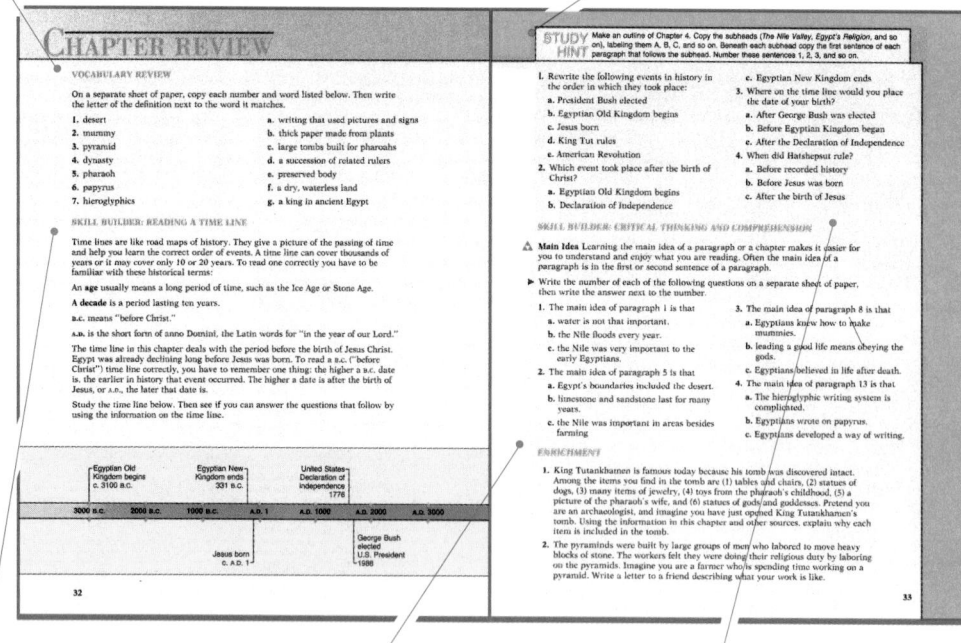

Skill Builders improve students' abilities to read and use maps, graphs, time lines, and diagrams.

Enrichment activities take students beyond their text to explore new facts and ideas.

A second section of Skill Builders introduce, apply, and reinforce critical thinking and comprehension skills. Symbols explain the kind of critical thinking skills being applied.

Student Edition

The wide variety of activities available in the review pages let you tailor review and testing to your students' needs and abilities.

Unit Reviews establish continuity by helping students see the relationship between Chapter content and Unit objectives.

Critical thinking and comprehension Skill Builders ask students to apply these skills to Unit concepts.

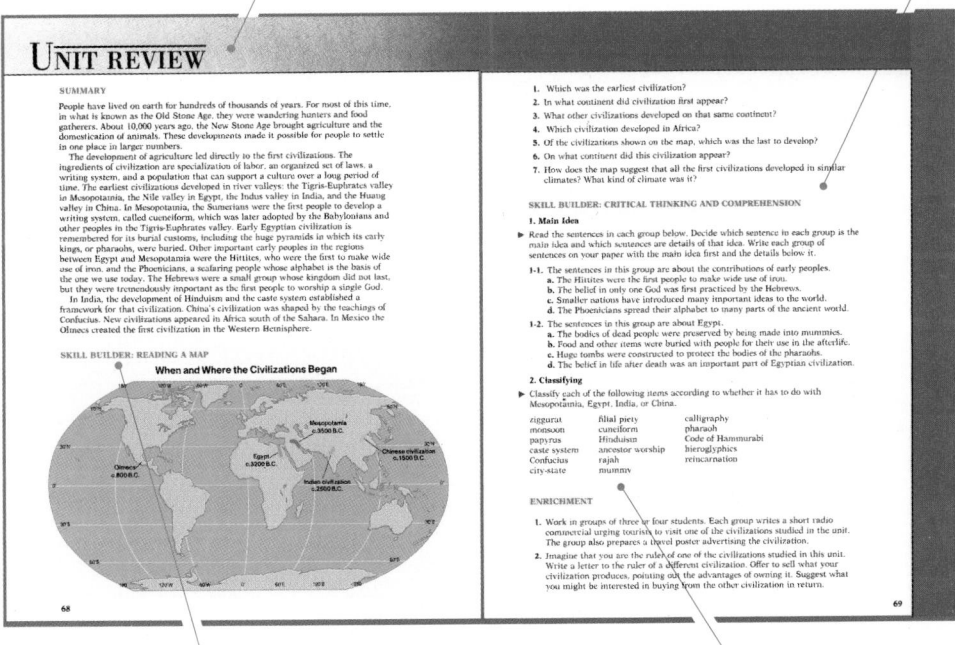

Map and graph Skill Builders give an overview of the Unit.

Enrichment activities challenge students' ability to bring together information from the Chapters and use it in new ways, sometimes using outside sources.

Student Edition

An unmatched level of teaching and management support.

The comprehensive Annotated Teacher's Edition provides maximum flexibility to suit your teaching style and your students' abilities. You'll find helpful annotated teaching suggestions plus complete lesson plans with clearly stated teaching objectives and an Answer Key.

Convenient on-page annotations provide background information, additional teaching suggestions, and questions on the Chapter.

Actual size: 8 × 10″

the gods told about the dead person's good qualities. Here is part of one of these messages:

Hail to Thee, Great God, Lord of Truth and Justice! . . . I bring unto you Truth . . . . I have not oppressed the poor man beyond that which he wrought [did] for himself . . . . I have not caused the slave to be ill-treated of his master. I have not starved any man. I have not made any to weep. I have not assassinated [killed] any man . . . . I have not committed treason against any. I have not [reduced in any way] the supplies of the temple . . . . I have not taken away milk from the mouths of sucklings [babies] . . . . I am pure. I am pure. I am pure.

From Our Oriental Heritage, by Will Durant

▷ What do you think a modern version of this message might say?

10. Wall paintings in the tomb told about the lives of the pharaoh's and their courts. Much of what is now known about Egypt comes from these tombs. Some tombs were carved out of hillsides in the desert. Other tombs were built in secret hiding places in the **pyramids** of ancient Egypt. A pyramid has a square ground plan with outside walls that form four triangles that meet in a point
▷ at the top. Why do you think the pyramids are still standing today?

EGYPT'S GOVERNMENT: What were the powers of the pharaohs, and how did these rulers govern Egypt?

11. The Egyptians believed that each pharaoh was a god on earth. The pharaohs had complete power over their people and government. As gods, they owned all the land and the crops that grew on it. Each pharaoh made all the laws and was the chief judge. The pharaoh also was the high priest who was able to gain the favor of the sun god and other gods for the people.

12. The pharaohs' duty was to care for the people and to protect them by using

▲ The pyramid of Khafre, the second largest of the great pyramids, has towered over the Egyptian desert for nearly 5,000 years.

great power wisely. Priests and high officials helped the pharaohs to govern Egypt. Some of these officials served the pharaohs at court. Others governed different parts of the kingdom. The Egyptian people gave a large amount of their crops to the pharaohs as taxes. They also had a duty to work for the pharaohs by helping to build religious temples and tombs.

EGYPTIAN CIVILIZATION: What were some of the greatest achievements of the Egyptians?

13. The Egyptians were among the first people to work out a system of writing. This writing, called **hieroglyphics** (hy-roh-GLIF-iks), used about 500 pictures and signs to stand for words and sounds. Egyptians used reed brushes and ink to write these hieroglyphics on scrolls, or rolls, of **papyrus** (puh-PY-rus). Papyrus was thick paper

28

made from plants that grew along the Nile River. Like the Sumerians, Egyptian priests set up schools in the temples to train the scribes.

14. The Egyptians were the greatest builders in the ancient world. Today the 80 pyramids that still stand along the Nile are known throughout the world. The huge pyramid of Pharaoh Khufu at Giza is still the

SKILL BUILDER/MAPS
Understanding Rivers

The Nile River brings lifegiving waters to the deserts of Egypt from the mountains of Central Africa.

1. Into what sea does the Nile River empty?
2. Does the Nile River flow northwards or southwards? How can you tell?
3. What two headwaters join to form the Nile in Nubia?
4. Which of the two Nile headwaters contributes a steadier flow of water throughout the year? Why?

Ancient Egypt

largest structure ever built. This pyramid is nearly 500 feet (152 meters) high, or about as high as a 50-story building. It covers as much land as 12 football fields. This great pyramid at Giza took 100,000 workers nearly 20 years to finish. About 2.3 million huge blocks of limestone were used to build it. Each of these limestone blocks weighed about 2.5 tons. The workers who built the pyramid had to push and pull these huge, heavy blocks of stone by using their muscle power. Most of the workers who built the pyramids were ordinary Egyptian farmers. They performed this labor as a religious duty for the pharaoh.

15. The Egyptians were skilled at measuring time. They developed one of the most accurate calendars in the ancient world. The year was divided into 12 months of 30 days each. The extra 5 days were used as holidays and religious feasts. The Egyptians used this calendar to tell them when the Nile would flood, when to plant crops, and when to harvest them. Egypt's calendar is the basis of the calendar used today.

16. The Egyptians also invented ways to measure land. Each year the Nile floods washed away many of the markers used to show the land boundaries. To remedy this situation, Egyptians developed skillful ways to **survey** (sur-VAY), or to measure, the land. How do people survey land today?

17. Some of the earliest discoveries in medicine were made by the Egyptians. They studied the human body and learned how to mend broken bones. They also discovered how to treat certain illnesses by using herbs. The Egyptians were one of the first people to perform surgery.

EGYPT'S KINGDOMS: What were the three major periods of Egypt's history, and what changes took place in Egypt in these years?

18. Historians divide Egypt's history into three major periods: the Old Kingdom, the Middle Kingdom, and the New Kingdom. The Old Kingdom in Egypt lasted from about 2700 B.C. to 2200 B.C. In this great period of Egyptian civilization, the largest

29

Annotated Teacher's Edition

Each Chapter has a step-by-step lesson plan that provides an overview followed by teaching objectives, lesson development and motivation, suggestions for building social studies skills, enrichment activities, and references to ancillary materials.

Lesson plans help you prepare students for the content and objectives of each Unit. You'll find a Unit overview, objectives, suggestions for motivation and lesson development, cooperative teaching strategies, writing activities, and answers to the Unit Review and Unit Test.

UNIT 1

Earliest Civilizations

Overview Most of human history, about a million years, took place in the Old Stone Age. About 10,000 years ago, the New Stone Age introduced agriculture, which was followed about 5,000 years ago by the development of civilization. The first civilizations appeared in fertile river valleys that were surrounded by desert or semi-arid lands: the Tigris-Euphrates valley in Mesopotamia, the Nile valley in Egypt, the Indus valley in India, and the Huang valley in China. Independently of the others, each civilization developed cities, bureaucracies, and writing systems. In the Middle East, additional contributions were made by the Hittites, Phoenicians, and Hebrews. Civilizations appeared somewhat later in sub-Saharan Africa and in Mexico.

Unit Objectives

1. To identify the changes in climate and geography that enabled humans to populate most parts of the earth.
2. To list the skills humans developed that enabled them to develop their civilizations.
3. To identify the characteristics common to all civilizations.

Developing the Unit

1. Motivation: Have students recall their earliest childhood memories.
Ask: How long ago did these experiences take place? Tell students that people have lived on the earth for thousands of years. Compared with this, our lives represent only a brief span of time in history.
Ask: Why is it important to study the people of the past?
Students should mention that important elements of our culture, such as our religions, our languages, and our government, were developed by people who lived many years ago. Studying the history of these people helps us better understand our culture and the culture of others.

2. Visual: Have students look at the photograph of the great pyramids. Point out that these are the largest structures that people have ever built, as tall as a fifty-story building and as big at the base as twelve football fields. They are also among the very oldest structures that are still standing.

3. Time Line: Point out that the intervals on this time line are in thousands of years. Have students calculate how much space on this time line would be required for the span of slightly more than 200 years that the United States has been independent. Point out also the break at the left of the time line. How wide would the page have to be if the extension to the left were in proportion to the rest of the time line? (about 10 miles)

Unit Activities:

1. Cooperative Learning: Before students begin this unit, assign each of them to a group and instruct them to use the group for study and review support. Tell them that you will give the groups class time to test each other on vocabulary, key events, key places, and key people as they study each chapter. Instruct students to do the chapter review materials on their own, but tell them to use their groups to review their answers before handing in their reviews to you.
2. Tell students to skim the unit for important dates and events from ancient history. Have them put these dates on a bulletin board time line. When the time line is complete, instruct student groups to make up five questions using the dates and information on the time line. Have groups exchange questions so that students can use their chronology skills.
3. Tell students to imagine they are ancient travel agents trying to lure tourists to one of the ancient civilizations discussed in this unit. Have them draw posters that illustrate the features that make these civilizations attractive places to live and visit. Students should re-read the appropriate chapters of their text to familiarize themselves with the unique characteristics of the civilization they plan to advertise.

Unit Review pp. 68-69.
Unit 1 Test.

UNIT 1

CHAPTER 4 Ancient Egypt

Overview About 3100 B.C., the villages of Egypt were united into one great kingdom that lasted for about 3,000 years. Ruled by dynasties of pharaohs who had complete power, Egypt flourished. Religion played an important role in Egyptian life. The Egyptians developed a system of writing and were the greatest builders of the ancient world. They could measure time and land, and they made valuable medical discoveries.

Objectives

1. To identify how the location of ancient Egypt helped the Egyptians to survive and flourish.
2. To list the achievements of the ancient Egyptians.
3. To identify ancient Egyptian religious beliefs.
4. To list the accomplishments of the three major periods of Egypt's history.

Developing the Chapter

1. Motivation: Have students look at the visuals in this chapter. Then ask the class to name the skills and knowledge needed to produce the products. Put their answers in a list on the chalkboard. After students have finished, tell the class they will learn about the people who produced some of these wonders in this chapter on the civilization of ancient Egypt.

2. Introduction:
a. Write the chapter's vocabulary words on the chalkboard. Have students write each word and its glossary meaning in their vocabulary notebooks. Then have them write a brief story using each of these words in their stories.
b. Have students read the chapter title and Objective question. To help them understand how long the Egyptian civilization endured, ask them how long American civilization has lasted so far. (More than 200 years) Then **Ask:** What strengths have allowed our civilization to continue this long? (Strong government, written laws, hardworking citizens, creative and talented people) What kinds of things threaten or have threatened the survival of our civilization? (Foreign enemies, powerful war weapons, pollution and misuse of our resources) Tell students that ancient Egyptian civilization had similar strengths and experienced similar threats.
c. Have students read the chapter.

3. Review and Recall: After the students have read the chapter:
a. Ask students to find evidence in the chapter to support the following generalization: Religion played an important part in the life of ancient Egyptians.
b. Have students list the achievements of Egyptians on the chalkboard. Then ask students to rank these achievements from most important to least important on a sheet of paper. Have volunteers share their rankings and the reasons for them with the class.

4. Building Social Studies Skills: Have students re-read the Spotlight on Sources excerpt on page . Then ask them to list the kinds of behavior that the Egyptians thought were important. (truthfulness, treating all people equally, charity, kindness, patriotism, loyalty, generosity)

5. Extension:
a. Have the class create a bulletin board display to illustrate what the inside of a pharaoh's tomb looked like. Students should use the visuals in this chapter to help them as well as library resources.
b. Have students use hieroglyphics of their own invention to describe the important events in the life of Queen Hatshepsut or King Tutankhamen. Their drawings should be accompanied by a brief written version of the queen's or king's life story.

Support Materials

Assignments can include:
1. Chapter Review pp. 32-33.
2. Workbook p.
3. Blackline Masters
4. Test 1-4.
5. Other (transparency and master source reading).

UNIT 1 CHAPTER 5

VOCABULARY REVIEW

1. treaty: A formal written agreement between nations about boundaries, trade, etc.
2. colonies: Settlements of people governed by a foreign nation.
3. alphabet: The letters of a written language arranged in their customary order.
4. Judaism: The Hebrew religion.
5. monotheism: The belief in one god.
6. cedar: A tall tree from the pine family known for its fragrance and durability.
Sentences will vary.

SKILL BUILDER: FOLLOWING DIRECTIONS

2. c, b, e, d, a

SKILL BUILDER: CRITICAL THINKING AND COMPREHENSION

1. Classifying

GROUP OF PEOPLE	MAJOR CONTRIBUTIONS
Hittites	horse-drawn chariots, iron-working
Phoenicians	the alphabet, trading colonies, purple dye
Hebrews	belief in one god, Old Testament

2. Main Idea
paragraph 3: One of the most important achievements of the Hittites was the discovery of how to make iron weapons and tools.
paragraph 6: The wars with the Egyptians had weakened the Hittite Empire.
paragraph 11: The Hebrews came from Mesopotamia into Palestine about 2000 B.C.

ENRICHMENT

1. Answers will vary. They should include references to hunger, disease, enemy armies, temptations such as idol worship, and doubt in their faith in God's promise.
2. Answers will vary. Examples could be the atom bomb, tanks, the machine gun, ironclad ships, and lasers.

UNIT 1 CHAPTER 6

VOCABULARY REVIEW

1. nirvana 2. caste system 3. rajah 4. monsoons 5. pariahs 6. Buddhism 7. Hinduism 8. reincarnation

SKILL BUILDER: READING A TIME LINE

1. c. Aryans settle in Ganges Valley e. Caste system begun b. Carthage founded f. Assyrians sack Israel a. Buddha born d. Buddha founds new religion 2. a. 1000 B.C. b. 722 B.C. c. 35-years-old d. 437 years e. Ninth century B.C.

SKILL BUILDER: CRITICAL THINKING AND COMPREHENSION

1. Classifying

RIVERS	MOUNTAINS	SURROUNDING WATERS
Ganges	Hindu Kush	Arabian Sea
Indus	Himalayas	Indian Ocean
		Bay of Bengal

2. Main Idea
a. Hindu beliefs strengthened the caste system
b. paragraph 14 c. first d. Hinduism

ENRICHMENT

1. Answers will vary, but should include menial jobs such as streetsweeping, dishwashing, emptying outhouses, and performing hard labor, such as digging ditches.
2. List should include: India, Burma, Thailand, Vietnam, China, Laos, Tibet, Nepal, Cambodia, Indonesia, Korea, and Japan.

UNIT 1 CHAPTER 7

VOCABULARY REVIEW

1. ancestor worship: To honor or reverence as divine beings with super powers, an individual or group one is descended from.
2. filial piety: A central idea of Confucius' teachings; that children and young people must honor and love their parents and all older family members.
3. Mandate of Heaven: The belief that each of China's dynasties received its power from the gods. The dynasty could rule only as long as it kept the mandate.
4. extended family: A family that includes several generations of relatives living together or near one another.
5. calligraphy: Fancy or elegant style of handwriting.

SKILL BUILDER: READING A MAP

1. China, Korea, Japan 2. Mesopotamia (Persia, or modern day Iran), India 3. India 4. Israel 5. the Persian Gulf, the Mediterranean Sea 6. India

SKILL BUILDER: CRITICAL THINKING AND COMPREHENSION

1. Classifying
Answers will vary, but might include some of the following:
Culture of China
a. Artisans and skilled crafts workers produced lovely jewelry and figures of animals carved in ivory and jade stone.
b. Bronze vases, often in the form of animals, were the greatest achievement of Shang art.
Trade of China
a. The chief goods traded were silk cloth, jade and ivory jewelry, wooden furniture, bronze vases, pottery, and iron tools.
b. During the Zhou Dynasty traders began to use coins as a way to trade for goods.
Leaders of China
a. China's first dynasty of rulers began in the Huang River Valley, where early farming villages were governed by local leaders.
b. The Zhou rulers helped develop a view of China's government called the Mandate of Heaven.
Geography of China

Check students' responses quickly and accurately with the easy-to-use Answer Key.

Annotated Teacher's Edition

An unmatched program of learning resources.

With the students' Workbook and Teacher's Resource Book you'll have everything you need to reinforce, motivate, enrich, and evaluate learning. Workbooks reinforce and extend reading and comprehension skills, thinking skills, history skills, and visual interpretation skills.

Actual size: 8¼ × 11″

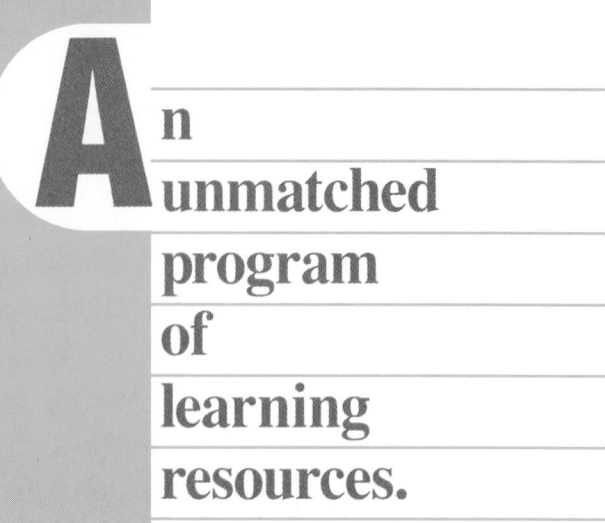

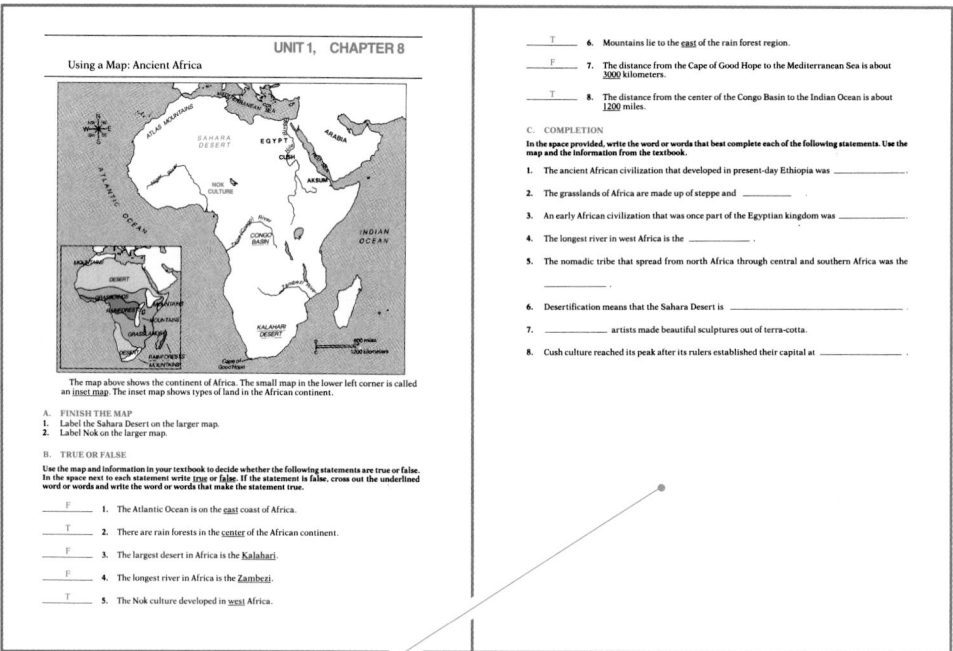

UNIT 1,   CHAPTER 8

Using a Map: Ancient Africa

The map above shows the continent of Africa. The small map in the lower left corner is called an inset map. The inset map shows types of land in the African continent.

A.   FINISH THE MAP
1.   Label the Sahara Desert on the larger map.
2.   Label Nok on the larger map.

B.   TRUE OR FALSE

Use the map and information in your textbook to decide whether the following statements are true or false. In the space next to each statement write true or false. If the statement is false, cross out the underlined word or words and write the word or words that make the statement true.

____F____ 1.   The Atlantic Ocean is on the east coast of Africa.

____T____ 2.   There are rain forests in the center of the African continent.

____F____ 3.   The largest desert in Africa is the Kalahari.

____F____ 4.   The longest river in Africa is the Zambezi.

____T____ 5.   The Nok culture developed in west Africa.

____T____ 6.   Mountains lie to the east of the rain forest region.

____F____ 7.   The distance from the Cape of Good Hope to the Mediterranean Sea is about 3000 kilometers.

____T____ 8.   The distance from the center of the Congo Basin to the Indian Ocean is about 1200 miles.

C.   COMPLETION

In the space provided, write the word or words that best complete each of the following statements. Use the map and the information from the textbook.

1.   The ancient African civilization that developed in present-day Ethiopia was _____.

2.   The grasslands of Africa are made up of steppe and _____.

3.   An early African civilization that was once part of the Egyptian kingdom was _____.

4.   The longest river in west Africa is the _____.

5.   The nomadic tribe that spread from north Africa through central and southern Africa was the _____.

6.   Desertification means that the Sahara Desert is _____.

7.   _____ artists made beautiful sculptures out of terra-cotta.

8.   Cush culture reached its peak after its rulers established their capital at _____.

Use the Workbooks for extra practice in reading, labeling, and interpreting maps and in reading and making graphs, charts, and time lines.

An Annotated Teacher's Edition for the Workbook (not shown) supplies answers.

Workbook

T12

The Teacher's Resource Book includes over 500 teaching aids all conveniently organized in an easy-to-use binder.

Writing Process Worksheets apply the steps of the writing process to world history topics.

Actual size: 8¼ × 11″

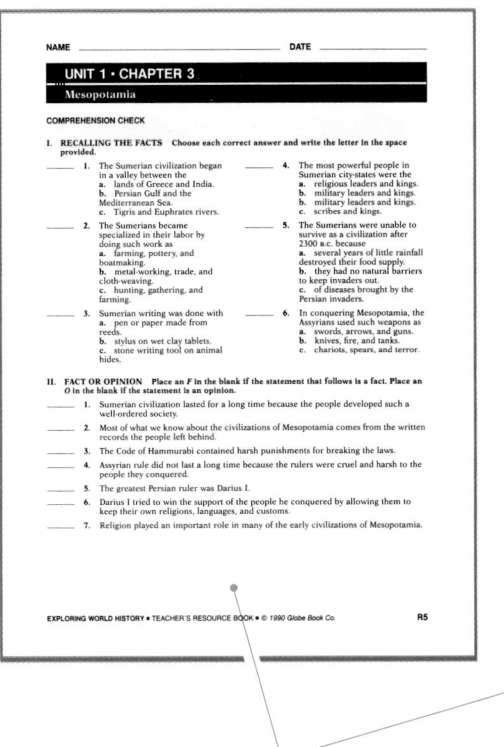

Activity Worksheets on Blackline Masters reinforce vocabulary; important people, places, and events; and comprehension of content.

NAME _____ DATE _____ SCORE _____

ASSIGNMENT 1

Reporting Facts

Archaeology is the study of the remains of ancient cultures. Discoveries made by archaeologists have provided many of the facts we now know about ancient times.

Facts can tell who, what, where, how, and why. Suppose you were asked to write about the archaeological discovery known as the Rosetta Stone. You would begin with a topic sentence that explained why you were writing. You would then write details that explained what the stone was, who discovered it and where, and why it is important.

Discover
- What is the topic sentence of the paragraph?
- What facts are used to support this main idea?

The discovery of the Rosetta Stone led to a breakthrough in the translation of the Egyptian picture writing known as hieroglyphics. The stone had a message written on it during the ninth year of the rule of Ptolemy V of Egypt in 196 B.C. The message was written in Greek and in two forms of hieroglyphics.

In 1799 the stone was discovered north of Alexandria, Egypt, by a Frenchman named Bouchard. A British physicist named Thomas Young tried for several years to figure out the message on the stone. He found Ptolemy's name written several times in hieroglyphics. Later, a French archaeologist named Jean Francois Champollion began trying to read the message. By 1822 he created a list of hieroglyphics and their Greek meanings using the words on the stone. This list broke the code of the Rosetta Stone and allowed modern historians to finally understand ....

Look at the Model

Understand
- How the writer uses facts to answer questions
- How the writer organizes facts in time order

1. What is the topic sentence of the report?
   _____
   _____

2. List three facts that tell <u>when</u>.
   _____

3. Why does the writer tell about Champollion after telling about Young?
   _____

W1

NAME _____ DATE _____

UNIT 1 · CHAPTER 3

Mesopotamia

COMPREHENSION CHECK

I. RECALLING THE FACTS Choose each correct answer and write the letter in the space provided.

_____ 1. The Sumerian civilization began in a valley between the
a. lands of Greece and India.
b. Persian Gulf and the Mediterranean Sea.
c. Tigris and Euphrates rivers.

_____ 2. The Sumerians became specialized in their labor by doing such work as
a. farming, pottery, and boatmaking.
b. metal-working, trade, and cloth-weaving.
c. hunting, gathering, and farming.

_____ 3. Sumerian writing was done with
a. pen or paper made from reeds.
b. stylus on wet clay tablets.
c. stone writing tool on animal hides.

_____ 4. The most powerful people in Sumerian city-states were the
a. religious leaders and kings.
b. military leaders and kings.
c. scribes and kings.

_____ 5. The Sumerians were unable to survive as a civilization after 2300 B.C. because
a. several years of little rainfall destroyed their food supply.
b. they had no natural barriers to keep invaders out.
c. of diseases brought by the Persian invaders.

_____ 6. In conquering Mesopotamia, the Assyrians used such weapons as
a. swords, arrows, and guns.
b. knives, fire, and tanks.
c. chariots, spears, and terror.

II. FACT OR OPINION Place an *F* in the blank if the statement that follows is a fact. Place an *O* in the blank if the statement is an opinion.

_____ 1. Sumerian civilization lasted for a long time because the people developed such a well-ordered society.

_____ 2. Most of what we know about the civilizations of Mesopotamia comes from the written records the people left behind.

_____ 3. The Code of Hammurabi contained harsh punishments for breaking the laws.

_____ 4. Assyrian rule did not last a long time because the rulers were cruel and harsh to the people they conquered.

_____ 5. The greatest Persian ruler was Darius I.

_____ 6. Darius I tried to win the support of the people he conquered by allowing them to keep their own religions, languages, and customs.

_____ 7. Religion played an important role in many of the early civilizations of Mesopotamia.

EXPLORING WORLD HISTORY ■ TEACHER'S RESOURCE BOOK ■ © 1990 Globe Book Co.   R5

NAME _____ DATE _____

UNIT 1 · CHAPTER 3

Mesopotamia

I. VOCABULARY REINFORCEMENT Pretend you are an archaeologist preparing a short speech for a group of middle school students on the subject of Mesopotamia and its early civilizations. In your speech, use each of the words listed below.

1. Fertile Crescent
2. dates
3. scribes
4. cuneiform
5. city-states
6. ziggurat
7. Code of Hammurabi
8. rites
9. satrapies

II. PEOPLE, PLACES, AND EVENTS Place the letter of the name of the group of people next to the statement that describes it. Letters may be used more than once.

a. Sumerians   c. Assyrians   e. Persians
b. Babylonians   d. Chaldeans

_____ 1. A warlike people who were skilled at metal-crafting

_____ 2. First people to build a civilization in Mesopotamia

_____ 3. In 550 B.C., their ruler, Cyrus the Great, began building an empire in the Middle East by conquering the Medes.

_____ 4. Their leader, King Nebuchadnezzar, ruled Mesopotamia after his people captured Nineveh in 612 B.C.

_____ 5. Civilization that lasted for nearly 1000 years

_____ 6. First people to develop a system of writing that was more than just pictures

_____ 7. They united their empire by building roads and setting up a unified system of laws, taxes, and money

_____ 8. First people to understand and use the principles of algebra and geometry

_____ 9. A group of nomads who settled in present-day Iran

_____ 10. Their king, Hammurabi, was the first ruler to organize laws into a complete system and write them down.

EXPLORING WORLD HISTORY ■ TEACHER'S RESOURCE BOOK ■ © 1990 Globe Book Co.   R5

Teacher's Resource Book

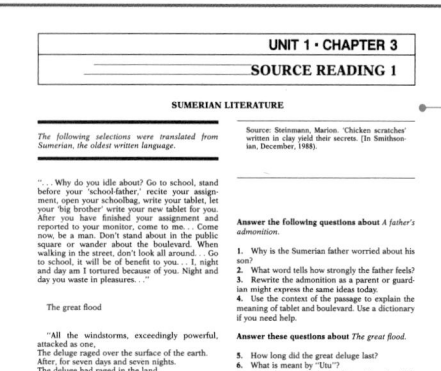

Forty-eight pages
of additional Primary Source
Readings enrich
your students' knowledge
of history.

Full-color Overhead
Transparencies of maps from
the text provide
life-size maps for students
and a teaching aid
for teachers.

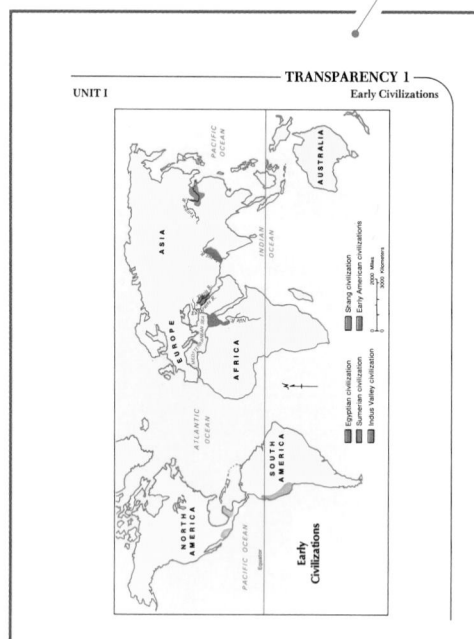

Accompanying Blackline
Masters let students work along with the
Overheads to reinforce
skills and content.

Teacher's Resource Book

A complete evaluation package includes Chapter Tests and Unit Tests on Blackline Masters. Tests are adaptable to students' needs and abilities. Answers to tests, and all Teacher's Resource Book activities, are found in the Answer Key provided.

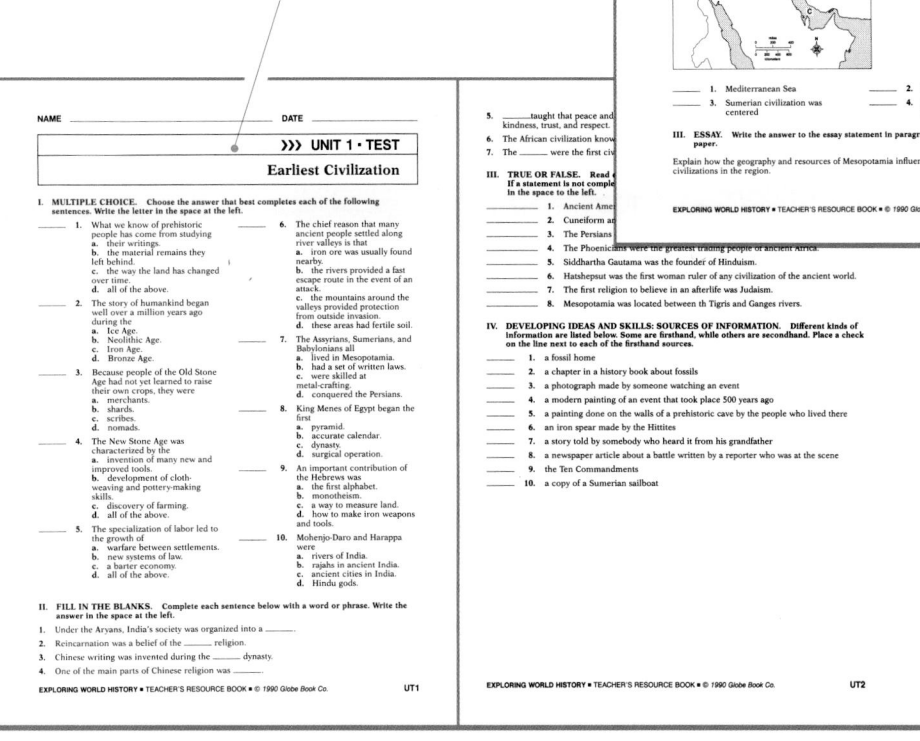

NAME _____ DATE _____

UNIT 1 · CHAPTER 3 Test

MESOPOTAMIA

I. FILL IN THE BLANKS. Complete each sentence below using a correct word or phrase. Write the answer in the space provided.

1. The system of writing created by the Sumerians used wedge-shaped symbols and was called _____

2. Each Sumerian city-state built a temple called a _____ to honor its god or goddess.

3. _____ was a great Babylonian king who had the laws of his civilization put into writing and displayed throughout Babylon.

4. The _____ were known for their military and metal-working skills.

5. The _____ were the founders of the first civilization.

6. The Persians were able to rule their huge empire by dividing it into provinces, or _____

7. The Assyrian Empire did not last long, because its leaders were _____

II. MAP QUESTION. Match the letters on the map of Mesopotamia to the descriptions below. Write each answer in the space at left.

_____ 1. Mediterranean Sea _____ 2. Persian Gulf
_____ 3. The Persians _____ 4. Babylon, the center of
_____ 3. Sumerian civilization was _____ 4. Babylonian rule
_____ centered

III. ESSAY. Write the answer to the essay statement in paragraph form. Use the back of the paper.

Explain how the geography and resources of Mesopotamia influenced the development of civilizations in the region.

EXPLORING WORLD HISTORY ■ TEACHER'S RESOURCE BOOK ■ © 1990 Globe Book Co.   CT5

NAME _____ DATE _____

>>> UNIT 1 · TEST

Earliest Civilization

I. MULTIPLE CHOICE. Choose the answer that best completes each of the following sentences. Write the letter in the space at the left.

_____ 1. What we know of prehistoric people has come from studying
a. their writings.
b. the material remains they left behind.
c. the way the land has changed over time.
d. all of the above.

_____ 2. The story of humankind began well over a million years ago during the
a. Ice Age.
b. Neolithic Age.
c. Iron Age.
d. Bronze Age.

_____ 3. Because people of the Old Stone Age had not yet learned to raise their own crops, they were
a. merchants.
b. shards.
c. scribes.
d. nomads.

_____ 4. The New Stone Age was characterized by the
a. invention of many new and improved tools.
b. development of cloth-weaving and pottery-making skills.
c. discovery of farming.
d. all of the above.

_____ 5. The specialization of labor led to the growth of
a. warfare between settlements.
b. new systems of law.
c. a barter economy.
d. all of the above.

_____ 6. The chief reason that many ancient people settled along river valleys is that
a. iron ore was usually found nearby.
b. the rivers provided a fast escape route in the event of an attack.
c. the mountains around the valleys provided protection from outside invasion.
d. these areas had fertile soil.

_____ 7. The Assyrians, Sumerians, and Babylonians all
a. lived in Mesopotamia.
b. had a set of written laws.
c. were skilled at metal-crafting.
d. conquered the Persians.

_____ 8. King Menes of Egypt began the first
a. pyramid.
b. accurate calendar.
c. dynasty.
d. surgical operation.

_____ 9. An important contribution of the Hebrews was
a. the first alphabet.
b. monotheism.
c. a way to measure land.
d. how to make iron weapons and tools.

_____ 10. Mohenjo-Daro and Harappa were
a. rivers of India.
b. rajahs in ancient India.
c. ancient cities in India.
d. Hindu gods.

II. FILL IN THE BLANKS. Complete each sentence below with a word or phrase. Write the answer in the space at the left.

1. Under the Aryans, India's society was organized into a _____.

2. Reincarnation was a belief of the _____ religion.

3. Chinese writing was invented during the _____ dynasty.

4. One of the main parts of Chinese religion was _____.

EXPLORING WORLD HISTORY ■ TEACHER'S RESOURCE BOOK ■ © 1990 Globe Book Co.   UT1

5. _____ taught that peace and kindness, trust, and respect.

6. The African civilization know _____

7. The _____ were the first civ

III. TRUE OR FALSE. Read e If a statement is not comple in the space to the left.

_____ 1. Ancient Ame

_____ 2. Cuneiform an

_____ 3. The Persians

_____ 4. The Phoenicians were the greatest trading people of ancient Africa.

_____ 5. Siddhartha Gautama was the founder of Hinduism.

_____ 6. Hatshepsut was the first woman ruler of any civilization of the ancient world.

_____ 7. The first religion to believe in an afterlife was Judaism.

_____ 8. Mesopotamia was located between th Tigris and Ganges rivers.

IV. DEVELOPING IDEAS AND SKILLS: SOURCES OF INFORMATION. Different kinds of information are listed below. Some are firsthand, while others are secondhand. Place a check on the line next to each of the firsthand sources.

_____ 1. a fossil home

_____ 2. a chapter in a history book about fossils

_____ 3. a photograph made by someone watching an event

_____ 4. a modern painting of an event that took place 500 years ago

_____ 5. a painting done on the walls of a prehistoric cave by the people who lived there

_____ 6. an iron spear made by the Hittites

_____ 7. a story told by somebody who heard it from his grandfather

_____ 8. a newspaper article about a battle written by a reporter who was at the scene

_____ 9. the Ten Commandments

_____ 10. a copy of a Sumerian sailboat

EXPLORING WORLD HISTORY ■ TEACHER'S RESOURCE BOOK ■ © 1990 Globe Book Co.   UT2

Teacher's Resource Book

Contents

Contents *(continued)*

Cooperative Learning As it Relates to World History

By Marsha Foley

Instructional Coordinator for Elementary Education, Indianapolis
Public School System, Indianapolis, Indiana

Students may interact with one another as they learn in three particular ways: individually to attempt to meet a previously set standard of performance, competitively to be the best, or cooperatively to work as a team with fellow students to reach common goals. Many teachers often structure their classrooms for students to work individually with little or no interaction among classmates. However, a great deal of research illustrates the numerous advantages of using the concept of cooperative learning within the classroom setting. Cooperative experiences can encourage:

Higher achievement and productivity

Increased self-esteem

The use of higher level reasoning and critical thinking skills

Increased employability

Greater psychological security and stronger peer relationships

The goal of cooperative learning is to promote positive interdependence among student learners. Students become partners in learning instead of competitors or passive audiences within the classroom. Cooperative learning effectively utilizes the structure of students working in heterogeneous groups to foster the learning of academic skills while promoting the development of valuable social skills. Students working within the structure assist and reinforce one another's learning.

Putting cooperative learning into practice within the world history classroom opens up a wide range of possibilities for both teacher and student. One particular world history lesson that uses cooperative learning involves sending historical figures through time. Students are divided into heterogeneous groups of three to four students. They are told to imagine that the following people have been carried through space and time:

Lyndon Johnson is sent to Germany during Adolph Hitler's reign.

Socrates is sent forward in time to replace Idi Amin of Uganda.

Mohandas Gandhi is transported a few years and miles to replace Mao Zedong in China.

Martin Luther King is sent decades back in time to replace Benito Mussolini.

The possibilities are endless. Each group of students would begin the exercise by preparing a chart of questions similar to the following:

How would each of the previously mentioned leaders react to their new assignment?

What obstacles would these people face if they tried to govern using methods that worked during their lifetime?

What personal strengths and weaknesses would each leader bring to his or her new situation?

Why would each leader succeed or fail?

What would be the response of the leader's new citizens?

Who would be most likely to oppose or support the transplanted leader?

In other words, students are to decide the values of each leader and the consequences of that leader using his or her normal methods to run a completely different country. Through research and discussion, students will fill in the charts and then report to the whole class what has been decided by each group. More discussion will follow and allow each student to see how the study of history enlarges and enlightens one's mind. Students may also learn that the transfer of knowledge from one situation to another can assist people in making better choices for the future.

Another form of cooperative learning involves the use of skits and newspapers. Students are again placed in heterogeneous groups of three or four people. Each group of students is given a specific period in history involving a main character and a given situation. Some such situations may include, for example:

Carrie Nation and her fight for prohibition.

Bishop Desmond Tutu and his struggle against South African apartheid.

Eleanor Roosevelt and her crusade for women's rights and racial equality.

Catherine the Great and her expansion of Russia's borders.

Prior to each skit presentation, students in the group will be asked to research the life of the individual who will be featured. General guide questions for students doing research may include, but are not limited to:

Who were the main influences on the historical figure?

What were some of the figure's personal quirks or traits, such as style of speaking, physical handicaps and style of dress?

How was that figure perceived during his or her lifetime?

Following the presentation of each skit, the entire class should discuss the relationship of the skit to present day. This type of cooperative learning will assist students in recognizing that "The subject of history is the life of peoples and humanity," as Count Leo Tolstoy described the past in *War and Peace*. Through the skits, history will be brought to life and interest will be peaked. Students will learn that personal willpower and individual struggle can change the course of history.

A corollary and complementary activity to the skits could be the creation of historical newspapers. News magazines and newspapers often publish a year-end edition that highlights the accomplishments and noteworthy events of the preceding year. Students may be placed in small groups and asked to produce such a newspaper for a given century or decade. Students will look at the index and general design of a local newspaper or a news magazine to get a feel for the various sections. Some examples of areas covered include death notices, comics, fashion, sports, hard news and feature stories, and even classified advertising. Each group may develop its newspapers along these lines, being sure to keep all news and other information relevant to the particular century or decade to which the group has been assigned. Upon completion, these newspapers will be shared with fellow classmates and perhaps displayed at school events where appropriate.

Of course, all of these activities require the full participation and active guidance of the teacher. Teachers' responsibilities in fostering these types of cooperative learning experiences include but are not limited to:

Making decisions of how students should be grouped
Providing specific objectives and goals
Detailing the assignment and goal structure to students
Observing the group's effectiveness
Evaluating student achievement

It is imperative to note that though only one product may result from a group effort, each student as a member of that group is responsible for what is learned. Teachers have the ability to teach students through cooperative teams that there are ways students can work together and learn within a nurturing, cooperative environment. In our global world, students need and deserve multiple experiences that foster cooperative learning and living.

For additional information on cooperative learning, the following sources may be helpful:

James L. Barth, *Elementary and Middle School Social Studies Curriculum Activities and Materials*, 1983.

Melanie Cook and Stephanie Hirsch, "Cooperative Learning in the Classroom," published in *Social Studies Supervisors Association*, Volume II, Number I, Spring 1987.

David Johnson, Roger Johnson and Edyth Johnson Holubec, *Revised Circles of Learning: Cooperation in the Classroom*. Edina, Minnesota, Interaction Book Company, 1986.

Toward Educating the "At-Risk" Child

By Dr. Gwendolyn C. Cooke

Principal, William H. Lemmel Middle School, Baltimore, Maryland

A growing number of our young people, particularly in urban schools, may suffer learning problems because of their home or community environment. These students in recent years have come to be classified as "at-risk" students. The Council of State School Officers (1987) defines at-risk students as young people who are often:

a. From impoverished backgrounds
b. Members of minority groups
c. From households where English is often a second language
d. Lacking in family and community support

More specifically, many of these students have not mastered basic skills consistent with their age group. They may have:

a. failed to meet the school's standard for promotion and may have been retained for one or more years.
b. been a school dropout or have had unexcused absences of 20 or more days during a calendar year.
c. suffered or are suffering health, social, or family problems that are impairing their ability to succeed in school.

These problems may include, but are not limited to, evidence of physical abuse, alcohol or drug abuse, pregnancy or parenthood, delinquent behavior or attempted suicide.

These students, in most cases, are not uneducable, rather they are often uneducated. In many cases they are just as intelligent as the achieving student. Responsibility for their growth may be debated, but we as educators influence these children during the school day. Consequently we play a major role in their development. We may have to adjust our teaching methods to reach these students. Otherwise, we may actually contribute to the problem.

A school system's failure to serve at-risk students may result from several factors. Low expectations for student performance, inadequate resources and uneven quality of teaching staff contribute to the at-risk student problem. Other factors may include absence of close home-school connections and the inadequacy of school programs. But teachers of at-risk students can and should try to address some of these problems.

HOW YOU CAN HELP

Teachers can address the factor of low expectations for student performance by making the classroom an inviting center for learning.

In such an environment, the display of student work is critical. Students assume a sense of responsibility for classrooms where their products are displayed. They challenge peers who attempt to vandalize or tamper with posted items. Other ways of encouraging a more creative atmosphere may include:

a. consistently referring to students by name when issuing directions or instructions.
b. using nonverbal means of positive reinforcement such as smiling or nodding your head in response to correct student behavior and academic performance.
c. establishing firm ground rules regarding acceptable and nonacceptable behavior.

Concommittant with disciplinary expectations is the choice of instructional strategies. In his research, Thomas Knight (1984) observed that the average high school student has an attention span of 12 to 15 minutes. Teachers can address this challenge by using two or three different approaches to learning within a class period. For example, ask students what kinds of activities interest them. Such activities could include role playing, simulations, or game formats modeled after television shows. Teachers could divide the students into smaller groups for cooperative learning or intensive instruction.

Students' responses to your "invitation for involvement" will vary. Some students will eagerly offer suggested activity choices. A few will refuse to participate. Several will challenge your authority to place this responsibility on them since you are "being paid to teach them." Others will rebel against the "new" structure. But teachers should be prepared for student opposition at this point. According to Purkey's research (1982) students who have not received many invitations from teachers or administrators to participate in shaping the learning environment have a difficult time recognizing and reacting to such invitations. Adult acknowledgement that students may have preferences for learning information may be alien to some students. They may compound this difficulty by acting as if they do not want to be invited to participate. School faculty and staff are often misled by this and may conclude that some students don't want to learn.

HOMEWORK HELPS

Close home-school connections can be established by the teacher requiring parents to sign homework every night that home assignments are given. Regular telephone calls to report "good news" help establish a rapport with the parent. Oftentimes, the only news a parent gets from his or her student's school is bad news. Invitations should be sent to parents when you have open house to display students' work. Another strategy may be a home visit, which is reasonable if you want to reach the at-risk student. Empathy may evolve from such a visit. Knowing what sort of home and community situations your students face may help you understand that student's behavior in your classroom. You may grow to know your student better, which will help when applying disciplinary actions or establishing parameters for assignments.

FILLING THE RESOURCE GAP

Inadequate resources may often exist in urban schools. But there are ways to compensate for a lack of resources. For example, why not invite guest speakers, achieving parents, social workers, or businesses patronized by teachers and students to adopt a class or team? Of course, you may not get a Eugene Lang, the businessman who promised a college education to a class of graduating sixth graders several years ago! But the adoption could take many forms. It could include simply having professionals come in and talk about what they do, while giving hands-on demonstrations. Business people could furnish supplies unique to their business, such as computers, which will help the educational process. Resources become less of a problem when you use this approach. Moreover, your sponsor can help make sure your existing resources are supplemented.

CHECK YOURSELF

Teachers must take time out to evaluate their effectiveness. You may do this with a peer or administrator. If you have set specific goals, make sure you have established target dates along with no more than four activities for each goal. Don't expect dramatic results in less than three months. Be surprised and grateful if the fruits of extra effort get dramatic results that quickly!

Working with at-risk students has its rewards. These students express their appreciation in many important ways: by sharing important items, by offering assistance, by giving gifts, and by demonstrating that they know you are accessible and that you care. Your contribution to them gives them an opportunity to become viable members of society. When at-risk students give back in these ways, you will know that you have begun helping them to become achieving, responsible adults.

For additional information on teaching the at-risk student, the following articles are suggested:

Council of State School Officers, *Assuring School Success for Students at Risk*, Annual Meeting paper, November 16, 1987, Asheville, North Carolina.

Jane Knight, *A Positive Atmosphere in the Classroom*, a paper presented in Frederick County, Maryland, February 24, 1984.

William Purkey "The Most Inviting Place in Town," *Inviting School Success*, Wadsworth Publishing Company, Belmont, California, 1978.

Scope and Sequence Chart for Critical Thinking Skills

UNIT/ CHAPTER	TITLE	Main Idea	Classifying	Summarizing	Generalizing	Sequencing	Spatial Relationships	Cause & Effect	Comparing & Contrasting	Drawing Conclusions	Predicting	Fact versus Opinion	Point of View	Making Judgments	Hypothesizing
1/1	Prehistoric Times	I													
1/2	Civilization Begins	R													
1/3	Mesopotamia	R													
1/4	Ancient Egypt	A													
1/5	The Ancient Middle East	A	I												
1/6	Ancient India	A	R												
1/7	Ancient China	A	R	I											
1/8	Ancient Africia	A	A	R											
1/9	Ancient America	A	A	R											
2/1	India's Early Empires		A		I										
2/2	China is Unified	A	A	A											
2/3	Ideas From India and China	A	A	A	R										
2/4	Emergence of Japan	A		A	A	I									
2/5	Australia and Oceania	A		A	A	R									
3/1	Government of Ancient Greece		A		A					I		I			
3/2	Life in Ancient Greece				A					R					
3/3	The Spread of Greek Culture			A	A	R	I			R					
3/4	Rome: From City to Empire			A	A				I						
3/5	The Height of the Roman Empire					A	R	I							
3/6	Life in Ancient Rome					A	A	R							
3/7	The Decline of the Roman Empire					A	A	R	R						
4/1	Christianity Spreads New Ideas						A	A	R						
4/2	The Rise and Fall of Carolingian Europe						A	A	R						
4/3	The Byzantine Empire						A	A	A	A					
4/4	Medieval Europe						A	A	A	A					
4/5	Manor and Town Life						A	A	A	A					
4/6	The Role of the Church in the Middle Ages							A	A						
4/7	The Closing of the Middle Ages		A					A	A						I
5/1	The Rise of Early Russia							A	A	A	I				

I = INTRODUCTION R = REINFORCEMENT A = APPLICATION

EXPLORING WORLD HISTORY
Scope and Sequence Chart for Critical Thinking Skills

UNIT/CHAPTER	TITLE	Main Idea	Classifying	Summarizing	Generalizing	Sequencing	Spatial Relationships	Cause & Effect	Comparing & Contrasting	Drawing Conclusions	Predicting	Fact versus Opinion	Point of View	Making Judgments	Hypothesizing
5/2	The Rise of Islam							A	A	A	R				
5/3	The Ottoman Empire							A	A	A	R				
5/4	African Empires								A	A	A	R			
5/5	Mogul India								A	A	A	R			
5/6	Isolationism in China and Japan								A	A	A	A			
5/7	Civilization of the Americas	A				A			A	A	A				
6/1	The Renaissance								A	A	A	I			
6/2	Protestant Reformation								A	A	A	R			
6/3	Western Monarchies and City-States								A	A	A	R			
6/4	Discovery and Settlement of Ottoman Empires										A	A	A	I	
6/5	The Holy Roman Empire										A	A	A	R	
6/6	The Rise of Russia and Prussia											A	A	R	R
7/1	Scientific Revolution											A	A	A	R
7/2	The Age of Reason	A	A	A	A									A	
7/3	American & French Revolutions	A	A	A	A										
7/4	Napoleon's Empire					A	A	A	A						
7/5	Freedom for Latin America					A	A	A	A						
8/1	Restoration of Europe					A	A	A	A						
8/2	The Growth of Democracy in Great Britain									A	A				
8/3	France, A Republic									A	A				
8/4	Czarist Russia									A	A				
8/5	The Spirit of Nationalism									A	A				
8/6	German States Unite											A	A	A	A
8/7	Italy is United											A	A	A	A
8/8	The Austrian Empire											A	A	A	A
8/9	Decline of the Ottoman Empire									A	A	A			A
9/1	Industry and Agriculture			A		A			A		A				
9/2	Modern Industry is Born			A				A			A		A		
9/3	New Ways to Communicate and Transport Goods	A						A				A			
9/4	Urbanism, Socialism, and Women's Rights														

I = INTRODUCTION   R = REINFORCEMENT   A = APPLICATION

Scope and Sequence Chart for Critical Thinking Skills

UNIT/CHAPTER	TITLE	Main Idea	Classifying	Summarizing	Generalizing	Sequencing	Spatial Relationships	Cause & Effect	Comparing & Contrasting	Drawing Conclusions	Predicting	Fact versus Opinion	Point of View	Making Judgments	Hypothesizing
9/5	Science and Medicine in the 1800's					A				A			A		A
10/1	Imperialism and Africa		A					A				A			
10/2	China and the West			A	A				A				A		
10/3	Japan's Power Grow	A				A				A			A		
10/4	Great Britain in India	A					A	A							A
10/5	Imperialism Spreads			A	A				A			A			
10/6	Economic Imperialism		A			A				A			A		
10/7	The World at War		A					A			A		A		
10/8	After World War I		A					A				A			A
11/1	The World, 1920–1939	A			A				A						
11/2	Russia Turns to Communism		A			A				A					A
11/3	Facism in Italy and Spain			A				A			A			A	
11/4	The Nazis in Germany	A			A			A				A			
11/5	Militarism in Japan		A			A			A				A		
11/6	Other Nationalist Struggles		A					A		A				A	
11/7	World War II				A			A			A				A
12/1	Effects of World War II		A			A			A						
12/2	The New Superpowers	A						A		A			A		
12/3	A Cold War			A				A					A	A	
12/4	Crisis and Change in Europe				A					A			A		A
12/5	Communism in China and Korea		A			A				A			A		
13/1	South Asia		A					A					A		A
13/2	The Middle East	A		A				A					A		
13/3	Conflict in Southeast Asia		A			A				A				A	
13/4	Freedom Movements in Africa			A			A				A				A
13/5	Latin America's Role		A	A									A	A	
14/1	Western Europe Prospers		A	A						A			A		
14/2	The Soviet Union Dissolves	A				A			A					A	
14/3	China Modernizes	A						A	A			A			
14/4	Japan Becomes an Economic Power				A			A			A				A
14/5	The United States Moves Ahead		A				A			A					A
14/6	The Challenge of the Future			A				A			A			A	

I = INTRODUCTION   R = REINFORCEMENT   A = APPLICATION

EXPLORING WORLD HISTORY SOCIAL STUDIES SKILLS LIST

Unit 1
Chapter 1. Sources of Information
2. Previewing
3. Reading a Table
4. Reading a Time Line
5. Following Directions
6. Reading a Time Line
7. Reading a Map
8. Making a Time Line
9. Studying for a Test

Unit 2
Chapter 1. Reading a Time Line
2. Using Context Clues
3. Interpreting a Map
4. Interpreting a Historical Time Line
5. Making an Outline

Unit 3
Chapter 1. Using Context Clues
2. Outlining
3. Using the Card Catalog
4. Making a Time Line
5. Interpreting a Diagram
6. Interpreting a Time Line
7. Reading a Map That Has Arrows

Unit 4
Chapter 1. Using an Encyclopedia
2. Reading a Map
3. Interpreting a Photograph
4. Reading a Time Line
5. Completing a Table
6. Reading a Map
7. Making a Time Line

Unit 5
Chapter 1. Interpreting a Time Line
2. Outlining
3. Using an Index
4. Comparing Maps
5. Interpreting a Time Line
6. Interpreting a Table
7. Creating a Table

Unit 6
Chapter 1. Outlining
2. Interpreting Primary Sources
3. Interpreting Time Lines
4. Reading a Map
5. Interpreting a Table
6. Reading a Biographical Time Line

Unit 7
Chapter 1. Using a Dictionary
2. Making a Table
3. Interpreting a Cartoon
4. Reading a Map
5. Time Line

Unit 8
Chapter 1. Introductory Paragraphs
2. Reading a Map
3. Using a Table
4. Outlining
5. Understanding a Cartoon
6. Completing a Chart
7. Completing a Time Line
8. Making a Time Line
9. Making a Chart

Unit 9
Chapter 1. Reading a Time Line
2. Using a Dictionary
3. Reading a Time Line
4. Using a Primary Source
5. Making a Time Line

Unit 10
Chapter 1. Writing Footnotes and Bibliographies
2. Interpreting Line Graphs
3. Interpreting Bar Graphs
4. Interpreting a Time Line
5. Reading a Map
6. Making an Outline
7. Creating a Time Line
8. Interpreting Cartoons

Unit 11
Chapter 1. Using a Graph
2. Diagrams
3. Outlining
4. Using Primary Sources
5. Reading a Time Line
6. Reading a Map
7. Making a Time Line

Unit 12
Chapter 1. Using Primary Sources
2. Reading a Circle Graph
3. Reading a Map
4. Creating a Time Line
5. Using Primary Sources

Unit 13
Chapter 1. Outlining
2. Interpreting a Time Line
3. Reading a Map
4. Using a Chart
5. Interpreting a Time Line

Unit 14
Chapter 1. Reading a Primary Source
2. Reading a Map
3. Reading a Primary Source
4. Making a Table
5. Reading a Line Graph
6. Reading a Map

Earliest Civilizations

Unit Overview. Most of human history, about a million years, took place in the Old Stone Age. About 10,000 years ago, the New Stone Age introduced agriculture, which was followed about 5,000 years ago by the development of civilization. The first civilizations appeared in fertile river valleys that were surrounded by desert or semi-arid lands: the Tigris-Euphrates valley in Mesopotamia, the Nile valley in Egypt, the Indus valley in India, and the Huang valley in China. Independently of the others, each civilization developed cities, bureaucracies, and writing systems. In the Middle East, additional contributions were made by the Hittites, Phoenicians, and Hebrews. Civilizations appeared somewhat later in sub-Saharan Africa and in Mexico.

Unit Objectives

1. To identify the changes in climate and geography that enabled humans to populate most parts of the earth.
2. To list the skills humans developed that enabled them to develop their civilizations.
3. To identify the characteristics that developed in the ancient Middle East with civilizations that developed in Egypt, India, China, Africa, and the Americas.

Unit Introduction

1. **Motivation:** Have students recall their earliest childhood memories.
Ask: How long ago did these experiences take place? Tell students that people have lived on the earth for thousands of years. Compared with this, our lives represent only a brief span of time in history.
Ask: Why is it important to study the people of the past?
Students should mention that studying the history of these people helps us better understand our culture and the culture of others. Discuss with students how we learn about the people who lived thousands of years or even hundreds of years ago.
2. **Visual:** Have students look at the photograph of the great pyramids. Point out that these are the largest structures that

people have ever built. To give an idea of their age, point out that they were already almost 3,000 years old when Jesus walked the earth 2,000 years ago. Ask students to speculate on how long it took to build them, how the job was done, and how many people were needed.
3. **Time Line:** Point out that the intervals on this time line are in thousands of years. Have students calculate how much space on this time line would be required for the span of slightly more than 200 years that the United States has been independent. Point out also the break at the left of the time line. How wide would the page have to be if the extension to the left were in proportion to the rest of the time line? (about 10 miles)

Unit Activities

1. **Cooperative Learning:** Before students begin this unit, assign each of them to a group. Instruct students to do the chapter review materials on their own, but tell them to use their groups to review their answers before handing in their reviews to you. Also assign each group to act as class specialist on one of the following areas of early human settlement: Mesopotamia, Egypt, other Middle East countries, India, China, Africa, or the Americas. As specialists, each group should become familiar with the achievements of the various civilizations that existed in their area. Students should use their textbooks as a starting point for this project and then consult encyclopedias and other library resources.
2. **Making a Time Line:** Have students make a bulletin board time line. When it is complete, instruct student groups to make up five questions about the time line.
3. **Making a Poster:** Tell students to imagine they are ancient travel agents trying to lure tourists to one of the ancient civilizations discussed in this unit. Have them draw posters that illustrate the features that make these civilizations attractive places to visit.

Support Materials

Assignments can include:
1. Unit Review, pp. 68–69
2. Unit 1 Test, UT1–UT2
3. Unit 1 ESL/LEP Worksheet 1, p. ESL 1
4. Unit 1 ESL/LEP Worksheet 2, p. ESL 2

UNIT 1

CHAPTER 1   Prehistoric Times

Overview   What we know of prehistoric times is the result of discoveries and studies made by archaeologists. They believe that humans first appeared over a million years ago. Early humans were hunters and gatherers who spread out from Africa as the Ice Age receded. The creation of tools and language and the discovery of fire helped early humans survive.

Objectives

1. To describe what prehistoric life was like.
2. To identify the changes in climate and geography that enabled humans to populate most parts of the earth.
3. To list the skills humans developed that greatly improved their lives.

Developing the Chapter

1. Motivation: Tell students that they are going to be detectives. Have students turn to the visual of an ancient door on page 4. Tell them that discoveries of such items reveal much about the people who used them.
Ask: What do you think early people needed doors for? To help students, discuss what we use doors for today (storage, privacy, safekeeping). Then ask students what the door tells them about prehistoric life.
Ask: Can we conclude that early humans who made this door led a wandering life? Why or why not? (No; nomads take their possessions with them. They do not need doors.

2. Introduction
a. Have students read the chapter title and Objective question. Tell students that the Objective question provides them with the definition of "prehistoric."
   Ask: What does prehistoric mean? (before written history)
b. Write the rest of the chapter vocabulary on the chalkboard. Have students write each word and its glossary meaning in their vocabulary notebooks.
c. Have students read the chapter.

3. Review and Recall: After the students have read the chapter:
a. **Ask:** Since prehistoric people left no written records, how do we know anything about them? (Prehistoric people did leave tools, bones, and other objects.)
b. Have students look at the map of Prehistoric Humans on page 6. Remind them that during the Ice Age, ice sheets locked up so much water that sea levels fell and "land bridges" connected the continents.
   Ask: How would early humans have traveled from Asia to North America? (by crossing a land bridge that connected the two continents)
c. Have students make a list of reasons why the discovery of fire is called the most important discovery made by early people (protected them from wild animals, enabled them to cook food, provided warmth, provided light). Then have them rank these reasons from most important to least important and explain the reasons for their rankings.

4. Building Social Studies Skills: Tell students to use their texts to find the causes of the following events:
a. People began to settle in what had been ice-covered northern regions of the world. (The last glacier retreated and the earth grew warmer).
b. People began to depend on small game, fish, and wild plants for their survival. (Mammoths and other large animals became extinct.)

5. Extension
a. Have students draw a mural entitled "Paleolithic Life," illustrating the tools these people used, their clothes, shelter, food, and daily activities.
b. In 1856, workers in Germany discovered bones that seemed to be human—the Neanderthal. Have students prepare a report on Neanderthal life.

Support Materials

Assignments can include:
1. Chapter Review, pp. 8-9
2. Workbook, p. 3
3. Blackline Masters, p. R1 and R2
4. Test 1-1, p. T1
5. Map Transparency 1 and Activity Sheet A1

CHAPTER 2   Civilization Begins

Overview   With the discovery of farming, humans gave up their nomadic lifestyles and established permanent settlements. Neolithic humans invented new tools and became skilled at cloth-making and pottery-making. As labor became more specialized, trade increased. And as settlements grew, laws, leaders, and armies were needed to govern and protect the people.

Objectives

1. To identify the characteristics common to all civilizations.
2. To list the skills developed by Neolithic humans
3. To compare life during the Neolithic Age with life during the Paleolithic Age.

Developing the Chapter

1. Motivation: Tell students to imagine they are on an archeological dig somewhere in the Middle East. Today's diggings have unearthed an unusual collection: a stone axe, a knife made from animal bone, a wooden hoe, and a pottery bowl. Put this list of items on the chalkboard.

Ask: Were the people who lived at this site from the Old Stone Age? How do you know? Students should recognize that there are items listed here that were beyond the skills of Old Stone Age people. Have students speculate about the people who lived at this site. Discuss how their way of life may have differed from that of Paleolithic people.

2. Introduction

a. Write the chapter's vocabulary words on the chalkboard. Have students use each word in a sentence to make sure they understand its meaning.
b. Have students read the chapter title, Objective question, and paragraph 1. Discuss and list on the chalkboard the four ingredients that a civilization has. Then tell students that as the chapter title suggests, this chapter is about the *beginning* of civilization.

Ask: Do you think the civilization that we will be reading about in this chapter will have all four ingredients? Why or why not?
c. Have students read the chapter.

3. Review and Recall: After the students have read the chapter:

a. Draw a chart on the chalkboard with these two column headings: "Life Before 8000 B.C." and "Life After 8000 B.C." Label the rows beneath these headings: Food, Clothing, Shelter. Then have students come to the chalkboard to fill in the chart. Ask students which style of life would have been easier.
b. Have students reread paragraph 9 and ask which Neolithic tool they think helped early humans the most. Have them explain their answers.
c. Ask students to explain how the specialization of labor gave rise to a barter economy. Review the meaning of a barter economy with them.

4. Building Social Studies Skills: Have students look at the map on page 14 of the earliest civilizations.

a. Which civilization was located near the Yellow River? (Huang He Valley)
b. Which desert lay to the west of the Nile Valley civilization? (Sahara Desert)
c. What do all of these civilizations have in common in terms of their location? (They were all located on rivers.)

5. Extension

a. Have students make a bulletin board display that illustrates specialization in America today. Tell students to cut out advertisements or draw pictures of businesses and stores in their area that are examples of specialization.
b. Divide students into five groups. Tell each group to draft a set of laws designed to avoid conflicts among one of the following groups: farmers, merchants, weavers, potters, and tool makers. After the groups are done, have them share their laws with the rest of the class.

Support Materials

Assignments can include:
1. Chapter Review, pp. 16-17.
2. Blackline Masters, pp. R3 and R4
3. Test 1-2, p. T2
4. Map Transparency 2 and Activity Sheet A-2

CHAPTER 3 Mesopotamia

Overview   The first civilization arose in a valley between the Tigris River and Euphrates River in Mesopotamia. Its founders were the Sumerians, who were skilled farmers and craftsmen. The Sumerians also developed the first system of writing. With no natural geographical defenses, Mesopotamia was subject to many invasions. The invaders maintained some aspects of Sumerian culture while contributing improvements of their own.

Objectives

1. To identify why Mesopotamia became the center of many early civilizations.
2. To list the contributions of the Sumerians.
3. To compare the rule of the Babylonians with that of the Assyrians and the Persians.

Developing the Chapter

1. Motivation: Tell students that early writing systems began as picture writing. People would draw pictures of the things they were writing about rather than use letters of an alphabet to make words. Have students try picture writing by asking them to put the following sentence into symbols: The man planted corn on the hill. Have them share their drawings with the class.

2. Introduction

a. Write the chapter's vocabulary words on the chalkboard. Then divide the class into four teams. To check their understanding of the vocabulary words, have each team define one of the words on the chalkboard.

b. Have students read the chapter title and the Objective question. Review with students the four ingredients of a civilization. Ask students to think of examples of how our own civilization fulfills these ingredients.

c. Have students read the chapter.

3. Review and Recall: After the students have read the chapter:

a. Place the heading "Accomplishments of the People of Mesopotamia" on the chalkboard and have students copy this heading into their notebooks. Then list Sumerians, Babylonians, Assyrians, and Persians under this main heading. Ask students to

volunteer information for each group and to put the data written on the chalkboard into their notebooks.,

b. Ask students to read the Spotlight on Sources excerpt from Hammurabi's Code on page 22.
   Ask: Why was Hammurabi's code important in the development of human society? Why do you think the laws were so harsh? (The code encouraged people to take responsibility for their actions and to think about the effect of their actions on other members of their society; answers will vary.)

c. Discuss with students which of the civilizations they read about in this chapter they would have wanted to be a part of. Tell students to support their answers with information from the text.

4. Building Social Studies Skills: Tell students to use the time line on page 18 to answer the following questions: How many years before Hammurabi began to rule did Sumerian civilization begin? (about 1700 years) Which civilization ruled Mesopotamia longer, the Babylonians or the Assyrians? (Babylonians) Which civilization produced the first written documents? (Sumerians)

5. Extension

a. Imagine that you are a reporter for a Mesopotamian newspaper covering the fall of the Assyrian Empire. Describe the actions of Assyrian rulers that led the people to revolt, the events of 612 B.C., and the outcome in your article.

b. Divide the class into two groups and have them hold a debate on whether the punishments contained in the Code of Hammurabi were fair and good for society.

Support Materials

Assignments can include:
1. Chapter Review, pp. 24-25
2. Workbook, pp. 4-5, 6
3. Blackline Masters, pp. R5 and R6
4. Test 1-3, p. T3
5. Source Reading, p. S1

CHAPTER 4   Ancient Egypt

Overview   About 3100 B.C., the villages of Egypt were united into one great kingdom that lasted for about 3,000 years. Ruled by dynasties of pharaohs who had complete power, Egypt flourished. Religion played an important role in Egyptian life. The Egyptians developed a system of writing and were the greatest builders of the ancient world. They could measure time and land, and they made valuable medical discoveries.

Objectives

1. To identify how the location of ancient Egypt helped the Egyptians to survive and flourish.
2. To list the achievements of the ancient Egyptians.
3. To identify ancient Egyptian religious beliefs.
4. To list the accomplishments of the three major periods of Egypt's history.

Developing the Chapter

1. Motivation: Have the students look at the visuals in this chapter. Then ask the class to name the skills and knowledge needed to produce the products. Put their answers in a list on the chalkboard.

2. Introduction

a. Write the chapter's vocabulary words on the chalkboard. Have students write each word and its glossary meaning in their vocabulary notebooks. Then have them write a brief story using each of these words in their stories.

b. Have students read the chapter title and Objective question. To help them understand how long the Egyptian civilization endured, ask them how long American civilization has lasted so far. (more than 200 years)

c. Have students read the chapter.

3. Review and Recall: After the students have read the chapter:

a. Have them turn to the map of Egypt on page 29 and answer the following questions: Describe the location of Egyptian lands made fertile by the Nile River. (The land immediately east and west from the Nubian border to the Mediterranean Sea) What was Egypt's climate like? (Hot and dry) How did Egyptians manage to farm in this kind of environment? (Spring rains in Ethiopia caused the Nile to flood, which brought water to the crops of Egypt's farmers) What geographic features protected Egypt from outside invaders? (The deserts that lay east, west and south of Egypt, and the seas)

b. Ask the students to find evidence in the chapter to support the following statement: Religion was important in the life of ancient Egyptians.

c. Review the major periods of Egypt's history by asking the following questions: Which kingdom was ruled by a new dynasty of pharaohs from Thebes? (Middle Kingdom) During which kingdom were the largest pyramids built? (Old Kingdom) What was the New Kingdom known for? (It was the time when Egypt was at its most powerful.)

4. Building Social Studies Skills: Have students re-read the Spotlight on Sources excerpt on page 27. Then ask them to list the kinds of behavior that the Egyptians thought were important (truthfulness, treating all people equally, charity, kindness, patriotism, loyalty, generosity)

5. Extension

a. Have the class create a bulletin board display to illustrate what the inside of a pharaoh's tomb looked like. Students should use the visuals in this chapter to help them as well as library resources.

b. Have students use hieroglyphics of their own invention to describe the important events in the life of Queen Hatshepsut or King Tutankhamen. Their drawings should be accompanied by a brief written version of the queen's or king's life story.

Support Materials

Assignments can include:
1. Chapter Review, pp. 32-33
2. Workbook, p. 6
3. Blackline Masters, pp. R7 and R8
4. Test 1-4, p. T4
5. Map Transparency 3 and Activity Sheet A3
6. Source Reading, p. S2

CHAPTER 5   The Ancient Middle East

Overview   Between 1600 B.C. and 1200 B.C., Asia Minor and the Fertile Crescent were occupied by three remarkable civilizations: the Hittites, the Phoenicians, and the Hebrews. The Hittites discovered how to make iron weapons and tools. The Phoenicians were skilled traders, shipbuilders, and sailors. They also spread their alphabet to many countries. The Hebrews were the first people to believe in one God. Judaism remains one of the world's great religions.

Objectives

1. To identify the contributions of the Hittites, Phoenicians, and Hebrews to civilization.
2. To compare the lives of the Hittites with the lives of the Phoenicians.
3. To explain how religion shaped the history of the Hebrews.
4. To identify the teachings of Judaism.

Developing the Chapter

1. Motivation: Begin the lesson by pointing out to students that not all peoples of early civilizations lived along river valleys and supported themselves by farming. Have students look at the map of the Hittites, Phoenicians, and Hebrews on page 36.
Ask: How do you think these people made their living? Students should recognize that the closeness of the sea made sea-related activities such as trading, fishing, and sailing important. Tell students that in this lesson, they will learn how these peoples survived and flourished.

2. Introduction

a. Have students skim the chapter and make a list of the vocabulary words. Tell them to use the glossary to find out what these words mean.
   Ask: For what do you think the Hittites were famous? (the making of weapons, skills as warriers) Follow the same procedure with the remaining vocabulary words.
b. Have students read the chapter title and Objective question. Ask students if they have heard of any of these civilizations. Most will be familiar with the Hebrews.

Discuss with students how the Jewish religion influences their lives and the lives of other Americans today.
c. Have students read the chapter.

3. Review and Recall: After students read the chapter:
a. Place these headings on the chalkboard and have students copy them into their notebooks: "Phoenicians," "Hebrews," and "Hitites." Now ask volunteers to describe the accomplishments of each group. Place this information on the chalkboard and have students copy it.
b. Summarize the lesson by asking students to name those features of present day culture that can be traced directly to the peoples studied in this chapter. Students should be able to recall the development of the alphabet, religion, codes of conduct, and so on from their reading.

4. Building Social Studies Skills: Have students skim the chapter and use all the dates mentioned to construct a time line entitled "The Ancient Middle East." When students have finished their time lines, have them practice their time line skills by asking them questions such as: Which civilization survived for the shortest amount of time? (Hittites) Which civilization founded a colony at Carthage? (Phoenicia) How long did the Kingdom of Israel last? (95 years)

5. Extension
a. Have students make a bulletin board map of the Ancient Middle East, including Egypt and Mesopotamia. Tell students to consult maps in this chapter and previous chapters for reference.
b. Have students write a short essay explaining which ancient Middle Eastern civilization they would have liked to have been a part of.

Support Materials

Assignments can include:
1. Chapter Review, pp. 40-41
2. Blackline Masters, pp. R9 and R10
3. Test 1-5, p. T5

UNIT 1

CHAPTER 6   Ancient India

Overview   Between 2500 B.C. and 500 B.C., India was ruled by two great civilizations. The Indus valley civilization lasted for about 1,000 years and was known for its large and elaborate cities and its skilled craft workers. During the years of Aryan rule, Indian society was changed into a caste system and Hinduism began. Buddhism grew out of an attempt to reform Hindu practices.

Objectives

1. To explain how India's geography affected the development of ancient civilizations.
2. To identify the achievements of the Indus valley civilization.
3. To list the ways in which the Aryans influenced Indian society and religion.
4. To compare the beliefs of Hinduism with those of Buddhism.

Developing the Chapter

1. Motivation: Have students turn to the visual of Mohenjo-Daro on page 42. Tell students that they are looking at the ruins of an Indian civilization that existed over 4,000 years ago.

Ask: What can you tell about this civilization from its architectural ruins? Students should notice that the early Indians made use of brick and built structures higher than one story. Their cities were laid out in grids, indicating they had a knowledge of geometry.

2. Introduction

a. Write the chapter's vocabulary words on the chalkboard. Have students write a paragraph about ancient India in which they use all of the vocabulary words.

b. Have students read the chapter title and Objective question. Ask students what comes to mind when they think of India today. Make a list of student responses on the chalkboard. Tell students that many of India's traditions go back thousands of years.

c. Have students read the chapter.

3. Review and Recall: After the students have read the chapter:

a. Have students examine the map of ancient India on page 44 and to locate the Indus and Ganges rivers. Ask students to explain why settlements grew up in these specific locations.

b. Discuss Aryan civilization with students.
   Ask: Why do you think the Aryans introduced the caste system: (Possible answer: They looked down on the people they conquered and needed a way to separate themselves from these people.)

c. Ask students to compare the main features and beliefs of Hinduism with those of Buddhism. Puts students' responses on the chalkboard.

4. Building Social Studies Skills: Tell students that an index is a useful tool for locating additional information on a specific subject. Guide students in using their textbook index by asking them to locate the pages in their text where they would find more information on India.

5. Extension

a. Have students use library resources to locate more information about the ancient cities of Harappa and Mohenjo-Daro. Then instruct a group of students to create a bulletin board display that illustrates scenes from daily life in one of these cities. For example, students should show what their houses looked like, what their crafts were like, and what kinds of work the people did.

b. Divide the class into four groups. Assign each group to be one of the four Aryan castes mentioned in the text. Instruct each group to make up rules for itself regarding its behavior, religious duties, work, and diet based on the information presented in this chapter. When groups are finished, have them compare their rules with those of the other castes.

Support Materials

Assignments can include:
1. Chapter Review, pp. 46-47
2. Workbook, p. 7
3. Blackline Masters, pp. R11 and R12
4. Test 1-6, p. T6

CHAPTER 7   Ancient China

Overview   Geographically protected from outside invaders, Chinese civilization began along the Huang River about 5000 B.C. The Shang were China's first dynasty of rulers. During this time, writing and a calendar were invented. The Zhou Dynasty replaced the Shang in 1027 B.C. New ideas of government were adopted, trade increased, and China's most important thinker, Confucius, began to spread his ideas of ethical behavior.

Objectives

1. To explain how geography helped shape ancient Chinese civilization.
2. To list the accomplishments of the Shang and Zhou dynasties.
3. To identify the role that family played in the development of Chinese civilization.
4. To identify the teachings of Confucius and the impact his teachings had on Chinese civilization.

Developing the Chapter

1. **Motivation:** Tell students that a tradition began in ancient China that continues in modern China today. According to this tradition, a person's family name always comes before his or her given name.
Ask: Why do you think the Chinese thought it important to state one's family name first? Tell students that from its beginnings China has been a family-centered society. Have them speculate on the effects this might have on the development of Chinese society as a whole.

2. **Introduction**
a. Write the chapter's vocabulary words on the chalkboard. Have students look up the meaning of these words in the glossary and use each one in a sentence.
b. Have students read the chapter title and Objective question. Then have them look at a wall map of the Far East. Ask them to identify some of the geographic features that mark China's borders with her neighbors. (Himalaya Mountains, Gobi Desert, Great Khinghan Mountains, and so on.)
Ask: How would borders like these help Chinese culture to survive? Students should recognize that borders like these present a deterrent to potential invaders.
c. Have students read the chapter.

3. **Review and Recall:** After the students have read the chapter:
a. Divide the class into three groups and assign each group to find the answer to one of the following questions: *Group 1:* "How did the geography of China affect its early settlement? *Group 2:* "What is known about the early Chinese?" *Group 3:* "How did dynasties rule China?"
b. Construct a chart on the chalkboard with the headings "Contributions of the Shang Dynasty" and "Contributions of the Zhou Dynasty." Ask volunteers to help you complete the chart. Then ask students which dynasty's contributions were more important and why.
c. Summarize the lesson by asking students to write a brief essay in which they answer this question: Why did the people of early China develop a great civilization?

4. **Building Social Studies Skills:** Explain to students that notetaking is an important skill that helps them master chapter content and study for a test. Guide students through taking notes on the section of the chapter entitled "China's Geography."

5. **Extension**
a. Many Shang farmers were sericulturists, or cultivators of silkworms that produced silk. Have a group of students use library resources to find out how silk is produced.
b. Have a group of students hold a panel discussion on whether the teachings of Confucius are useful guides for the people of our civilization to follow today.

Support Materials

Assignments can include:
1. Chapter Review, pp. 54-55
2. Blackline Masters, pp. R13 and R14
3. Test, p. T7
4. Source Reading, p. S3

Overview   Ancient Africa's civilizations developed in the northern part of the continent. By 250 B.C., Cush was famous as an iron-making center. Skilled craftsworkers made the kingdom a center of trade. Trade was also important in Aksum. The Aksumites adopted many Greek ways and made their kingdom a center of Christianity. In West Africa, the Nok culture used iron-making to improve farming and hunting. Their most lasting achievement, however, was their art.

Objectives

1. To describe the geography of Africa.
2. To list the achievements of the Cush civilization.
3. To identify the Aksumites as ancestors of Ethiopians.
4. To compare the contributions of the Aksumites with those of the Nok people.

Developing the Chapter

1. Motivation: Ask students to think of recent inventions that have changed American life drastically and have made their lives different from when their parents or grandparents were children. Put their answers on the chalkboard. Tell them that over 2,500 years ago another invention changed life dramatically for the people of ancient Africa. That invention was iron-making. Have students speculate about what these early people might have made out of iron.

2. Introduction

a. Write the chapter's vocabulary words on the chalkboard. Have students write each word and its glossary meaning in their vocabulary notebooks.

b. Have students read the chapter title and Objective question. Tell students that the location of ancient African civilizations can be found by looking at the map on page 58.

 Ask: What do these civilizations have in common in terms of their location? Students should see that they were all located in the northern part of the continent and most were in the east.

c. Have students read the chapter.

3. Review and Recall: After students have read the chapter:

a. Have students turn to the map of Ancient Africa on page 58. Ask them to identify the deserts of Africa and describe what the climate and geography of the desert are like. Next ask them to describe where Africa's steppe and grasslands are located. Have them explain what the land and climate are like in these regions. Do the same with Africa's tropical rain forests.

b. Have students re-read paragraph 4. Ask them to explain what is happening to the steppe south of the Sahara today. Discuss how this change will affect the lives of the people who live in this area.

4. Building Social Studies Skills: Explain to students that knowing where to locate information in the library is an important skill in preparing research reports. Describe the purpose and use of the card catalogue. Then ask students what subject headings they would look under if they were doing research reports on the following topics: Nok art, ivory products made by the Aksumites, the Cush city of Meroë.

5. Extension

a. Using the information presented in the chapter, have students draw an imaginary map of Meroë that shows the location of important sights and activities of the city. Tell students to imagine they work for the Meroë tourist bureau. Have them write a brief tour guide for Meroë that tells what sights tourists should see.

b. Using library resources, have students find out what the iron weapons and tools of the ancient African civilizations looked like and how they were made.

Support Materials

Assignments can include:

1. Chapter Review, pp. 60-61
2. Workbook, pp. 8-10
3. Blackline Masters, pp. R15 and R16
4. Test 1-8, p. T8
5. Map Transparency 4 and Activity Sheet A4
6. Source Reading, p. S4

CHAPTER 9   Ancient America

Overview   The first people came to North American from Asia about 30,000 years ago, but it took many thousands of years to settle the vast land. The earliest civilization began in Mexico among the Olmecs about 3,500 years ago. In North America, the early people developed very different cultures because they lived so far apart. The geography of the land and the lack of metal-working skills kept farming areas and cities from developing as rapidly in ancient America as they did in Asia and Africa.

Objectives

1. To identify how the first people came to North America.
2. To describe the way of life and the contributions of the Olmec civilization.
3. To explain why so many different cultures developed among the peoples of North America.
4. To compare life in ancient America with life in ancient Asia and Africa.

Developing the Chapter

1. Motivation: Have students look at the Olmec stone head pictured on page 65 and tell students that this sculpture had religious importance.

Ask: How is this sculpture similar to or different from the religious sculptures we see today? Have students speculate about the religious beliefs of the people who carved this sculpture.

2. Introduction

a. Write the chapter's vocabulary words on the chalkboard. To make sure students understand their meanings, have students write a sentence using each of the words.

b. Have students read the chapter title and Objective question. Then have students turn to the map on page 64.

Ask: What parts of the Americas were settled by the ancient Americans? Students should recognize that all parts of the North and South American continents, including Central America, were settled by the ancient Americans.

c. Have students read the chapter.

3. Review and Recall: After students have read the chapter:

a. Refer students to the map "Ancient Americas" on page 64. Help students locate the Bering Strait and trace the movement of the first inhabitants as they traveled southward through the North American continent to South America.

Ask: What caused the first inhabitants to move in a southerly direction through these continents? Students should recognize that the first inhabitants headed south in search of a better climate and environment.

b. Have students compare the cultures of ancient American peoples with ancient Asian and African peoples.

Ask: Why did it take longer for farming and cities to develop in the Americas? Students should recognize that it was due partly to less advanced technology in the Americas and partly to the kind of land the ancient Americans had to work with.

4. Building Social Studies Skills: Have students use the dates provided in the section on Middle America to construct a time line on the chalkboard. The time line should include the dates 5000 B.C., 1500 B.C., 1 B.C. and the events associated with these dates. Then ask students questions using the time line.

5. Extension

a. Divide students into five cooperative groups. Assign each group to research one of the following ancient American civilizations: the Mayans, the Aztecs, the Incas, the Eskimos, the Anasazi.

b. Many states in the United States have geographic names that can be traced to the tribes that settled the North American continent. Have students make a list of some of these names.

Support Materials

Assignments can include:
1. Chapter Review, pp. 66-67
2. Blackline Masters, pp. R17 and R18
3. Test 1-9, p. T9

UNIT 2

Civilizations Grow And Spread

Unit Overview   The greatest contributions of the early civilizations of India and Southeast Asia were the development of Hinduism and Buddhism. From the formation of the Maurya empire in 321 B.C. to the end of Gupta rule about A.D. 500, India grew in size and experienced a golden age in art, music, science, and literature. from the unification of China in 221 B.C. to the collapse of the Song dynasty in A.D. 1279, the Chinese experienced periods of disunity and harmony known as the dynastic cycle. During the rise and fall of the Han, Sui, Tang, and Song dynasties, China expanded its territory, established Confucianism, and developed trade with Southeast Asia, parts of Europe, and India. During the same period, the island civilization of Japan evolved from a clan society to a centralized government ruled by an emperor to government by shoguns. Meanwhile, the isolated region of Oceania was developing unique island civilizations and cultures.

Unit Objectives

1. To show how strong leadership can foster the economic and intellectual growth as well as the political stability of an empire.
2. To explain how ideas are spread from one culture to another.

Unit Introduction

1. **Motivation:** Show students examples of ancient architecture or sculpture (perhaps from Buddhist monasteries) from India, China, Japan, Southeast Asia, Korea, and from the islands of Oceania. Identify the cultures whose works of art are being examined. Have students locate these countries on the Atlas map on page 727. After students have examined the art,
Ask: What do these works of art say about the cultures that produced them? What similarities and/or differences can you see among the works of art?

2. **Visual:** Direct students' attention to the unit opening visual of the Great Wall (p. 71). Ask them to speculate on why the Chinese built a wall around China's northern borders.

3. **Time line:** Have the class read the events on the time line (pp. 70–71). Encourage students to refer to the unit time line to help *them put* events in perspective as they study the unit.

Unit Activities

1. **Cooperative Learning:** Assign each of five groups of students a chapter of the unit. Tell students from each group that they are responsible for reading the chapter content before it is assigned to the class as a whole. The groups are to function as "ambassadors" from the cultures discussed in their assigned chapters. As each chapter is studied by the class as a whole, students will consult the ambassadors from the other chapters to see how other cultures compare to the one being studied by the class.

2. **Research:** Have five groups of students research traditional customs and rituals still followed today by one of the cultures from Unit 2. Tell students to take notes as they research and to bring these notes to class. Hold a class discussion on their findings.

3. **Drawing Conclusions:** Have students complete the following cause and effect chart as they read through the unit. After students complete the chart, instruct them to review what they have written and then draw a conclusion about the formation of early empires. Have them share their conclusions with their classmates.

Cause	Effect
Trade	
Conquest	
Strong leadership	
Migration	

Support Materials

Assignments can include:
1. Unit Review, pp. 108–109
2. Unit 2 Test, pp. UT3–UT4
3. Unit 2 ESL/LEP Worksheet 1, p. ESL 3
4. Unit 2 ESL/LEP Worksheet 2, p. ESL 4

CHAPTER 1   India's Early Empires

Overview   From about 320 B.C. to about A.D. 650, India was ruled by two powerful empires. These were the Maurya and Gupta empires. The strong leadership of these empires helped ancient India to grow and prosper. The stability under the Guptas in particular allowed for the development of a Golden Age in art, music, and literature.

Objectives

1. To explain why the Maurya Empire prospered.
2. To describe how the emperor Asoka ruled.
3. To list some of the achievements of the Golden Age of the Guptas.

Developing the Chapter

1. Motivation: Begin the lesson on India's early empires by playing a word association game with the students. On 3 × 5 index cards, write the words *planet, number, hospital*. Give one word-card to each of three students. Have these students give the class a maximum of three clues for each word. Write each of the clues on the chalkboard. When a word is identified, write it in bold letters above the appropriate clues. After the three words have been identified, tell the class that these three words have something in common—the early empires of India. Have the students guess what this connection might be. Then have them read the introduction to Chapter 1 to find out if their guesses were correct.

2. Introduction:

a. Write the chapter's vocabulary words on the chalkboard. Have students read aloud each word and its glossary definition.
b. Have students read the chapter title and Objective question.
c. Have students read the chapter.

3. Review and Recall: After the students have read the chapter:

a. Have students hypothesize about what might have happened to the Maurya and Gupta empires if they did not have strong armies. (Students should point out that strong armies helped to build India's early empires. For example, without the support of a strong army, the Gupta leaders might not have been able to keep the peace and a Golden Age might never have occurred.

b. Have students examine the photograph of Asoka's pillar on page 72.
Ask: What did Asoka use pillars for? (He had his edicts carved on them.) What else about Asoka does this pillar show? (IT shows his devotion to Buddhist beliefs, which guided his rule of India.)

4. Building Social Studies Skills: Ask students to trace the map of the Maurya and Gupta empires on page 74 onto a sheet of paper. As a class activity, have students identify possible trade routes in ancient India. In preparation for this task, remind students that ancient India's main trade partners were East Africa, China, Southeast Asia, and the kingdoms of the Persian Gulf. Also mention geographic features such as rivers, oceans, and mountains that would help or hinder the development of trade routes. Once all the trade routes have been drawn on their maps, ask individual students to label the routes and describe the course of each trade route using arrows.

5. Extension:

a. Have students do research on how a bureaucratic government works. Have them share information with the class.
b. Two Chinese Buddhist pilgrims left records of the prosperity and good government of the Gupta empire Ta-Hsien traveled for 10 years during the reign of Chandragupta II, and Huen-Tsang spent 8 years in the empire of Harsha, the last of the great Gupta kings. Have students research the travels of these pilgrims and report to the class.

Support Materials

Assignments can include:

1. Chapter Review, pp. 76-77
2. Workbook, p. 11
3. Blackline Masters R19 and R20
4. Test 2-1, p. T10

CHAPTER 2   China is Unified

Overview   From 221 B.C. to A.D. 1229, the Qin, Han, Sui Tang, and Song dynasties contributed to the cultural, economic, social, and political development of China. China developed a basic government structure, expanded its territory, grew prosperous through trade and increased industry, and opened itself to outside ideas and peoples. But China did not undergo such changes without much internal fighting and many revolts. Still, its people managed to produce beautiful art and new ideas and inventions.

Objectives

1. To explain how Shi Huang Di united China.
2. To explain what is meant by a dynastic cycle and how it applies to China's early history.
3. To compare the accomplishments of each dynasty from Qin to Song.

Developing the Chapter

1. Motivation: Show students pictures of the Eiffel Tower, the Egyptian pyramids, and the Verrazano Narrows Bridge.

  Ask: What do these structures say about the societies that built them?

Refer students to the picture of the Great Wall of China on page 78. Tell them that the wall was built 2,200 years ago.

  Ask: How do you think the wall was built? Tell them that over a period of 20 years it took a million people to build the wall. The builders not only put the bricks in place, they also made the bricks! Have students speculate about what the people who built this wall may have been like.

2. Introduction:

a. Have students restate the chapter title as a question. (How was China united?)

  Ask: What do you think helps to unite a nation? (Strong leaders, well-organized government, laws . . .)

b. Have students write each vocabulary word and its Glossary definition in their vocabulary notebooks. Then have them classify the words according to the following categories: *political* (civil service, dynastic cycle), *economic* (Silk Road, prosperity, aims), *cultural* (polo, monochrome, porcelain), and *scientific* (seismograph).

3. Review and Recall: After the students have read the chapter:

  Have students create a chart comparing the achievements of the early Chinese dynasties. Here is a sample entry:

Dynasty	Period of Rule	Achievements
Qin (Shi Haung Di)	247-210 B.C.	Unified China by organizing the government and by building roads and bridges

4. Building Social Studies Skills: Have students illustrate the dynastic cycle in early Chinese history by creating a time line showing the rise and fall of the dynasties covered in this chapter. Have them label powerful dynasties at the top of the time line in one color and weak dynasties at the bottom in another color.

5. Extension:

a. Have students compare Chandragupta Maurya (p. 73) to Shi Huang Di.
   Ask: What common steps did each of these leaders take to unify their empires? Which of these men do you think was a better leader? Why?

b. The Yuan Dynasty was founded by Kublai Khan in 1260 and lasted until 1368. Have students find out about the accomplishments of the Yuan Dynasty and report their findings to the class.

Support Materials

  Assignments can include:

1. Chapter Review, pp. 86-87
2. Blackline Masters R21 and R22
3. Test 2-2, p. T11
4. Map (transparency R22 and activity sheet A5

CHAPTER 3   Ideas From India and China
           Spread

Overview   Ideas and practices from ancient India and China greatly influenced the developing cultures of Southeast Asia and Korea. India, through trade and missionaries, and China, through invasion and conquest, brought their cultural ideas and religion to these neighboring lands. Southeast Asians and Koreans absorbed Indian and Chinese ideas without sacrificing their own traditions and ways of life.

Objectives

1. To describe life in early Southeast Asia.
2. To identify the cultural influences of India and Southeast Asia.
3. To explain how the Khmer Empire rose and fell.
4. To identify the effects of Chinese rule in Vietnam and Korea.

Developing the Chapter

1. **Motivation:** Ask students of different ethnic backgrounds how they celebrate a particular holiday. Discuss with the class the similar and different ways in which different groups of people celebrate holidays in the United States. Point out to students that the United States is not the only country whose culture has been influenced by other cultures. Then have students read the introduction to Chapter 3

2. **Introduction:**
a. Direct the students to the atlas map of Asia on page 727. Have them locate India and China on the map.
   Ask: Which neighboring lands do you think were influenced by India and China? (Southeast Asian countries) Which land do you think were influenced by China alone (Korea and Japan)
b. Assign seven students a vocabulary word from Chapter 3. Have them look up the glossary definition. Then have them write a sentence on the chalkboard in which they use the vocabulary word. Students try to guess the meaning of each vocabulary word from the sentence.

3. **Review and Recall:** After the students have read the chapter:
a. **Ask:** What were the two greatest influences of India on Southeast Asia? (religion and trade)
b. Have students quiz each other about the chapter content.
c. Have students compare the effects of ancient Chinese rule in Vietnam with the effects of ancient Chinese rule in Korea. (Both groups adopted Chinese script and religion, yet both managed to maintain their own traditions.)

4. **Building Social Studies Skills:** Refer students to the map titled "The Spread of Buddhism" on page 90. Ask them to trace the route marked 5th and 6th centuries A.D., starting in Sri Lanka, moving through Southeast Asia, and ending in southeast China. Ask students to imagine they are travelers on this route during the year A.D. 585. Have them write an entry in a travelogue describing the governments, the economy, and the way of life of some of the kingdoms they pass thorough. (The Guptas ruled India in the late sixth century A.D., the Chenla ruled Southeast Asia, and the Sui Dynasty of China ruled northern Vietnam. Student descriptions should reflect the characteristics of rule under these governments discussed in the first three chapters of this unit.)

5. **Extension:** The Khmer Rouge is a group of communist-backed guerrillas in modern Cambodia. Tell students that *rouge* means red in French. Have students do research and report on the Khmer Rouge.
Ask: Given the history of Cambodia, why do you think this group adopted the name Khmer Rouge? (To associate its cause with the time when Cambodia was a powerful empire.)

Support Materials

Assignments can include:
1. Chapter Review, pp. 94–95
2. Workbook, pp. 12-14
3. Blackline Masters R23 and R24
4. Test 2-3, p. T12
5. Source reading S5.

Overview   The Japanese adopted Chinese script in the early centuries A.D. Little is known about early Japanese history before then. Japan borrowed much from China, including ideas of religion and government. At first, Japan's government centered around the emperor. Later, Japanese culture truly developed when the royal court became the center of political life. But by the twelfth century government by shogun had become the style of rule and the emperor had lost much of his power.

Objectives

1. To describe the political, cultural, and economic climate of early Japan.
2. To list the cultural influences of China on early Japan.
3. To trace the change in forms of leadership in early Japan.

Developing the Chapter

1. Motivation: Refer students to the photograph of the samurai on page 98. Then have students read the "Daily life in…" feature on page 97.
Ask: What impression do you have of early Japanese history based on this photograph and this description? Direct students to read the chapter to find out if their conclusions are correct.

2. Introduction:
a. Have students read the chapter title. Give the meaning of the word *emergence* (to come forth, into view or notice)
b. Have students read the subheads to preview Chapter 3.

3. Review and Recall: After the students have read the chapter:
a. **Ask:** Which vocabulary word best shows how Japan blended its ancient beliefs with ideas from China? (Shinto)
b. Write these statements of fact and opinion about early Japanese history on the chalkboard. Have students label each statement *fact* or *opinion*.
b-1. The earliest people who settled in Japan were probably the Ainu. (Opinion: Although the facts point in this direction, this statement has yet to be proved.)

b-2. Without the Chinese influence Japan never would have developed culturally. (Opinion).
b-3. The religion of early Japan was based on the worship of *kami*, or anything sacred or special in nature. (Fact)
c. Have students analyze how government by shoguns evolved. (It was a blend of early Japanese ways and Chinese ideas: the idea of a central government came from the Chinese, but the practice of making the head of the most powerful clan the head of government was distinctly Japanese.)

4. Building Social Studies Skills: Have students determine how land elevation influences where people settle by comparing the contour map of Japan on page 99 with a population density map of Japan. You might show the population density map by means of an overhead projector or make copies of the map to distribute to the class.

5. Extension:
a. No one knows what Japan was like before the early centuries A.D. Have students write their version of early Japanese history based on the knowledge they have gained of Asian history in the centuries B.C. from Unit One.
b. *Mahayana Buddhism*, which made Buddha a god and held out the promise of salvation not only through one's own efforts but also through the help of spiritual beings, spread to Japan as early as the A.D. 600s. Eventually religious leaders adapted some Buddhist teachings to Shinto practices and the two religions have existed side by side ever since. Have students do library research on how Shinto was influenced by Buddhist teachings in the sixth century and report their findings to the class.

Support Materials

Assignments can include:

1. Chapter Review, pp. 100–101
2. Workbook, pp. 15 and 18
3. Blackline Masters R25 and R26
4. Test 2-4, p. T13
5. Source reading S6

CHAPTER 5 The Peoples of Australia and Oceania

Overview   The islands of Australia and Oceania probably were settled by people from Southeast Asia who walked across land bridges to New Guinea during the Ice Age. From New Guinea, people migrated to other Pacific Islands. In 1768, the British sent Captain James Cook to find the "great southern continent"—now known as Australia. Cook made great contributions to the European knowledge of the Pacific.

Objectives

1. To locate Australia and the three main island groups of Oceania.
2. To describe how Australia and the islands of Oceania were discovered and settled.
3. To explain how historians and archeologists have learned about the cultures of the Pacific islands.
4. To identify the contributions made by Captain James Cook to European knowledge of the Pacific.

Developing the Chapter

1. Motivation: Refer students to the photograph of outrigger canoes on page 102. Have them imagine taking a trip across an ocean in these canoes. Ask them to describe what such a trip would be like. Refer them to the map of Oceania on page 104. Explain that the islands of the Pacific Ocean were first settled about 40,000 years ago by people who traveled the ocean on outrigger canoes.

2. Introduction:
a. Have students read the chapter title and Objective question.
   Ask: Which southern Pacific islands are covered in this chapter? (Australia and Oceania) Refer them to the Atlas map on page 722.
   Ask: What imaginary line separates the northern Pacific islands from the southern ones? (equator) Which northern Pacific islands have you already studied in this unit? (Japanese islands)
b. Write the vocabulary words on the chalkboard. Have students look up the glossary definition for each vocabulary word.

c. Ask students to write a paragraph answering the Objective question in which they use the vocabulary words. Then have them read the chapter to find out if their answer was correct.

3. Review and Recall: After the students have read the chapter:
a. Distribute an outline map of Australia and Oceania. Ask students to label the three island groups—Melanesia, Micronesia, and Polynesia—as well as Australia. Based on their reading of the chapter, have students draw arrows on the map to trace the course of settlement of these areas.
b. Ask students to review the paragraphs that they wrote in response to the Objective question in preparation for reading the chapter. Now that they have read the chapter, instruct them to rewrite the paragraph by adding information that more completely answers the Objective question.

4. Building Social Studies Skills: Have students create a time line for the settlement of the Pacific islands covered in Chapter 5.

5. Extension
a. Have interested students make a scale model of an outrigger canoe. They may use the photograph on page 102, the description given in the "Daily life in …" feature, or a chosen library source as a guide.
b. Ask students to write an imaginary journal entry of either Captain James Cook or a member of his crew for the day on which Cook first visited the islands of Oceania.

Support Materials

Assignments can include:

1. Chapter Review, pp. 106–107
2. Workbook, pp. 16–17
3. Blackline Masters R27 and $28
4. Test 2-5, p. T14

UNIT 3

CLASSICAL CIVILIZATIONS

Unit Overview Athens and Sparta were the leading city-states of ancient Greece. The Golden Age of Greece came to an end with Sparta's victory in the Peloponnesian Wars. Alexander the Great brought together the cultures of Greece and Asia during the Hellenistic Age. The Romans borrowed from the Greek and Etruscan cultures and built a vast empire. The western half of the Roman Empire finally succumbed to barbarian invasions in A.D. 476; the eastern half thrived for another thousand years as the Byzantine Empire.

Unit Objectives

1. To outline the features of daily life in ancient Greece and Rome.
2. To explain the spread of Greek culture throughout the western world.
3. To explain the decline and fall of the Roman Empire.
4. To identify the important and lasting cultural contributions of ancient Greece and Rome.

Unit Introduction

1. **Motivation:** Ask students if they have ever heard the expression "Beware of Greeks bearing gifts." Then show students a picture of the Trojan horse. Explain that, according to legend, Greek soldiers gained entry into the fortified city of Troy by leaving a huge hollow wooden horse at the city gates, supposedly as a gift. Inside the horse lay concealed many Greek soldiers. When the horse was brought into the city, the concealed soldiers came out under cover of darkness and opened the gates to the Greek army. Troy was destroyed. Tell students that we know about the Trojan War, which is supposed to have taken place about 3000 years ago, from the writings of the ancient Greek poet Homer and the ancient Roman poet Virgil. Also have students speculate on why ancient Greece and Rome are often referred to as "classical" civilizations.

2. **Visual:** Direct students' attention to the unit opening visual of the Parthenon (p. 111). Show them a picture of the Lincoln Memorial, and ask volunteers to point out the similarity of construction between the buildings.

3. **Time line:** Have the class read the events on the time line (pp. 111–112). Ask students if they are familiar with any of the events shown, and have them share their knowledge with the class. Encourage students to refer to the unit time line as they study the unit to help them put events in perspective.

Unit Activities

1. **Cooperative Learning:** Have students work in small groups to construct an illustrated time line highlighting major events from the rise of the Greek city-states to the fall of Rome. Encourage students to use pictures cut out from old magazines or drawn by students to illustrate the time line.

2. **Research:** Have students do library research on the religious beliefs of the ancient Greeks and Romans. Ask them to compare and contrast the role played by religion in the lives of those ancient peoples with the role that religion plays in the world today. Students might choose to compare and contrast the creation stories in classical mythology with the story of creation in Genesis and/or scientific theories of the origin of the universe, addressing such questions as: How do theories and myths differ? How are they alike?

3. **Creative Writing:** Ask students to imagine that they are one of the following historical characters: Pericles, Alexander the Great, Julius Caesar, Queen Zenobia, Caligula, or Marcus Aurelius. Then have them write a diary entry for the character they have chosen. Students might want to do additional library research on the historical character of their choice as a preparation for writing. Encourage students to use their imaginations in speculating on what the characters might have thought and felt about the historic events in which they participated.

Support Materials

Assignments can include:

1. Unit Review, pp. 164–165
2. Unit 3 Test, pp. UT5–UT6
3. Unit 3 ESL/LEP Worksheet 1, p. ESL 5
4. Unit 3 ESL/LEP Worksheet 2, p. ESL 6

CHAPTER 1   Government of Ancient
             Greece

Overview   The idea of democratic
government began in the independent city-
states of ancient Greece around 600 B.C. While
the people of Athens took an active role in
law-making, Sparta remained an aristocracy.
The Athenian leader Pericles worked hard to
prevent war between Athens and its
militaristic neighbor, Sparta.

Objectives

1. To outline the development of independent
   city-states in ancient Greece.
2. To explain the origins of democracy in
   ancient Greece.
3. To compare and contrast the governments
   of Athens and Sparta.

Developing the Chapter

1. **Motivation:** Show students the map of
   ancient Greece on page 129. Locate the
   Mediterranean Sea, the Greek peninsula, and
   the numerous islands comprising Greece.
   Point out that Greece is a mountainous land
   with an indented coastline.
   Ask: What influence might geography have
   had on the history of Greece? What sort of
   government might have developed in such a
   land?

2. **Introduction**
   a. Write the chapter vocabulary words on the
      chalkboard. Have students write each word
      and its glossary definition in their
      vocabulary notebooks. Then have students
      use each vocabulary word in a sentence.
   b. Have students read the chapter title and
      Objective question.
   c. Have students read the chapter.

3. **Review and Recall:** After the students
   have read the chapter:
   a. Have them define the term "city-state" and
      explain how ancient Greek city-states
      developed.
   b. Have them ask each other questions about
      the chapter's content. For examples, have
      them ask how the Council of Five Hundred
      in Athens differed from the Assembly in
      Sparta.
   c. Have students reread each subhead
      question and answer it.

   d. Have students reread and answer the
      chapter's Objective question.
   e. Have students look at the Chapter Time
      Line. Ask them to summarize the changes
      that took place in the government of
      ancient Greece between 510 B.C. and the
      Age of Pericles. Have them discuss these
      changes orally or in a written exercise.

4. **Building Social Studies Skills:** Explain to
   students that generalizing is an important
   skill that helps them to draw conclusions
   from a group of facts. Review the discussion
   of ancient Sparta and help students draw
   valid generalizations, based on the chapter
   information about what was most important
   to Spartans. Then assign Skill Builder:
   Generalizing, page 117 of the Chapter Review.

5. **Extension**
   a. Divide students into two groups. Have one
      group imagine that they are citizens of
      ancient Sparta and the other, citizens of
      ancient Athens. Ask students to imagine
      that the two city-states are discussing the
      possibility of uniting under a single
      government. Have the two groups debate
      the pros and cons of combining their very
      different societies.
      Ask: What form of government would be
      best for the new state? Why?
   b. Have students prepare a chart comparing
      and contrasting the societies of ancient
      Athens, ancient Sparta, and the present-
      day America. The chart might include such
      topics as law-making, military service, art,
      religion, and education.
   c. Ask students to predict which city-state,
      Athens or Sparta, would develop the
      greatest civilization. Students should give
      reasons for their prediction in a brief
      written essay.

Support Materials

Assignments can include:

1. Chapter Review, pp. 116–117
2. Blackline Masters R29 and R30
3. Test 3-1, p. T15

CHAPTER 2   Life in Ancient Greece

Overview   Ancient Greeks worked mainly as farmers and shopkeepers. Slaves and foreigners, who did much of the hard labor, were not permitted to become citizens. The family was the most important unit in ancient Greece. Greek girls did not go to school, and women rarely left the home. In Sparta, however, women worked in the fields as well as in the home, and the mothers of soldiers were honored. The Greeks were greatly interested in music, art, theater, athletics, and philosophy. Plato was the most famous of the philosopher-teachers. The music, art, and theater of the ancient Greeks were greatly influenced by gods and the myths that surrounded them.

Objectives

1. To outline the daily life of the ancient Greeks.
2. To identify the religious and philosophical beliefs of the ancient Greeks.
3. To identify the roles played by men, women, children, foreigners, and slaves in ancient Greek society.

Developing the Chapter

1. **Motivation:** Have students imagine that they have been chosen to select items for a time capsule to be opened in 2000 years. The purpose of the time capsule is to give future generations an idea of how the people of today think and behave.
Ask: What items would you select for the time capsule, and what idea would these items give to future generations about your everyday life? Then have students speculate on how we may have learned what we know about everyday life in ancient Greece.

2. **Introduction:**
a. Write the chapter vocabulary words on the chalkboard. Have students write each word and its glossary definition in their vocabulary notebooks.
b. Have students read the chapter title and Objective question.
c. Have students work in small groups or pairs. Assign the following topics to the groups: 1. The Role of Women in Ancient

Greece; 2. the role of Slaves and Metics in Ancient Greece; 3. The Role of Gods in Ancient Greece; and 4. The Role of Games and Sports in Ancient Greece. Tell students to research their topic as they read the chapter, and to take notes in preparation for a later class discussion.
d. Have students read the chapter.

3. **Review and Recall:** After the students have read the chapter:
a. Have them share their notes on their group topics in a class discussion.
b. have them ask each other questions about the chapter's content.
c. Have students reread each subhead question and answer it.
d. Have students reread and answer the chapter's Objective question.
e. Have students reread paragraphs 9 and 10. Ask them to compare and contrast the educational system in ancient Greece with our own educational system.

4. **Building Social Studies Skills:** Explain to students that outlining is an important skill that will help them to organize and understand information. Guide students through the first steps in preparing an outline on the role of women in ancient Greece. Then assign Skill Builder: Outlining, page 124 of the Chapter Review.

5. **Extension:**
a. Have students prepare a brief report on the lives and teachings of Socrates, Plato, and Aristotle. Ask students to discuss how the teachings of these ancient philosophers compare with their own beliefs.
b. Have students prepare an illustrated bulletin board on the major Greek gods and goddesses.

Support Materials
Assignments can include:
1. Chapter Review, pp. 124–125
2. Workbook, p. 19
3. Blackline Masters R31 and R32
4. Test 3-2, p. T16
5. Source Reading S7

CHAPTER 3   The Spread of Greek Culture

Overview   In the fifth century B.C., Greece was split apart by warfare between the allies of Sparta and the allies of Athens. Less than a century later, Alexander of Macedonia had conquered much of the known world. His empire blended the best features of eastern and western cultures. Classical art and learning thrived and spread during the Hellenistic Age.

Objectives

1. To outline the highlights of Greek culture during the Golden Age of Greece (480 B.C.-339B.C.)
2. To identify the causes and effects of the Peloponnesian Wars.
3. To outline the accomplishments of Alexander the Great.
4. To explain the changes Greek culture underwent during the Hellenistic Age. (323 B.C.-31 B.C.)

Developing the Chapter

1. **Motivation:** Tell students that, according to legend, a king name Hiero once came to Archimedes, the Greek mathematician, and commanded him to determine whether the royal crown was made of pure gold. Ask student to speculate on how Archimedes might have solved the problem. (Archimedes placed the crown in water and measured the amount of water that spilled over. If the crown were pure gold, it would displace the same amount of water as an equal weight of gold. If a lighter metal had been added, the density would be greater and more water would spill.) Point out that the ancient Greeks were very curious about the world around them and made many important contributions to science and philosophy.

2. **Introduction**
a. Write the chapter vocabulary words on the chalkboard. Have students write each word and its glossary definition in their vocabulary words. Ask volunteers to use each vocabulary word in a sentence.
b. Have students read the chapter title and Objective question.
c. Have students read the chapter.

3. **Review and Recall:** After the students have read the chapter:
a. Have them ask each other questions about the chapter's content.
b. Have them reread each subhead question and answer it.
c. Have them reread and answer the Objective question.
d. Have students look at the time line on page 126.
   Ask: What changes took place in the ancient world between the fighting of the Persian Wars and the death of Alexander.

4. **Building Social Studies Skills:** Explain to students that using a scale of distance is an important skill that helps them understand the locations of and distances between places they are learning about. Guide students through using the scale of distance on the map of Alexander's empire on page 130. Then assign Skill Builder: Using Map Scale and Compass Directions To Follow a Route, page 130 of the chapter text.

5. **Extension**
a. Have students prepare a report on the growth of science in the Hellenistic Age. You may want to divide the class into groups researching advances in mathematics, physics, and medicine. Have students share their findings orally or by means of a bulletin board display.
b. Have students research the rise and fall of the Macedonian Empire. Findings may be presented in the form of an imaginary interview or a series of newspaper headlines.

Support Materials

Assignments can include:

1. Chapter Review, pp. 132–133
2. Workbook, pp. 20–22
3. Blackline Masters R33 and R34
4. Test 3-3, p. T17
5. Source Reading S8

CHAPTER 4   Rome: From City to Empire

Overview   In the 7th century B.C., the Etruscans conquered the villages around Rome and built a city of wood and brick. Around 509 B.C., the Romans drove out the Etruscans and set up a republic. Over the next two and a half centuries, the mighty Roman army conquered all of Italy. Rome won control of many lands from Carthage in the three Punic Wars. Julius Caesar was made dictator for life in 44 B.C. His assassination later that year marked the end of the republic.

Objectives

1. To explain how the city of Rome gained control of the Mediterranean world.
2. To describe the structure of the Roman government and army during the years of the republic.
3. To identify the causes and results of the Punic Wars.
4. To outline the life and accomplishments of Julius Caesar.

Developing the Chapter

1. Motivation: Show students a picture of present-day Rome. Tell them that Rome has been called the "Eternal City." Ask students if they know the meaning of "eternal," and have them speculate on how Rome earned its nickname. Then tell them that Rome, which has ruled much of the western world for almost five centuries, has been an important city for over 2000 years. Have students speculate on the qualities that made a nation important by discussing past and future roles of the United States.

2. Introduction

a. Write sentences on the chalkboard that use each vocabulary word from the chapter. (You might want to use the phrases from the Chapter Vocabulary exercise on page 138 as a guide.) Have students try to determine the words' meanings from context clues.

b. Have students read the chapter title. Solicit definitions of *city* and *empire*. Ask students how an empire differs from an ordinary nation.

c. Have students read the chapter.

3. Review and Recall: After the students have read the chapter:

a. Ask them to compare and contrast the government of the Roman Republic with our own system of government. Have them explain why Rome was not a true democracy.

b. Have them reread and answer the chapter's Objective question.

c. Have them make up a crossword puzzle using words and ideas from the chapter. After they have written all the Down and Across clues, they might exchange, and try to solve, each other's puzzles.

4. Building Social Studies Skills: Explain to students that making generalizations is an important skill that helps them group facts into general statements. Guide students by helping them make a generalization about the 100 year of Etruscan rule discussed in paragraph 2 on page 135. (For example, "Etruscan rule was beneficial to Rome," "Etruscans brought improvements to Rome.") Then have students make generalizations abut events covered in the chapter, such as the Roman class system (paragraph 3), the Roman army and weapons (paragraphs 5 and 6), etc.

5. Extension

a. Have students do research on the march of Hannibal and his elephants from Spain to Italy. Ask students to imagine that they are soldiers in Hannibal's army. Have them write diary entries or letters home describing their experience crossing the Alps. Some students may wish to prepare a map showing the route of the march.

b. have students write a series of newspaper headlines tracing the career of Julius Caesar. Some students may wish to write editorials for or against Caesar's appointment as dictator for life.

Support Materials

Assignments can include:

1. Chapter Review, pp. 138–139
2. Blackline Masters R35 and R36
3. Test 3-4, p. T18
4. Map Transparency 6 and Activity Sheet A6
5. Source Reading S9

CHAPTER 5   The Height of the Roman Empire

Overview   Under the capable leadership of Augustus, the Roman Republic came to an end and the Roman Empire was born. During the Augustan Age, the powerful Roman army expanded the empire's boundaries and brought an end to the civil wars that had long plagued Rome. Roads were built linking the territories of the empire, trade prospered, and the standard of living rose sharply through the realm. Rome enjoyed two centuries of peace and prosperity known as the Pax Romana which came to an end following the reign of Marcus Aurelius.

Objectives

1. To explain how the Roman Republic was transformed into an empire.
2. To outline the changes that took place in Rome during the reign of Augustus.
3. To outline the accomplishments of the emperors who reigned during the Pax Romana.

Developing the Chapter

1. **Motivation:** Show students the picture of Augustus on page 140. Explain that Octavian was the adopted son of Julius Caesar. Shortly after Caesar's death, Octavian became emperor and established a military dictatorship in Rome.
Ask: Why might the Roman people have been willing to give up their republic in favor of a dictatorship? Point out that Augustus promised to end the destructive civil wars that had long plagued Rome. Ask students to comment on the observation that people are sometimes willing to sacrifice their personal freedoms to enjoy peace.

2. **Introduction**
a. Write the chapter vocabulary words on the chalkboard. Have students write the words and their glossary definitions in their vocabulary notebooks.
b. Have students read the chapter title and Objective question. Ask them to speculate on the steps a powerful empire might take in order to ensure long-lasting peace and prosperity.

3. Have students read the chapter. Tell them to take notes on the accomplishments of Roman rulers as they read.

3. **Review and Recall:** After the students have read the chapter:
a. Write these names on the chalkboard and have students list important facts about these people: Marc Antony, Cleopatra, Octavian, Nero, Caligula, Hadrian, Marcus Aurelius.
b. Have students read the Spotlight on Sources feature (p. 143) aloud. Have them discuss the feature question orally or answer it in a written exercise.

4. **Building Social Studies Skills:** Explain to students that summarizing is an important skill that tests their understanding of main ideas and events in the materials they have read. Then ask students to summarize the changes that took place in Rome under the reign of Augustus.

5. **Extension**
a. Ask students to imagine that they are Roman Senators considering the appointment of Octavian to the position of emperor for life. Have students debate the idea of changing Rome from a republic to an empire. Some students may wish to write editorials for or against the appointment of an all-powerful military dictator.
b. Have students write a biographical report on one of the following: Nero, Caligula, Hadrian, or Marcus Aurelius.
c. Have students prepare oral or written reports on the philosophy of stoicism.
Ask: How did Marcus Aurelius apply the theories of the ancient Greek philosophies to the practical problems of governing the Roman Empire?

Support Materials

Assignments can include:
1. Chapter Review, pp. 146–147
2. Workbook, pp. 23–25
3. Blackline Masters R37 and R38
4. Test 3-5, p. T19
5. Map Transparency 7 and Activity Sheet A7

CHAPTER 6   Life in Ancient Rome

Overview   Rome was the center of the civilized world from the 100s B.C. to the A.D. 200s. The aristocracy was at the top of the strict class system. Members of the working class toiled long hours while conquered peoples served the ruling aristocracy as slaves. Roman women were active at home and in the workplace. Wealthy Romans enjoyed relaxing in public baths and watching chariot races and gladiator contests. The Romans made many contributions in the fields of art, literature, science, and law.

Objectives

1. To explain the structure and function of the class system in Roman society.
2. To outline the daily life of Roman aristocrats, workers, women, and slaves.
3. To list major Roman contributions in the fields of architecture, science, medicine, law, and literature.

Developing the Chapter

1. **Motivation:** Refer students to the picture of the Colosseum on page 152. Have students read the photo caption (the Colosseum was completed almost 2000 years ago, was shaped like a football stadium, and could seat 45,000 people). Ask students to speculate on how the Colosseum was used. Then tell them that the Colosseum was used for public exhibitions in which armed men fought against wild animals or other men, often to the death. Ask students to speculate on the character of a society in which mortal combat was accepted as a popular form of mass entertainment.

2. **Introduction**
a. Write the chapter vocabulary words on the chalkboard. Have students write each word and its glossary definition in their vocabulary notebooks.
b. Have students read the chapter title and Objective question.
c. Have students read the chapter.

3. **Review and Recall:** After the students have read the chapter:
a. Have them ask each other questions about the chapter's content.

b. Have them reread each subhead question and answer it.
c. Have them reread and answer the Objective question.
d. Have them read aloud the discussion of women's role in Roman society (paragraph 12). Then have volunteers answer the question at the end of the paragraph.

4. **Building Social Studies Skills:** Explain to students that note-taking is an important skill that helps them master chapter content and study for a test. Then assign students a section of the chapter on which to take notes. (You might wish to guide students through taking notes on the first section of the chapter.)

5. **Extension**
a. Divide students into five groups. Assign each group one of the Romance languages to research: French, Spanish, Italian, Portuguese, or Romanian. Have each group prepare a list of at least ten words in their assigned language that clearly reflect Latin roots. Then have the entire class identify some English words that are derived from Latin.
b. Ask students to imagine that they are either aristocrats, merchants, or slaves in ancient Rome. Then have each student write a diary entry describing a typical day in his or her life. Ask students to share their writings with the rest of the class.
c. Have students prepare a bulletin board display depicting Roman contributions to Western civilization. The display might focus on such areas as art, architecture, science, law, and literature.

Support Materials

Assignments can include:

1. Chapter Review, pp. 154–155
2. Workbook p. 26
3. Blackline Masters R39 and R40
4. Test 3-6, p. T20

CHAPTER 7   The Decline of the Roman
                   Empire

Overview   By the close of the third century
Roman military leaders were setting
government policy and choosing emperors
from their own ranks. By then the great
Roman roads had fallen into disrepair and
trade had significantly decreased. Inhabitants
of the empire at that time faced severe food
shortages, heavy taxes, and ongoing inflation.
By the fifth century, the western half of the
empire had been overrun by invading
Germanic tribes and Huns from central Asia.
Although the great Roman Empire had come
to an end, the eastern half of the empire
thrived for another thousand years as the
Byzantine Empire.

Objectives
1. To outline the political, economic, and
   social factors that led to the decline of
   Rome.
2. To identify the steps taken to strengthen
   the faltering government and to delay the
   decline of Roman civilization.
3. To explain the role of barbarian invasions
   in the fall of Rome.

Developing the Chapter

1. Motivation: Show students the map of the
barbarian invasions on page 162 of the
Chapter Review. Ask students to define the
word "barbarian." Point out that people
throughout history had tended to look on
outsiders with different beliefs and customs
as inferior or uncivilized. Discuss the concept
of ethnocentrism—that is, the notion that
one's own culture is superior to all others. Ask
students to discuss why the United States is
more or less likely than other nations to be
guilty of ethnocentrism.

2. Introduction
a. Write the chapter vocabulary words on the
   chalkboard. Ask students to speculate on
   the meaning of the words. Then have them
   write each word and its glossary definition
   in their vocabulary notebooks.
b. Have students read the chapter title and
   Objective question.
   Ask: What are some reasons why great
   nations might weaken?

c. Have students look at the time line on page
   156 of the chapter. Ask them to speculate
   on how the actions of Diocletian and
   Constantine may have hastened the decline
   of the Roman Empire.
d. Have students read the chapter.

3. Review and Recall: After the students
have read the chapters:
a. Have them ask each other questions about
   the chapter's content.
b. Have them reread each subhead question
   and answer it.
c. Have them reread and answer the Objective
   question.

4. Building Social Studies Skills: Explain to
students that reading a map that has arrows is
an important skill that helps them to
understand historical events. Use the map of
the barbarian invasions on page 162 to
demonstrate how various groups invaded the
Roman Empire from different directions.
Then assign Skill Builder: Reading a Map
That Has Arrows on page 162 of the Chapter
Review.

5. Extension
a. Have students research the causes and
   effects of monetary inflation. Then have
   them write a report on how inflation
   contributed to the decline of the Roman
   Empire.
b. Have students prepare a chart comparing
   political, social, and economic conditions
   in the Roman Empire with those in the
   present-day United States. Students may
   wish to write a chapter of an imaginary
   textbook of the future entitled "The Decline
   of the American Empire."
c. Have students prepare biographical reports
   on Diocletian, Constantine, or Attila.

Support Materials
Assignments can include:
1. Chapter Review, pp. 162–163
2. Blackline Masters R41 and R42
3. Test 3-7, p. T21

Europe's Early Development

Unit Overview   After the collapse of the Roman empire in the west, the Christian church was the only unifying element in western Europe. Political unity eventually was achieved by the Frankish empire of Charlemagne, but the unity was only temporary. In eastern Europe the Byzantine empire was more successful in maintaining the traditions of Rome. In the ninth and tenth centuries, feudalism gradually took shape in western Europe, restoring a degree of order. In succeeding centuries, the church reached the height of its prestige and influence. At the same time, a gradual increase in trade led to the increase in both size and number of cities and, correspondingly, of the middle class. Various events and trends during the fourteenth century further strengthened the middle class at the expense of the feudal nobility and the church, indicating that the Middle Ages were giving way to a newer order.

Unit Objectives

1. To show how forms of government changed during the Middle Ages.
2. To explain the influence and importance of Christianity during the Middle Ages.
3. To list important leaders in Europe and the Byzantine Empire.

Unit Introduction

1. **Motivation:** Explain to students that at the beginning of the Middle Ages, life was very different from today. Point out that in Europe most people served a noble person in peace and war. The church was extremely important in daily life. Tell them that by the late Middle Ages, life had changed in many ways.

2. **Visual:** Ask students if they can tell what is happening in the picture. Drop hints that it is like a sporting event. It is, in fact, the concluding event of a medieval tournament, a melee, in which two teams of knights fight each other as if they are on an actual battlefield. Have students identify the two teams, the tournament officials, and the different groups of spectators. Tell students that fighting was the medieval knight's reason for existence. Tournaments were organized late in the Middle Ages to keep the knights amused at a time when the need for real fighting was declining.

3. **Time Line:** Have students calculate how long a span of time is covered by this line (about 1400 years). Have them find three places where there is a space of at least 200 years between events, and ask them to speculate on the kinds of conditions that might have led to these gaps.

Unit Activities

1. Have students work together to make a mural. The mural should consist of a series of maps that cover Europe and the Near East, including North Africa. For each chapter, have students make a map and fill it in with important places and events. When they are finished with the unit, the mural should provide them with information for making comparisons about life in the Middle Ages.

2. Have students compare and contrast the manor-based economic system with the economic system based on money that replaced it. Ask them to include several reasons why they think that the manor-based economy died out in Europe. Have them research information on the history of banking in Europe, common trade practices, and guilds as they developed in Europe during the Middle Ages.

3. Have students write abut the effect of Christianity on various aspects of life in the Middle Ages. These should include daily life, politics, wars, education, the growth of monasteries, and the structure of the church itself. Encourage students to look at the crusades and the schism and to compare the state of the church at the end of the Middle Ages with the early Christian community at the time of Jesus.

Support Materials

Assignments can include:
1. Unit Review, pp. 216–217
2. Unit 4 Test, pp. UT7–UT8
3. Map Transparency 10 and Activity Sheet A10.
4. Unit 4 ESL/LEP Worksheet 1, p. ESL 7
5. Unit 4 ESL/LEP Worksheet 2, p. ESL 8

CHAPTER 1 Christianity Spreads New Ideas

Unit Overview Nearly 2000 years ago, Christianity began with the life and teachings of Jesus. Despite opposition from the Romans before A.D. 313, Christianity grew very rapidly. By A.D. 395, missionaries had spread the teachings of Jesus throughout the Roman Empire, and it had become the empire's official religion. Within 400 years, Christianity grew from a small group of believers to one of the world's major religions.

Objectives

1. To explain how Christianity grew and became a major religion.
2. To identify the ideas of Jesus, the founder of Christianity.
3. To explain the organization of the early Christian church and monasteries.

Developing the Chapter

1. Motivation: Explain that Christianity includes many churches including Catholic, Orthodox, Lutheran, Baptist, Methodist, Episcopalian, and others. Point out that this very large world religion was begun by the ideas and teachings of one person, Jesus, who lived nearly 2,000 years ago. Ask students to think of a person who has influenced great numbers of people in modern times. Point out that even though communication at the time of Jesus was very slow, making it difficult for him and his followers to reach people, they were still successful in spreading Jesus' word.

2. Introduction

a. Write the chapter's vocabulary words on the chalkboard. Have students choose a word and look up its meaning. Then have them read the word and its definition to the class.

b. Read the chapter title and Objective question aloud. Have the students make inferences based on the chapter title and the Objective question.

c. Have students read the chapter.

3. Review and Recall: After students have read the chapter:

a. Have them look at the map on page 170 and discuss the early spread of Christianity. Ask them to identify the birthplace and major centers of Christianity, and to discuss the importance of the Mediterranean Sea to Christianity's growth.

b. Have each student read the first sentence of one of the numbered sections and use it to make up a question. Then have students answer each other's questions.

c. Read the Objective question aloud and have students discuss it, checking the accuracy of inferences made earlier.

d. Have students read the two Spotlight on Sources sections. Then have them compare and contrast the two descriptions of Christian life.

4. Building Social Studies Skills: Explain to students that preparing a research report is a good way to learn more about a topic. Point out that the encyclopedia is an excellent source of information. Then have students research and write about one of the following people: Peter, Paul, Constantine, or Benedict. The reports should focus on the importance of each person to the development of Christianity.

5. Extension

a. Divide students into two cooperative groups. Have one group research the development of the Western church that became centered in Rome. Have the other group research the Eastern church that became centered in Constantinople. Then have the groups compare their findings and discuss the similarities and differences between the two.

b. Help students find one of Jesus' parables in the Bible (Possible parables: Matthew 13, Matthew 20, 1-16; Mark 4, 2-9; Luke 14, 7-14; Luke 12, 23-28) Have students read the parable and discuss its meaning. Ask them to tell why they think Jesus chose to speak in parables.

Support Materials

Assignments can include:

1. Chapter Review, pp. 172–173
2. Blackline Masters R43 and R44
3. Test 4-1, p. T22.

CHAPTER 2   The Rise and Fall of Carolingian Europe

Overview   The first great empire in Europe after the fall of Rome was formed by the Carolingian dynasty of the Frankish kingdom. It began around A.D. 750, and Charlemagne was its greatest ruler. Charlemagne ruled from A.D. 768 until his death in A.D. 814. After his death, the empire eventually divided into three parts. Outsiders hastened this breakup, particularly the Vikings, or Northmen.

Objectives

1. To explain conditions in Europe before the Caroligian dynasty.
2. To compare Europe before and after the rule of Charlemagne.
3. To identify the groups of people who hastened the destruction of Charlemagne's empire.

Developing the Chapter:

1. Motivation: Explain that after the fall of the Roman Empire, European lands were divided and life became chaotic and dangerous. There were no schools, most people could not read, and there were no strong central governments. Point out that uniting the small kingdoms of Europe in the eighth century was a huge task, but Charlemagne was able to accomplish it.

Ask: In the conditions of the time, what kind of ruler do you think would be most effective? What characteristics in a person would most likely contribute to success as a ruler? Why are they important?

2. Introduction:

a. Write the chapter's vocabulary words on the chalkboard. Have students write each word and its glossary meaning in their vocabulary notebooks.
b. Have students read the chapter title and Objective question.
c. Have students read the chapter.

3. Review and Recall: After students have read the chapter:

a. Have them ask each other questions about the chapter's content.
b. Have them look at the map on page 176 and identify the areas attacked by the Vikings.

c. Have students re-read and answer the Objective question for this chapter.
d. Have them read the Spotlight on Sources feature and discuss what seem to be the major reasons for the Viking invasions.

4. Building Social Studies Skills: Explain to students that a time line is a helpful way to see the order in which events have taken place and to understand how they are related. Show them a simple example of a time line. Then have them make a time line for the Franks that begins in A.D. 500 and ends in A.D. 824. The time line should include Clovis, the soldiers' baptism, Carolingian dynasty, Charlemagne, the rescue of Leo III, Charlemagne as Roman emperor, the death of Charlemagne, and the breakup of the empire.

5. Extension:

a. Have students compare a map of Charlemagne's empire with a current map of the same area. Encourage them to notice differences and similarities. Have them discuss whether the divisions of territory in the Middle Ages influenced the formation of modern countries or not.
b. Ask students to discuss why it is important that Charlemagne founded schools and monestaries and saved copies of ancient Roman writings. Have them consider what life might be like without opportunities for education.
c. Discuss with students the reasons why the Caroligian monarchy did not last. Ask: Should Charlemagne have anticipated what happened? What might he have done differently? What difference would it have made?

Support Materials

Assignments can include:

1. Chapter review, pp. 178–179
2. Workbook, p. 27
3. Blackline Masters R45 and R46
4. Test 4-2, p. T23
5. Map Transparency 8 and Activity Sheet A8
6. Source Reading, p. 5–10.

CHAPTER 3   The Byzantine Empire

Overview   The Roman Empire was divided into eastern and western halves in A.D. 330. The eastern half became the Byzantine Empire and lasted for nearly 1,000 years after the fall of Rome. Its capital, Constantinople, became a very wealthy trading center and the seat of the eastern Christian church. Its most important ruler was Justinian, who ruled from A.D. 527 to A.D. 565. He added huge amounts of territory to the empire and is famous for his law code, the Justinian Code. His wife, Theodora, also had a strong voice in the government.

Objectives

1. To explain how the Byzantine Empire came into existence.
2. To list important achievements of the emperor Justinian.
3. To explain the importance of Theodora.
4. To show the effect of Christianity on the people of the Byzantine empire.

Developing the Chapter

1. **Motivation:** Have students look at the picture of Hagia Sophia. Tell them that it was originally built as a Christian church around A.D. 535. In 1453, it was converted into an Islamic mosque when the Turks conquered Constantinople. Point out the artwork and decoration. Explain that this is one of the finest examples of Byzantine art and architecture and is now a museum in Istanbul, Turkey. When the Turks converted Hagia Sophia, they covered the original Christian mosaics with plaster, but much of this original decoration has been restored in the twentieth century.

2. **Introduction:**
a. Write the vocabulary words on the chalkboard. Have students choose a word and look up its meaning. Then have them read the word and its definition to the class. Have students use each word in an original sentence to be sure that they understand its meaning.
b. Read the chapter title and Objective question aloud.
c. Have students read the chapter.

3. **Review and Recall:** After students have read the chapter:
a. Have students look at the map on page 182. Ask them to compare the Byzantine Empire in 527 with the Empire at the time of Justinian's death.
b. Have students re-read each subhead question and answer it.
c. Have students re-read and answer the chapter's Objective question.

4. **Building Social Studies Skills:** Explain to students that preparing a research report will help them learn more abut a topic. Have them research and write about the Justinian Code. Ask them to find out what its important points are. Then ask them to list basic ideas from the Code that are used in modern European civil law.

5. **Extension:**
a. Have students compare and contrast the rules of Justinian and Charlemagne (king of the Franks from A.D. 768–814). How was life different from people in these two places and times? For what was each ruler most famous? In which area and in what ways was the culture more advanced? Put a chart on the chalkboard with the headings "Justinian" and "Charlemagne." Ask students to complete the chart, comparing the empires each of them ruled and their similarities and differences as rulers.
b. Have students find more information about the Empress Theodora. Ask them to discuss the ways in which she influenced the course of the Byzantine empire under Justinian. Have them think of other examples of powerful and influential women in government.
c. Ask students to find and bring to class color photographs or slides of Byzantine mosaics. A group can prepare a report on mosaics, telling how they are assembled; what makes a good mosaic; where they are found; and what kinds of subjects they depict.

Support Materials

Assignments can include:

1. Chapter Review, pp. 184–185
2. Blackline Masters R47 and R48.
3. Test 4-3, p. T24.

CHAPTER 4   Government in the Middle Ages

Overview   During the Middle Ages in Europe, feudalism was the primary form of government. The most important leaders were William the Conqueror and Henry II in England, Philip II in France, Eleanor of Aquitaine in both England and France, and Otto the Great in the Holy Roman Empire. These strong leaders gradually centralized power in their countries.

Objectives

1. To explain the feudal system in western Europe during the Middle Ages.
2. To list the important rulers and their achievements in England, France, and Germany.

Developing the Chapter

1. **Motivation:** Present the class with the following information: The United States Constitution was written in 1788 by the Constitutional Convention, a group of delegates representing the thirteen states of the new nation. Together the convention delegates designed the framework for the new government, and they did such a good job that the framework is still in use. In the Middle Ages, by contrast, there was never anything resembling a Constitutional Convention. Forms of government were not planned. Instead, they evolved slowly out of the chaos that followed the collapse of the Carolingian monarchy. Gradually a form of government took shape that met the needs of its time. This form of government was called feudalism.

2. **Introduction:**
a. Having students use a thesaurus. Ask them to find a synonym or antonym for two of the vocabulary words. Then have them read what they have found to the class.
b. Have students read the chapter title and Objective question.
c. **Ask:** What can you tell me about those people called knights, who were once so important in Europe? After eliciting such information as that they rode horses and wore armor, point out that they also played a key role in feudalism.

3. **Review and Recall:** After the students have read the chapter:
a. Have them ask each other questions about the chapter's content.
b. Have students read each subhead question and answer it.
c. Have students re-read and answer the chapter's Objective question.
d. Have students look carefully at the chapter's time line. Help them understand the relative chronological order in the three areas discussed.

4. **Building Social Studies Skills:** Explain to students that life was very different in the Middle Ages than life is today. Have them write a report that compares and contrasts the lives of people their age in the Middle Ages with their own lives. Suggest that they consider such things as education, work, pleasure, and role in the family.

5. **Extension:**
a. Have students compare Theodora from the Byzantine Empire with Eleanor of Aquitaine. What common effects did these two women have on their husbands, governments, and lands? How were they different?
b. One of the conflicts during the reign of Henry II centered around Thomas à Becket. Have students research and write about this man and his conflict with Henry.
c. Have students work in small cooperative groups to compare Charlemagne's and Otto's relationship with the popes of their time.
d. Perhaps the greatest contribution of Henry II was the foundation he laid of the English legal system. Ask a group of students to prepare a report on the legal reforms in the reign of Henry II. Students should also point out how these reforms have carried through to today's courts of law in America.

Support Materials

Assignments can include:

1. Chapter Review, pp. 192–193
2. Blackline Masters R49 and R50
3. Test 4-4, p. T25.

CHAPTER 5   Manor and Town Life

Overview   During the Middle Ages in Europe, village life centered around the manor. The manor included a castle and the lands and people that surrounded it. The lord lived in the castle, which was usually a fortress, and the peasants lived around the castle. After A.D. 1000, when trade began to grow, the middle class gained importance and towns became common. Status in society shifted from owning land to having money. Groups of merchants banded together to form guilds and corporations.

Objectives

1. To explain how people lived in medieval manors and medieval towns.
2. To show how trade caused the growth of towns in the Middle Ages.
3. To explain the importance of the rise of the middle class.
4. To identify important cultural aspects of life in the Middle Ages.

Developing the Chapter

1. Motivation: Point out to students that many of the business practices that are common today had their roots in the Middle Ages. Explain that the fist partnerships started in the Middle Ages, and the use of credit was common. Guilds, which is some ways were similar to labor unions, also existed. Finally, the idea that one's life could change and improve through work began at this time.

2. Introduction:
a. Write the chapter's vocabulary words on the chalkboard. Have each student look up one or two words and find out the origin of the word.
b. Have students read the chapter title and Objective question. Read the first paragraph and ask students how they would like to live in the place described.
c. Have students read the chapter.

3. Review and Recall: After the students have read the chapter:
a. Have students look at the map on page 198 and discuss the major centers of life in medieval times. Ask them to discuss the relationship between these towns and important trade routes.
b. Have each student read the first sentence of one of the numbered sections and use it to make up a question. Then have students answer each other's questions.
c. Have students re-read and answer the chapter's Objective questions.
d. Have students look carefully at the picture of Siena. Ask them to discuss what life in Siena might have been like based on what they have read in the chapter.

4. Building Social Studies Skills: Explain to students that notetaking is an important skill that can help them better understand what they have read. Taking notes is also an excellent way to prepare for a test. Guide students through taking notes on the first section of the chapter.

5. Extension:
a. Have students write a story about going to a medieval trade fair. Have them try to imagine the sights, sounds, and smells they might encounter. Ask them to describe several events they might participate in.
b. Have students research the importance of guilds during the Middle Ages. Ask them to find out information about the major guild organizations. Ask individual students also to compare these organizations to (1) modern trade organizations, such as associations of bookstores, jewelry stores, or hardware stores; (2) local organizations, such as the chamber of commerce; and (3) labor unions, particularly craft unions such as those for electricians or plumbers.
c. Have students research the Knights Templar and find out the role they played in early European banking.

Support Materials

Assignments can include:
1. Chapter Review, pp. 200–201
2. Workbook, pp. 28–31
3. Blackline Masters R51 and R52
4. Test 4-5, p. T26
5. Map Transparency 9 and Activity Sheet A9
6. Source Readings, pp. 511–512

CHAPTER 6   The Role of the Church in the Middle Ages

Overview   In Europe, during the Middle Ages, the church played an important part in the lives of all people. Members of the clergy had tremendous influence. The church became wealthy and powerful. Orders of friars were established by Francis of Assisi and others. They lived simple lives and did good words. Other church leaders became great feudal lords, and conflicts arose between the pope and the Holy Roman Emperor.

Objectives

1. To explain the influence of the church on the everyday lives of people in the Middle Ages.
2. To explain why the church was so powerful.
3. To show why the people of the Middle Ages joined the crusades.

Developing the Chapter

1. **Motivation:** Ask students to think of who the most powerful people in our society are. What work do they do? Why are they powerful? Discuss these questions and then point out that in the Middle Ages in Europe, the most powerful institution was the church, and its leaders were the most powerful people. Have students discuss how this is different today.

2. **Introduction:**
a. Write the chapter's vocabulary words on the chalkboard. Have students write each word and its glossary meaning in their vocabulary notebooks.
b. Have students read the chapter title and Objective question.
c. Have students read the chapter.

3. **Review and Recall:** After the students have read the chapter:
a. Have students read the Spotlight on Sources. Ask them to discuss what they think about the crusades and if they can imagine this kind of event happening today. Why or why not?
b. Have students look carefully at the chapter visuals. For each one, ask them to explain the material from the chapter that the visual illustrates.
c. Have students re-read and answer the chapter's Objective questions.
d. Have students read the Art and Artifacts feature aloud. Ask them to study the visuals. Have them discuss which style of architecture they prefer and why.

4. **Building Social Studies Skills:** Have students find more information about Francis of Assisi. Suggested sources are encyclopedias, biographies, and his own writings, such as *The Little Flowers of St. Francis*. Point out to students that some of the descriptions of Francis's life may be biased or attempting to prove a point. Have them discuss the issue of fact versus opinion when reading biographies.

5. **Extension:**
a. Have students research and write a report on the Children's Crusade. Ask them to include details about the children, their motives for going on the crusade, and what happened to them.
b. Have students compare life in a monastery to that of a typical lord's castle in the Middle Ages. What was similar and what was different? Encourage students to learn about the vows that were taken by monks and the daily discipline and order of their lives. How might this contrast with secular life?
c. Have a group of students prepare a report on a Gothic cathedral. Individual students should report on the various characteristics of the cathedral, such as its floor plan, construction principles (the Gothic arch, flying buttresses), steeples and towers, stained glass, and sculpture. Students can describe a specific cathedral (Chartres, Paris, Canterbury), or they can present the general characteristics of the type.

Support Materials
Assignments can include:
1. Chapter Review, pp. 208–209
2. Workbook, pp. 32–33
3. Blackline Masters R53 and R54
4. Test 4-6, p. T27.

CHAPTER 7 The Closing of the Middle Ages

Overview During the late Middle Ages in Europe, the medieval way of life gradually came to an end. Land power was replaced by money power. Trade was opened up tremendously by the crusades. Peasants no longer had to rely on the nobles for their livelihood. Conflicts in the church also weakened the power of the clergy. Cities became the new focus of wealth and power in Europe.

Objectives

1. To explain how economic life in western Europe was changed by the crusades.
2. To identify factors that led to the end of feudalism in western Europe.
3. To explain why the power of the church declined in the late Middle Ages.

Developing the Chapter

1. **Motivation:** Explain that the fourteenth century was the time of one of the worst disasters in European history—the Black Death. It was also when gunpowder was first used in Europe. Gunpowder changed war forever and made it more destructive and deadly. It was also a time of upheaval in many other areas, including religion, government, and economics. Have students discuss how the twentieth century is similar.

2. **Introduction:**
a. Write the chapter's vocabulary words on the chalkboard. Have students use each word in a sentence in their vocabulary notebooks.
b. Read the chapter title and Objective question aloud.
   Ask: What do you think would happen if half the people in town suddenly died? How would the lives of the people who survived be affected? Students probably will think first of the sorrow caused by so many deaths. Ask them how this might affect their attitudes toward things they have previously taken for granted. If students do not raise the subject themselves, lead the discussion to the question of a shortage of people. How

could half as many people do the same jobs as the former larger number? Are there any jobs that would no longer be necessary, or that would be less important? Lead the discussion to the conclusion that survivors will be in a much stronger position to choose the kind of work they want to do and where they want to do it.
c. Have students read the chapter.

3. **Review and Recall:** After students have read the chapter:
a. Have students discuss how the invention of gunpowder would have changed warfare in the Middle Ages.
b. Have students re-read each subhead question and answer it.
c. Have students re-read and answer the chapter's Objective question.
d. Have students look at the picture of Pope Boniface VIII. Ask them to discuss elements that led to conflicts between the church and various secular leaders.

4. **Building Social Studies Skills:** Explain to students that the ability to draw conclusions from information is very important. Have them read Boccacio's description of the plague in the chapter. Then ask them to discuss how aware of disease and germs the people of his time were. Have students explain the reasons for their conclusions.

5. **Extension:**
a. Have students work in groups to compare and contrast the Catholic Church in the fourteenth century with the early Christian community during and just after Jesus' time.
b. Have students work together to research the Black Death. If possible, have them find first-hand descriptions of this terrifying and horrible event. Ask them to compare the Black Death to other epidemics in more recent times.

Support Materials

Assignments can include:
1. Chapter Review, pp. 214–215
2. Workbook, p. 34
3. Blackline Masters R55 and R56
4. Test 4-7, p. T28
5. Source Readings, p. S13.

UNIT 5

The Rise of Asia, Africa and the Americas

Unit Overview   Early Russian culture was strongly influenced by Byzantine traditions, but 200 years of foreign rule isolated Russia from the West. Meanwhile, the religion of Islam was spreading throughout the Middle East as large and powerful trading empires were developing independently in Africa. By the eleventh century, "conquests in the name of Allah" had been made throughout Asia Minor; by the 1200s, throughout northern India and China; and in 1452, Constantinople itself was conquered, signifying the end of the Byzantine Empire. The Chinese drove out the Mongols in 1368 and, with the founding of the Ming Dynasty, began an isolationist policy that lasted 300 years. Japan, also an isolationist nation, enjoyed 250 years of rule by shogun. It, like China, built a strong and rich culture. Across the seas in the early Americas, three great civilizations—the Maya, Aztec and Inca—developed and prospered.

Unit Objectives

1. To describe the early civilizations of Asia, Africa and the Americas.
2. To explain how religion played a central role in the rise and growth of early civilizations.
3. To compare and contrast the rise of civilizations during periods of trade and cultural exchange and during periods of isolation.

Unit Introduction

1. **Motivation:** Begin this unit by having students examine a contemporary world map and compare it to index maps of the early civilizations in Asia, Africa and the Americas. Notice in particular rivers, oceans, and trade routes. Discuss the benefits and liabilities of isolation and contact with other cultures in these early civilizations and the importance of trade and exchange of culture and religion. Have students think about and discuss America's modern-day trade with these areas of the world.
Ask: What products do we import from Asia, Africa, and Central and Latin America? Are there philosophies, art forms, and scientific or technological findings from early

civilizations that are important to the United States today?

2. **Visual:** Direct students' attention to the unit opening visual of Machu Picchu (p. 219). Tell students that Machu Picchu is one of the greatest ancient cities ever found. Its ruins unearthed by American explorer Hiram Bingham in 1911, Machu Picchu had fine stone houses, golden temples, and terraced hillsides. Incas called gold, which they thought was holy, "tears of the sun," and they had plenty of it. Ask students to speculate on what brought about the downfall of the great Inca Empire. (the discovery of that gold by outsiders)

3. **Time Line:** Have students read the unit time line (pp. 218-19) to survey events in the rise of Asia, Africa and the Americas.
Ask: Which empire arose first? Which developed latest? Encourage students to refer to the unit time line to help them put events in perspective as they study the unit.

Unit Activities

1. **Cooperative Learning:** Divide students into three groups. Assign Asia to one group, Africa to another, and the Americas to the third. Have students compare and contrast the rise of civilizations during times of autonomous government, government under foreign rule, and during periods of isolation.

2. **Research:** Many powerful religious and political leaders emerged within early civilizations. Have students choose a leader from one of the civilizations: Suleiman I, Genghis Khan, Mohammad I, Mansa Musa, Askia the Great, Akbar, Tamerlane, Shah Jahan, Marco Polo, or Ie Yasu. Have students research the leader and give an oral report to the class on their findings; or have them write a speech that the leader might have given to his constituency.

Support Materials

Assignments can include:

1. Unit Review, pp. 272–273
2. Unit 5 Test, pp. UT9–UT10
3. Unit 5 ESL/LEP Worksheet 1, p. ESL 9
4. Unit 5 ESL/LEP Worksheet 2, p. ESL 10

T57

UNIT 5

CHAPTER 1   The Rise of Early Russia

Overview   A Russian kingdom based in Kiev was established when people from the north conquered the Slavs in the 9th century. Early Russian culture was strongly influenced by Byzantine religious, artistic, architectural, educational, and legal traditions. After 200 years of foreign rule, Ivan the Great expelled the Mongol conquerers in the late 15th century. The czars in Moscow gradually assumed absolute power while the lives of the peasants grew increasingly harsh.

Objectives

1. To explain the evolution of the Russian state.
2. To compare and contrast the influences of Byzantine and European cultural traditions on Russia.
3. To identify the effects of autocratic rule on Russian society.

Developing the Chapter

1. **Motivation:** Show students pictures of a Gothic or Romanesque cathedral, a Byzantine church (such as Saint Sophia), and St. Basil's Cathedral in Moscow (p. 220). Ask students to compare and contrast the architectural features of these buildings. Explain that people in early Russia traded more with Asia and the Byzantine Empire than with their neighbors to the west. Ask students to speculate on how Eastern influences may have shaped early Russian culture to create a society very different from that of Western Europe.

2. **Introduction**

a. Write the chapter vocabulary words on the chalkboard. Have students write each word and its glossary definition in their vocabulary notebooks.

b. Have students read the chapter time line.
 Ask: What period of time does the term "early Russia" refer to?

c. Have students read the chapter title and Objective question. On the basis of the Objective, have students make a prediction about Russia in 1584.

 Ask: Would you expect to see Russia keeping pace with its Western neighbors and playing an important role in world affairs? Why or why not?

d. Have students read the chapter.

3. **Review and Recall:** After the students have read the chapter:

a. Have them make a list of the ways in which the Rus (Northpeople) invaders improved life for the Russian people.

b. Have students examine the map of early Russia on page 222. Ask them to discuss the effect of geography on the development of Russian political and cultural history.
 Ask: How did Russia's borders change between A.D. 800 and 1584?

c. Have students debate which rulers, the Mongols or the early czars, did more damage to Russia and its people. Remind students to use facts from the chapter to support their points of view.

4. **Building Social Studies Skills:** Explain to students that a time line is a tool for organizing and clarifying the order of events in history. Then assign Skillbuilder: Reading a Time Line on page 224.

5. **Extension**

a. Have students prepare a mural that illustrates the Mongol conquest and domination of Russia. The mural can be divided into a series of panels, each showing a stage or event in the Mongols' conquest of Russia.

b. Have students prepare oral or written reports on the life of the serfs during the reign of the czars. How were their lives changed by the Mongol invasion? Ask students to compare and contrast peasant life in Russia with that in England and Western Europe. (The feudal system began and ended later in Russia. Russian serfs were virtual slaves and were generally poorer and had fewer legal rights.)

Support Materials

Assignments can include:
1. Chapter Review, pp. 224-225
2. Blackline Masters R57 and R58
3. Test 5-1, p. T29
4. Source reading S14

Overview   The religion of Islam began nearly 1,400 years ago in the city of Mecca in Saudi Arabia. Muhammad, who called himself a prophet, preached the word of Allah (God). Muhammad's teachings are found in a book called the Koran, which says that there is but one Allah and that people must follow the Five Pillars of Islam to be rewarded after death. Muslims built an empire by conquering many countries in the name of Allah.

Objectives

1. To explain where, when, and how Islam began.
2. To explain the main beliefs of Islam.
3. To describe how Islam is a way of life as much as a religion.
4. To identify accomplishments of Islam.
5. To explain how Islam spread to other parts of the world.

Developing the Chapter

1. **Motivation:** Islam is the last of the three great monotheistic religions (the others are Christianity and Judaism). Talk about the Five Pillars. Ask students how they would feel living with Islamic rules (e.g., women wearing veils, praying five times a day, followers fasting during the holy month of Ramadan, etc.). Have students compare and contrast the rules of the faith of Islam with the rules of Christianity and/or Judaism. Make a chart on the chalkboard to display differences and similarities discussed.

2. **Introduction**
a. Have students read the chapter Objective.
b. Have students look at the map on page 229 to find Saudi Arabia and the cities of Mecca and Medea. Have them trace the path of Islamic conquests as Muslims "spread the word."
c. Have students write each vocabulary word and its meaning in their notebooks.

3. **Review and Recall:** After students have read the chapter:
a. Have them use the vocabulary words in an oral sentence.
b. Have them reread each subhead question and answer it.

c. Have them identify important places on the map: The Red Sea, Mecca, Medina, Damascus, Egypt, Persia.

4. **Building Social Studies Skills:** Explain to students that research and report writing are important skills for expanding and clarifying imformation. Have them use encyclopedias and other sources to write a short report on the Five Pillars of Islam.

5. **Extension**
a. Hold a debate on the status of women in the Islamic religion. Students may want to do extra library research to prepare for the debate.
b. Have students write a personal opinion paragraph about whether "conquest in the name of God" is ever justified. Tell them to cite examples from holy wars past and present (e.g., the Crusades, the Iran-Iraq war) to support their position. Then hold a class discussion on this issue.
c. Have students look for photographs of Muslim art and architecture to show to the class. Muslims borrowed Roman architectural devices but also created their own style in the introduction of the mosque and the use of tapestries and arabesque patterns in decoration. Ask students to point out Roman influences in the examples of Muslim architecture they have chosen.
d. Read aloud and discuss a story from the *Arabian Nights*. Tell students that the *Arabian Nights*, a collection of about 200 folk tales from Arabia, Egypt, India, Persia, and other countries, is probably the most famous example of Arabic literature in the Western world.

Support Materials

Assignments can include:
1. Chapter Review, pp. 232-233
2. Workbook, pp. 35-37
3. Blackline Masters R59 and R60
4. Test 5-2, p. T30
5. Map Transparencies 11 and 12 and Activity Sheets A11 and A12

CHAPTER 3 The Ottoman Empire

Overview Turkic peoples began invading the Middle East in the eighth century, gradually converted to Islam, and adopted other parts of the Muslim culture. During the eleventh century, the Seljuk Turks seized Baghdad and went on to conquer much of Asia Minor in the name of Allah. The Ottoman Turks replaced the Seljuk empire and expanded Islamic control by conquering the Christian city of Constantinople, signifying the end of the Byzantine Empire. Suleiman I led the Ottomans into their Golden Age as they continued to expand into Europe, North Africa, and Russia.

Objectives

1. To identify the highlights and leaders of Turkic expansion from the eighth through the seventeenth century.
2. To compare and contrast the Seljuk Turks with the Ottoman Turks.
3. To explain the influence of Allah in Turkic expansion.
4. To describe the Golden Age of the Ottomans under Suleiman I.

Developing the Chapter

1. **Motivation:** Have students review and compare the maps from Chapter 2 on pages 229 and 230. Note the expansive path of the Turkic conquests. Explain that while trade and power were important motivators, the expansion was empowered by the Muslim belief, "conquest in the name of Allah." Have students explain how they feel about political expansion and control in the name of religion. Use Christianity and Judaism as examples.

2. **Introduction**
a. Write the chapter vocabulary words on the chalkboard. Have students write each word and its glossary definition in their notebooks.
b. Direct students' attention to the chapter visuals. Have students preview the chapter by reading the photo captions and examining the art.
   Ask: How powerful were the Ottoman Turks? (very powerful) From what clues did you draw your conclusion? (The Turks conquered the Christian stronghold of Constantinople. The Ottoman Empire lasted from the time of Genghis Khan to the sixteenth century.)
c. Have students read the chapter Objective and the subhead questions. Have students look at the chapter time line.
d. Have students read the chapter.

3. **Review and Recall:** After the students have read the chapter:
a. Hold a "Vocabulary Bee" using the new vocabulary words and the vocabulary words from chapters 1 and 2.
b. Have them reread and answer the Objective question and the subhead questions.
c. Hold a class discussion on the important Turkic leaders and their contributions: Togrul, Alp Arslan, Mahik Shah, Mohammad I, Selim I, and Suleiman I.

4. **Building Social Studies Skills:** Explain to students that reading a map is a skill that will help them to master information. Have students use the unit maps and/or maps from an encyclopedia or atlas as an aid in drawing, coloring, and coding their own maps of the Turkic conquests. Tell them to include the invasion paths of the Turks in the Middle East, Asia Minor, Palestine, Persia, Anatolia, Greece, and Constantinople.

5. **Extension**
a. Divide students into small groups. Have each group research and write a report comparing and contrasting Suleiman I with a contemporary "visionary" leader such as John F. Kennedy, Martin Luther King, Jr., Pope John XXIII, or Indira Gandhi.
b. Tamerlane posed a temporary setback for the Ottomans when he seized western Anatolia in 1402. Have students research Tamerlane's campaigns against the Turks and report their findings to the class.

Support Materials

Assignments can include:
1. Chapter Review, pp. 238-239
2. Blackline Masters, R 61 and R 62
3. Test 5-3, p. T31

CHAPTER 4   African Empires

Overview   The Sahara Desert served as an early highway of trade in salt and gold between the Berbers of North Africa and the people of the Sudan. Many people grew rich from this early trade, and towns and cities grew into large and powerful empires. The influences of Islam spread across the continent, and art, architecture, and academics flourished. Between A.D. 500 and 1500, civilization prospered and new empires in Africa grew and collapsed and grew again. In the fifteenth century, the arrival of the Europeans influenced and changed this course of growth.

Objectives

1. To locate the early civilizations that developed south of the Sahara and to describe their achievements.
2. To identify how the great trading empires developed in early West Africa.
3. To describe the golden age of Timbuktu.
4. To compare the city-states of West and East Africa with the great African empires.

Developing the Chapter

1. Motivation: Preview the chapter maps on page 246 and the Atlas map on page 725. Have students imagine traveling across the Sahara Desert. Explain that people in West Africa lived simple farming lives until the salt and gold trade began. Have students speculate on how life would change for these simple farmers as a result of a flourishing trade. Also have students locate Africa's early empires. Students should note that the location of these cultures is south of the Sahara Desert. Explain how the Sahara served as a barrier that cut off the early Africans from contacts across the Mediterranean.

2. Introduction
a. Write the names of the major early African trading and cultural cities on the chalkboard. Have students copy the names in their notebooks and take notes on them as they read the chapter.
b. Have students read the chapter Objective and the subhead questions.
c. Have students read the chapter time line and photo captions. Tell them to preview

the historical period by examining the chapter visuals.
d. Have students read the chapter.

3. Review and Recall: After the students have read the chapter:
a. Have them reread and answer the chapter Objective and subhead questions.
b. Have them compare and contrast early African empires.
c. Have them identify early African rulers.
d. Ask them to compile a list of dates and characteristics for each early West African kindgom covered in the chapter—Ghana, Mali, and Songhai.

4. Building Social Studies Skills: Have students create their own time line of an early African empire of their choice. Instruct them to include the following items on their time line: the name of the capital city, the name of the ruler, and something for which the city or ruler is remembered.

5. Extension
a. Have a few students borrow some albums of African folk songs (in Swahili, if possible) from the local library. As a class, learn an African folk song.
b. Divide students into cooperative groups. Review the People in History feature on Mansa Musa. Then have the groups plan a modern-day pilgrimage to Mecca. Have them answer the questions why, when, where, and how in their plans. Have each group share its plans with the rest of the class.
c. Ask students to compare life in the early kingdoms of West Africa with life in Western Europe at this time. Students should note that Ghana, Mali, and Songhai had achieved a level of sophistication still unknown in western Europe.

Support Materials

Assignments can include:
1. Chapter Review, pp. 246-247
2. Workbook, p. 38
3. Blackline Masters R63 and R64
4. Test 5-4, p. T32

CHAPTER 5   Mogul India

Overview   Mogul Turkic invaders took advantage of a long period of political unrest in India. In 1186 Qutb ud-Din Aibak conquered Delhi and the surrounding areas and established a large kingdom known as the Delhi Sultanate. Hindu temples were destroyed, Indians were forced to convert to Islam, and Qutb and later sultans lived lavishly off Indian lands, taxes, and profits. Hindus and Turks were uneasy neighbors. Later, new Muslim invaders from Mongolia took control of most of northern India. The area became known as the Mongol or Mogul Empire. During this period India experienced political and religious conflict.

Objectives

1. To explain how Muslim invaders succeeded in conquering northern India.
2. To compare the Delhi Sultanate to the Mogul Empire.
3. To identify differences and similarities in Islam and Hindu lifestyles.

Developing the Chapter

1. **Motivation:** Talk to the students about the differences in Islam and Hindu religion and lifestyle. Ask them how they would feel if a large religious group invaded the United States and forced its religion and lifestyle on Americans while growing rich and powerful from U.S. resources. Explain that this is what happened when Muslim invaders conquered Hindu India, making the people convert to Islam.

2. **Introduction**
a. Write the chapter vocabulary words on the chalkboard. Have students define the words as they read the chapter.
b. Have students read the chapter Objective and the subhead questions.
c. Have students read the chapter.

3. **Review and Recall:** After the students have read the chapter:
a. Have them reread and answer the chapter Objective and subhead questions.
b. Have them read aloud The Arts & Artifacts feature and look at the picture of the Taj Mahal on page 252. Ask them to recall specifics of the life of Shah Jahan, his marriage, the Taj Mahal, and his death. Then have them answer the feature questions in a classroom discussion.
c. Have them quiz each other on the definitions of the new vocabulary words.
d. Have them make a table or chart of the similarities and differences between Muslims and Hindus (reference paragraphs 8 and 9, page 250).

4. **Building Social Studies Skills:** Explain that keeping a journal is a good way to develop your writing skills. Have each student write a "diary entry" telling how he or she might have felt as a Hindu living under the rule of Qutb ud-Din Aibak.

5. **Extension**
a. Have students use reference books and their textbooks to prepare a report that compares the Indian caste system with Apartheid in South Africa.
b. Discuss the Spotlight on Sources. Talk further about memoirs, asking students if they have read the memoirs of a famous person and, if so, to share anecdotes from these memoirs with the class. Read some examples from other famous memoirs to the class. Have students write a brief memoir of their own about an important event in their life.
c. Divide students into two groups. Have one group research women's role in Hindu society and have the other group research women's role in Muslim society. Ask students to act out or role-play their findings.
d. Remind students that much of the work of the artists of ancient India reflected the beliefs of Hinduism and Buddhism.
  Ask: Was religion an influence in the works of artists in other civilizations you studied? Have students answer the question in a written report based on library research.

Support Materials

Assignments can include:
1. Chapter Review, pp. 254-255
2. Blackline Masters R65 and R66
3. Test 5-5, p. T33

CHAPTER 6 Isolationism in China and Japan

Overview After a Mongol invasion and dynasty in northern China during the thirteenth century, the Mongols were driven out and China returned to native rule with the 1368 founding of the Ming Dynasty. This dynasty lasted 300 years and brought a period of prosperity, trade, and cultural achievement to China. Chinese trade with Europe and other nations ceased in the 1400s when the nation became isolationist. The Ming Dynasty ended when the Manchus of Manchuria conquered China in 1644. Around the same time, Ieyasu started a line of shoguns that ruled Japan for 250 years. These strict and forceful leaders brought peace and prosperity to Japan, where art, culture, and education flourished. China and Japan each built strong and rich cultures; but because of their isolationist policies, these nations fell behind the Western world in science and technology.

Objectives

1. To identify early trade routes of China and Japan.
2. To explain why China and Japan chose isolationism.
3. To list cultural achievements of both nations.
4. To describe China under foreign rule.

Developing the Chapter

1. **Motivation:** Talk with students about kabuki. Have them brainstorm about what it would have been like for a common peasant to be able to share Japanese life and culture with family and friends in the intimate surroundings of a small, outdoor theater production of music, dance, and acting. **Ask:** What might a kabuki play have been about? Point out that the Japanese and Chinese are immensely proud of their culture and traditions. Ask students how isolationism might have fostered this pride.

2. **Introduction**
a. Write the chapter vocabulary words on the chalkboard. Have students write the words in their notebooks and define them as they read the chapter.

b. Have students read the Objective question and the subhead questions.

3. **Review and Recall:** After the students have read the chapter:
a. Have them reread and answer the Objective and subhead questions.
b. Have them list the cultural achievements of China and Japan.
c. Have them describe China under foreign rule.

4. **Building Social Studies Skills:** Explain to students that outlining is an important tool for organizing information. Assign an outline of China's dynasties from 1200 to 1600. Guide students through the Yuan Dynasty as an example.

5. **Extension**
a. Divide students into three cooperative groups. Assign each group a Japanese skill: samurai, karate, or judo. Have students research the skill and explain how it fits into the Japanese philosophy of "simple living and discipline."
b. Have students find source material from Confucius. Have them write a "saying" based on Confucianism and share it with the class.
c. Ask students to explain the role played by the Mongols in both India and China. (You may wish to divide students into groups— one to research India, the other China.) Create a comparison/contrast chart on the chalkboard as the roles are discussed. (Sample answers: Mongols in India united more of the region, gave Hindus greater freedom, reduced taxes under Akbar, and started schools. They gave India its most brilliant period in which all facets of culture flourished. In China, Mongols restored peace and order, increased trade between East and West, and built roads.)

Support Materials

Assignments can include:
1. Chapter Review, pp. 262-263
2. Workbook, p. 39
3. Blackline Masters R67 and R68
4. Test 5-6, p. T34
5. Source Reading S15

CHAPTER 7 Civilizations of the Americas

Overview   Three great civilizations—the Maya, the Aztec, and the Inca—developed and prospered in the early Americas. While these civilizations were isolated from each other they held in common the importance of corn and sun, of religion and the foundation of great cities. Stonework, art and jewel work, and the rudiments of writing, counting, and calendars can be traced to these early civilizations.

Objectives

1. To list the achievements of the Maya, Aztec, and Inca civilizations.
2. To compare and contrast the early civilizations of the Americas.
3. To explain the importance of religion and gods in these early civilizations.

Developing the Chapter

1. Motivation: Talk about the terrain, the conditions, and the lack of technology in the early Americas. Have students imagine how cities were built, roads were made, and canals were dug without benefit of the wheel, draft animals, or sophisticated machinery and tools. Then refer students to the unit opening visual of Machu Picchu on page 219. Discuss the knowledge of engineering and mathematics required to produce the city. Point out to students the high mountains surrounding Machu Picchu. Ask students what this tells them about the environment of the ancient Incas.

2. Introduction

a. Write the chapter vocabulary words on the chalkboard. Have students write the words in their notebooks and define them as they read the chapter.
b. Have students read the chapter Objective and the subhead questions.
c. Have students read the chapter.

3. Review and Recall: After the students have read the chapter:

a. Hold a vocabulary "Bee" using all the new words in Unit 5.
b. Reread and have volunteers answer the chapter Objective question and the subhead questions.

c. Have them name, locate, and give one accomplishment of each of the three early civilizations.

4. Building Social Studies Skills: Explain to students that note-taking is an important skill for mastering chapter content and studying for a test. Guide students through note-taking on the section on the Maya civilization. Then have students take notes on the Aztecs and Incas.

5. Extension

a. Divide students into cooperative groups. Have each group locate a story in a library book from or about one of the early civilizations. Have students share the story with the rest of the class orally, dramatically, or as a game.
b. Divide the class into three groups and have each group research the achievements of the Maya, Aztecs, or Incas. Once they have done the research in their groups, call upon volunteers to report their findings. Place student responses on the chalkboard in chart form, and have students copy the completed chart into their notebooks for use as a study aid.
c. Many states in the United States have geographic place names that are Indian words or names. Have students construct a list of such names based on library research.
d. Have students research and draw the early Mayan calendar.
e. Corn was an essential part of life for the early Maya, Aztecs, and Incas. Have students do further research on its importance and share with the rest of the class a story of its cultivation and trade and its use in a recipe.

Support Materials

Assignments can include:
1. Chapter Review, pp. 270-271
2. Workbook, pp. 40-42
3. Blackline Masters R69 and R70
4. Test 5-7, p. T35
5. Source Reading S16

The Birth of Modern Europe

Unit Overview   In the 1300s to about 1600 the Renaissance spread from Italy to the rest of Europe, bringing a rebirth of learning. In the same period the Reformation brought the birth of Protestant faiths. Government changed too, as Europe moved from feudalism toward centralized governments. Strong governments and the curiosity that the Renaissance nurtured led to the Age of Exploration. Meanwhile, by the 1600s the Holy Roman Empire had declined. A few years later, Europe erupted in the Thirty Years War. In the years that followed, both Russia and Prussia rose to become world powers.

Unit Objectives

1. To identify key features of the Renaissance and its connection to the Age of Exploration.
2. To compare the rise of western monarchies with the later rise of Russia and Prussia.
3. To describe developments in religion that led to the Reformation and the decline of the Holy Roman Empire.

Unit Introduction

1. Motivation: Have students review what they know abut the Middle Ages in Europe. **Ask:**How was society organized? What was religious life like? How much did people know about the world around them? Then ask them to imagine what might happen to the feudal world if these events occurred: (a) Outspoken people begin to question the power of the Catholic Church. (b) Certain kings become more powerful than other kings. (c) People want to find a new way to travel to the East for spices.

2. Visual: Ask students for ideas in response to the question in the student's book. Help them to realize that the picture expresses several important themes of the period of time they will study in Unit 6. The style of the painting is typical of the early Italian Renaissance painting, with its detailed rendering of people, buildings, and clothing. Venice was a powerful city-state and an important center of art, trade, commerce, and transportation during the Renaissance.

3. Time line: Ask the students to identify the first and last date mentioned on the time line. Explain that most of the events they will study in this chapter fall between 1400 and 1600. Point out that Dante's *Divine Comedy* and other achievements that belong to the spirit of the Renaissance took place well before 1400. For this reason, scholars do not always agree on exact dates for the Renaissance.

Unit Activities

1. Cooperative Learning: Divide students into teams. Each team should choose one historical event discussed in the unit to illustrate. Ask students first to review everything in the unit about that event. They can divide their teams into researchers and artists. The researchers should find out details about the event that would make the illustration more interesting and authentic. Set a target date for each group to show their illustrations and comment on what they learned.

2. Completing a Chart: Draw the outline of a chart on a large sheet of paper and attach it to the bulletin board. Write these headings across the top: France, Spain, Russia, Germany, Great Britain. Then write these headings on the side: Government, Relations with Other Nations, Strengths, Religion. Have students work in groups to complete the chart as they study Unit 6. Each group is responsible for one country. After the chart is complete, ask students to draw at least one conclusion from the chart.

Support Materials

Assignments can include:

1. Unit 6 Review, pp. 324–325
2. Unit 6 Test, pp. UT11–UT12
3. Unit 6 ESL/LEP Worksheet 1, p. ESL 11
4. Unit 6 ESL/LEP Worksheet 2, p. ESL 12

CHAPTER 1   The Renaissance

Overview   From the 1300s to about 1600, Europe experienced a rebirth in learning known as the Renaissance. During this time, people sought to revive the achievements of the ancient Greeks and Romans while at the same time exploring new ideas. The Renaissance began in Italy and spread throughout Europe. It brought great achievements in art, literature, and philosophy.

Objectives

1. To list the main features of the Renaissance.
2. To name major artists and writers of the Renaissance.
3. To describe the influence of the Medici family on Renaissance Italy.

Developing the Chapter

1. Motivation: Read aloud the biography of Isabella d'Este below. Then ask students if they think d'Este was unusual. If so, why?

Isabella d'Este was born in 1474 to a noble family. As a child she received an education that included Greek, Latin, music, dancing, and embroidery. At age 16, Isabella married a man who became the ruler of Mantua. She became a patron of the arts and collector of paintings, music, and books. She herself wrote over 2,000 letters in which she expressed her ideas about art, politics, and the famous people of the day with whom she was acquainted. Isabella was so talented, witty, and intelligent, she was known as "first lady of the world."

2. Introduction

a. Write sentences on the chalkboard using each vocabulary word from the chapter. (You might want to use the sentences in the Chapter Review as a guide.) Have students try to determine the words' meanings from context clues.
b. Tell students that the word renaissance means "rebirth." Ask what they think was reborn in the 1300s.
c. Have students read the Objective question. Then ask them to read the chapter.

3. Review and Recall: After students have read the chapter:

a. Divide the class into teams to play "Who Am I?" based on the people discussed in the chapter. The person pretending to be a Renaissance figure must answer yes-and-no questions posed by the other team until the team guesses the identity of the figure. The team that makes the most correct guesses wins.
b. Have students re-read each subhead question and answer it.
c. Have students make up a crossword puzzle using words and ideas from the chapter. After they have written all the Down and Across clues, they might try to solve each other's puzzles.

4. Building Social Studies Skills: Have students look closely at the map on page 280. **Ask:** What is the map about? If you wanted to travel from Milan to Rome, in which direction would you travel? About how far is Genoa from Florence? What bodies of water might you use to travel from Venice to Barcelona?

5. Extension

a. In small groups, have the students plan a Renaissance art exhibit. (You might bring to class some art books to help them.) Within the group, students can decide whether each member will concentrate on a particular artist or a certain work of art. Together the group should decide which works of art to include in the exhibit and they should write a catalogue telling about each one.
b. Have students plan and perform a skit about the Renaissance. They should assume that the audience has no knowledge about the period; the skit should provide information.

Support Materials

Assignments can include:

1. Chapter Review, pp. 282–283
2. Workbook, p. 43
3. Blackline Masters, R71 and R72
4. Test 6-1, p. T36
5. Source Readings S17 and S18.

CHAPTER 2   Protestant Reformation

Overview   By the late 1400s, corrupt practices had become common among the clergy of the Catholic Church, the most powerful institution in Europe. These included bribery of church officials and the sale of indulgences. Martin Luther issued the 95 theses as a protest against the sale of indulgences. His action began the Protestant Reformation. A variety of new Protestant churches emerged. The Catholic Church reacted against the Reformation and reformed itself in the Counter-Reformation.

Objectives

1. To describe the situation that led to the Reformation.
2. To identify Martin Luther's actions that sparked the Reformation.
3. To explain how political and church leaders reacted to Luther's ideas.

Developing the Chapter

1. **Motivation:** Have students list the Protestant churches in their community. Ask them to share what they know about the beliefs and origins of each church. Tell them they are going to read a chapter about a time when the Roman Catholic Church was very powerful. Changes in the church were as significant as a political revolution.

2. **Introduction**
   a. Write the chapter's vocabulary words on the chalkboard. Have students write the words and their glossary meanings in their vocabulary notebooks.
   b. Have students read the chapter title and objective question. Solicit a definition of **reform**. Ask what they think the chapter will be about.
   c. Have students read the chapter.

3. **Review and Recall:** After the students have read the chapter:
   a. Have students identify the main idea in each subsection.
   b. Have students reread and answer the chapter's Objective question.
   c. Name these people and have students tell something about them: Erasmus, Martin

Luther, Pope Leo X, Emperor Charles V, John Calvin, Theresa of Avila.
   d. Ask students to review the reading by Erasmus on page 287.
   Ask: What was Erasmus objecting to in the behavior of the clergy? (greed) What abuses of church practice did this lead to? (bribes, sale of indulgences) What happened as a result? (efforts at reform; eventually, the Reformation)

4. **Building Social Studies Skills:** Have students practice their outlining skills by preparing an outline of two or more subsections of this chapter. (You might want to review with them the information on making an outline on page 282 before they begin.)

5. **Extension**
   a. Have students form groups to research and write a newspaper about the Diet of Worms. The newspaper should include at least one article, one editorial, and one feature story. Ask the students to share ideas of what makes interesting news reporting before they begin. For example, the reporters might include interviews with Luther himself or with persons holding opposing views.
   b. Have individuals or groups of students make a series of illustrations to accompany this chapter. The students should write a caption to go with each illustration. Illustrations might include: a cathedral or church, Luther nailing his theses to the church door, Luther speaking at the Diet of Worms, the Peasant's War, Theresa of Avila visiting a convent.
   c. Provide students with a blank map of Europe. One the map have them locate the places mentioned in the chapter.

Support Materials

   Assignments can include:

1. Chapter Review, pp. 288–289.
2. Workbook, p. 44.
3. Blackline Masters R73 and R74.
4. Test 6-2, p. T37.

UNIT 6

CHAPTER 3   Western Monarchies and City-States

Unit Overview   After the age of feudalism, new government arrangements developed in Europe. In Italy, City-States gained power. In Spain, a strong monarchy gradually emerged; by the 1500s Spain had become the most powerful country in Europe. In England, a limited monarchy developed: the king or queen shared power with an elected Parliament. France was ruled by an absolute monarch.

Objectives

1. To compare the government of England, Spain, and France with the government of Italy.
2. To identify important rulers in Europe up to the 1600s.
3. To describe key developments in political history in Europe to the 1600s.

Developing the Chapter

1. Motivation: Direct students to the picture of the palace of Versailles on page 297. Tell them that the palace was commissioned by King Louis XIV of France and took 35,000 workers and 27 years to build. It cost Louis half the taxes collected each year to maintain the court there.

Ask: How might the palace be seen as symbolic of King Louis's rule in France?

2. Introduction

a. Write the chapter's vocabulary words on the chalkboard. Have students copy the words and use the glossary to find their meanings. Then ask students to classify the words in their own categories (for example, government leaders; military terms).

b. Have students read the chapter title. Ask them to read the Objective question and review what sorts of governments existed in western Europe during feudalism.

c. Have students read the chapter.

3. Review and Recall: After students have read the chapter:

a. Prepare flash cards to help students review the chapter. On one side of each card, write England, France, Spain, or Italy; on the other side, write a feature of the country's

political history as discussed in this chapter. Pairs of students might use the flash cards together, or you could show them to the whole class and let students volunteer answers.

b. Have students re-read each subhead question and answer it.

c. Have students read the "A Geographic View of History" feature aloud. Ask them to look closely at the map. Then have them discuss the feature questions orally or answer them as a writing exercise.

4. Building Social Studies Skills: Have students read this excerpt written by a French Bishop in the late 1600s:

> "The royal throne is not the throne of a man, but the throne of God himself…It appears from …this that the person of the king is sacred, and that to attack him in any way is sacrilege…Therefore, the royal power is absolute."

Bishop Jacques Bousset, *Politics Drawn from the Words of Holy Scriptures*

Ask students to restate the quotation in their own words.

Ask: Would King Louis XIV have approved of these ideas? Would members of Parliament in England have approved? Explain your answers.

5. Extension

a. Have students find out more about court life at Versailles. They might prepare a written or oral report based on their findings.

b. Assign parts and have students read aloud all or part of *St. Joan* by George Bernard Shaw. Afterwards, discuss the usefulness of the play as a source of information about Joan of Arc and her times.

Support Materials

Assignments can include:

1. Chapter Review, pp. 298–299
2. Blackline Masters R75 and R76
3. Test 6-3, p. T38

T68

CHAPTER 4   The Discovery of Overseas Empires

Overview   Through the daring of early explorers, Europeans began to learn more about the world far from their shores. Portugal and Spain led the way. Spain set up colonies in the rich lands it found in the Americas. This inspired other European nations to do the same. Through its explorations and settlements, Europe learned a great deal about the Earth and its inhabitants.

Objectives

1. To explain how Portugal found an all-water route to Asia.
2. To tell why Columbus set sail west from Spain.
3. To explain why European countries set up colonies in the Americas.
4. To list results of European exploration and settlement of the Americas.

Developing the Chapter

1. Motivation: Lead a discussion about space exploration today.

Ask: What sort of people become astronauts? How do they prepare for their voyages? Would you consider becoming an astronaut? Why or why not? What would be your greatest fear in space travel? What would you expect to be your greatest achievement? Explain to students that space travel today is something like sea exploration in the 1400s. Much was unknown and frightening; yet some people still braved the unknown to satisfy their curiosity or desire for adventure.

2. Introduction
a. On the chalkboard write a sentence using each of the vocabulary words. Have students try to define the vocabulary word from the context. Use the glossary to look up those words the class does not know.
b. Have students read the chapter title and Objective question.
c. Have students read the chapter.

3. Review and Recall: After students have read the chapter:
a. Have them play a game of "Twenty Questions" abut people, places, or events discussed in the chapter.

b. Have students re-read each subhead question and answer it.
c. Have students read the "Art and Artifacts" feature aloud. Ask them to observe the photographs carefully and comment on them. Use the feature questions to stimulate a discussion, or assign them as a writing exercise.

4. Building Social Studies Skills: Have students study the chapter timeline.

Ask: What years are covered by the timeline? Who was the first explorer to voyage around the world? Which happened first—Cortez conquered Mexico or Columbus landed at San Salvador? Use material in the chapter to add at least three more events to the time line.

5. Extension
a. Have interested students learn facts about the ships used by early explorers. Then have them prepare a model or diagram of a typical ship.
b. Divide the class into two groups. Have the students in one group imagine they were Cortez or one of his soldiers. Have the students in the other group imagine they were Montezuma or one of his followers. Then ask the students to write a description of the first meeting between Cortez and Montezuma. The description should reflect the point of view of the "Spanish" or "Aztec" writer.
c. Have students prepare a television news broadcast about one of the events discussed in this chapter. They could include on-the-spot news reporters, interviews, and an anchor report.

Support Materials

Assignments can include:

1. Chapter Review pp. 308–309
2. Workbook pp. 45–47
3. Blackline Masters R77 and R78
4. Test 6-4, p. T39
5. Map Transparencies 13 and 14; and Activity Sheets A13 and A14
6. Source readings 519 and 520.

CHAPTER 5   The Holy Roman Empire

Overview   The Holy Roman Empire covered much of eastern and central Europe by the 1300s and was ruled by the *Habsburgs* for much of that time. But the empire had a number of difficulties in ruling the lands. Conflicts with the pope weakened the emperor. Local princes challenged the emperor's authority. In the 1600s, political and religious disputes erupted into the Thirty Years War, which devastated German.

Objectives

1. To list the factors that weakened the Holy Roman Emperor.
2. To describe the causes of the Thirty Years War.
3. To identify results of the Thirty Years War.

Developing the Chapter

1. Motivation: Have students read aloud the first half of the introductory paragraph on page 310. Lead a discussion about how they would feel in that situation. Then ask what strategies they might try, as club president, to get the club members to listen.

Ask: How might those strategies be adapted for use by a government leader in a similar situation?

2. Introduction

a. Write the chapter's vocabulary words on the chalkboard. Have students write each word and its glossary meaning in their vocabulary notebooks.
b. Have students read the chapter title and Objective question. Suggest they work together to form answers to the question. List their suggestions on the chalkboard. Refer to the suggestions after students have read the chapter so they can compare their answers with actual events.
c. Have students read the chapter.

3. Review and Recall: After students have read the chapter:

a. Have them review the chapter time line. Let them take turns describing the events named on the time line.
b. Have students ask each other questions about the chapter content.

c. Have students look closely at the picture on text page 313. Have students make up a title for the picture. Ask them to write a new caption for the picture.
d. Have students re-read each subhead question and answer it.

4. Building Social Studies Skills: Have students review the excerpt from Grotius on text page 313. Help them to restate Grotius's ideas in their own words. Then ask them to write a paragraph expressing their own opinions of Grotius's ideas. Remind them to give reasons for their opinions.

5. Extension

a. Have students use an encyclopedia or other source to learn more about the Thirty Years War. Then have them make a map showing some of the major areas of fighting during the war. Help them make a map key to identify symbols used on a map.
b. Have students work in small groups to prepare "conversations" among some of the people discussed in this chapter—for example, Emperor Maximilian I, Emperor Henry IV, Pope Gregory VII, Emperor Charles IV, and King Gustavus Adolphus of Sweden. They could write out or perform the "conversation."
c. Have students design a board game based on the information in this chapter. They should decide how many people can play, the object of the game, how to win, and other playing rules.
d. Have students look up the family tree of the Habsburgs. Most large encyclopedias have this information. They might transfer one or more branches of the tree to a chart and briefly explain to the class what their chart shows about how the influence of the Habsburgs spread.

Support Materials

Assignments can include:

1. Chapter Review pp. 314–315
2. Blackline Masters R79 and R80
3. Test 6-5, p. T40

UNIT 6

CHAPTER 6   The Rise of Russia and Prussia

Overview   The Romanovs in Russia and the Hohenzollerns in Prussia transformed their countries into world powers. Peter the Great and Catherine the Great used absolute power to westernize Russia and expand its territory. In Prussia, the Great Elector and Frederick William I turned a backward land into a centralized nation with a strong military.

Objectives

1. To identify the changes brought to Russia by Peter the Great and Catherine the Great.
2. To define "enlightened despot" and distinguish the ideal from the reality in Russia and Prussia.
3. To describe the changes brought to Prussia by the Great Elector and Frederick William I.

Developing the Chapter

1. Motivation: Direct students to the picture on page 316. Tell them that Peter also made laws governing the clothing people should wear. His goal was to make Russia more like western countries. Ask students how they would feel if they were no longer allowed to wear their favorite fashions. (You might name specific articles of clothing or hairstyles to make the situation more real the them.)

Ask: Why do you think clothing and hair styles are so significant? What do these things have to do with who we are or how we want people to think of us?

2. Introduction

a. Write the chapter's vocabulary words on the chalkboard. Have students look up each word in the glossary. Then have students suggest sentences using the words. These sentences should show an understanding of the word.

b. Have students read the chapter title and locate Russia and Prussia on the map on page 319.

c. Have students read the Objective question.

d. Have students read the chapter.

3. Review and Recall: After students have read the chapter:

a. Have them work as a class to fill in a chart about the four rulers discussed in the chapter. The finished chart should contain the main characteristics of the reign of each ruler.

b. Have students re-read and answer the chapter's Objective question.

c. Ask students questions about the chapter content.

4. Building Social Studies Skills: Have students make notes about the main ideas and accomplishments of the Great Elector and Frederick William I. (Or ask them to review the relevant parts of the chart they prepared in the Introduction activity.) Then ask them to write a paragraph comparing and contrasting the reigns of the two Prussian rulers.

5. Extension

a. Have students find out more about the city of St. Petersburg. They should find out how the city was built and how it has changed since it was built. Have them present their findings to the class.

b. Divide the class into two groups to conduct a debate. Have each group prepare one side of this statement: Catherine the Great did more good than harm for Russia.

c. Have students imagine that they lived in Prussia at the time of Frederick William I. Have them draw a political cartoon showing their point of view about Frederick William's rule in general or about one specific policy. You might want to make a bulletin board display of the cartoons.

Support Materials

Assignments can include:

1. Chapter Review pp. 322–323.
2. Workbook pp. 48–50.
3. Blackline Masters R81 and R82.
4. Test 6-6, p. T41.
5. Map Transparency 15 and Activity Sheet A15.

Natural Rights and Revolution

Unit Overview: During the late 1500s, scientists began to develop new ways of working based on experimentation. The world's place in the universe began to be understood for the fist time. Philosophers were influenced by the advances in science and sought ways to put scientific reasoning to work in solving problems of society. People began to question the rights of the aristocracy. A sweeping series of revolutions took place. In America, the British colonies rebelled against the king and won a War for Independence. In France, a revolution resulted in the displacement of the monarchy with a new republic that promised greater equity for all citizens. The countries of Latin America rebelled and won independence from Europe in the early 1800s.

Unit Objectives

1. To describe how scientists and philosophers developed new ways of thinking in the 1600s and 1700s.
2. To explain how new ideas inspired leaders to effect changes in societies of the 1700s and early 1800s.
3. To compare the revolutions in North America, France, and Latin America in the late 1700s and early 1800s.

Unit Introduction

1. Motivation: Bring into class a photograph of yourself when you were a teenager and one of yourself today.

Ask: Why do people look and act differently when they grow older? (growth, learning more about themselves, and so on) Lead the discussion to Europe in the late 1700s and 1800s. Tell students that people in Europe at this time were starting to think and act differently.

2. Visual: Ask students what emotions are shown in the expressions of people in the unit opener painting. They may notice fear, respect, admiration, and distrust. Explain that Napoleon, the central figure in the painting, was a military leader who conquered much of Europe during the early 1800s.

Ask: What reactions do people normally have to strong leaders? Encourage students to give examples of public figures of today who inspire varying reactions.

3. Time line: Ask students to look over the unit time line for familiar names. Identify unfamiliar figures for the students and explain that they will be learning about the importance of these people's work in their study of Unit 7.

Ask: What activities seem to be most prominent in the early part of the time line? Students should notice that writings and scientific discoveries seem to be important in the early part of the time line. Next draw attention to the latter part of the time line. Students should notice that various countries achieved independence during the late 1700s and 1800s.

Ask: Do you think there could be a cause and effect relationship here? How might the early scientific discoveries and writing on philosophy have affected political life?

Unit Activities

1. Cooperative Learning: Have the students work together to create news sheets of facts about life in the 1800s. Divide the class into five groups and assign each group one of these topics: art, music, fashion, furnishings, men, or women. Each group will produce one news sheet. Students in each group should divide up tasks as follows: research, writing, artwork, and print and layout. Set target dates for each group to distribute its news sheet to the class.

2. Research: Have the students do research to write a short biography of one of the following personalities of the eighteenth century. *Thinkers*: Isaac Newton, Jean Jacques Rousseaur; *Radicals*: Miguel Hidalgo, Samuel Adams, Robespierre; *Military Leaders*: George Washington, Napoleon, Simon Bolivar. Have the students conclude their biographies by explaining in what way this person represents the spirit of his time.

Support Materials

Assignments can include:

1. Unit Review, pp. 366–367
2. Unit 7 Test, pp. UT13–UT14
3. Unit 7 ESL/LEP Worksheet 1, p. ESL 13
4. Unit 7 ESL/LEP Worksheet 2, p. ESL 14

CHAPTER 1   Scientific Revolution

Overview   In the 1500s and 1600s a Scientific Revolution took place in Europe. Ideas about nature were no longer accepted without being tested through careful measurement and experimentation. This new approach led to a rapid increase in scientific knowledge and opened new fields of science. The important work of Galileo, Newton, and other scientists of this period changed the way people viewed the world around them.

Objectives

1. To explain how and why scientists changed their way of thinking during the 1500s and 1600s.
2. To identify the contributions made by scientists during the Scientific Revolution.
3. To describe how a better understanding of the laws governing the universe helped many branches of scientific knowledge to grow.

Developing the Chapter

1. **Motivation:** Ask students to think of machines they use often. Some examples might be hair dryers, cars, televisions, and computers. Discuss what their lives would be like without these machines. Tell the students that many of these machines would not have been conceived without the scientific discoveries made in the 1500s and 1600s. Have students read the introduction to Chapter 1.

2. **Introduction:**
   a. Have student read the chapter title. Ask them to define **revolution**. Have the students look at the time line on page 328 to find out when the Scientific Revolution took place. **Ask:** What might have caused such a rapid change in science at this time? (Students might refer to the Renaissance or the religious upheaval of the times.) Then have them read the Objective question. Direct them to look at the chapter subheads for a clue about the kind of discoveries and changes made during the period.
   b. Ask the students to find the definitions of the vocabulary terms in the Glossary on pages 728-738 and write them in their notebooks.

Ask: Which method of reasoning do you think a modern scientist would use? (inductive reasoning)

3. **Review and Recall:** After the students have read the chapter:
Have the students apply their understanding of the scientific method by asking them to describe how each of the following phenomenon might have been explained before and after the Scientific Revolution—the phases of the moon and the refraction of light in a glass. (Students should note that before the Revolution, scientific ideas were formed chiefly from observation, while after the revolution observations were tested to see if they were accurate.)

5. **Building Social Studies Skills:** Have students determine where on the time line on page 324 the following discoveries would be placed. (a) 1628: William Harvey discovers how blood circulates in the human body; (b) 1780–81: Lavoisier discovers the true nature of fire; (c) 1665: Leeuwenhoek reveals the structure of living matter.

5. **Extension:**
   a. Have a colleague who teachers chemistry or physics demonstrate in a laboratory setting some of the discoveries made by early scientists such as Isaac Newton and Antoine Lavoisier.
   b. Have each student choose one discovery from the chapter to research further. They should imagine that they are the scientist and write a letter describing their own reaction to the discovery and explaining its importance.

Support Materials

Assignments can include:

1. Chapter Review, pp. 332–333
2. Workbook p. 51
3. Blackline Masters, R83 and R84
4. Test 7-1, p. T43.

CHAPTER 2   The Age of Reason

Overview   During the Enlightenment in the late 1600's and the 1700's, the ideas of the Scientific Revolution influenced other areas of thought. Enlightenment thinkers believed that reason could be used to solve human problems and help to improve people's lives. Some used scientific reasoning to develop theories of government and the nature of society. New ways of thinking about rights and authority encouraged some monarchs to initiate reforms.

Objectives

1. To compare Thomas Hobbes's view of society and the role of government with that of John Locke.
2. To identify the ideas of the French philosophes.
3. To explain how the ideas of the Enlightenment spread and influenced society.

Developing the Chapter

1. **Motivation:** Open the lesson by playing a current popular song that shows a sharp contrast to the ordered and balanced tone of the music of the 1700s. Then play Bach's *Brandenburg Concerto No. 4.* Ask the students to compare Bach's music to the contemporary song. Tell students that the concerto is an example of a style of music developed in the late seventeenth century. This style emphasized balance of form and clarity of sound. The presence of order in music reflected an appreciation of order and reason in all aspects of life in the 1600s and 1700s.

2. **Introduction** Have students infer from the Objective question and from the Motivation discussion the meaning of the chapter title, "The Age of Reason."

3. **Review and Recall:** After the students have read the chapter:

a. Read the portion of the *Declaration of Independence* which begins "We hold these truths to be self-evident…" Identify the document and when it was written. **Ask:** Which Enlightenment ideas do you recognize in this document? (The document was primarily influenced by the ideas of John Locke, although students also

might recognize the idea of Rousseau's social contract.)

b. Have students look through the chapter for the names of the philosophers discussed. Write the names in a list on the chalkboard, then have volunteers name one idea or contribution for each thinker.

4. **Building Social Studies Skills:** Have students analyze Voltaire's view of equality cited in Spotlight on Sources. After they have read the excerpt once, **Ask:** What about the human condition does not make much sense to Voltaire? (one humans's dependence on another) Which lines show Voltaire's wit? ("But man…—what?") (c) Which of the two— slavery or royalty— do you think Voltaire would object to? (slavery)

5. **Extension**

a. Rousseau's philosophy was influenced by his personal experiences. Have students write a paragraph or two describing how their experiences so far have influenced their own view of the world and human nature. They might also compare their own philosophy with that of Rousseau.

b. The witty use of words was prized during the Enlightenment. Have students look up some sayings from the 1700s in *Bartlett's Familiar Quotations*. They should choose saying that they feel express the spirit of the Enlightenment especially well and turn them into posters.

Support Materials

Assignments can include:

1. Chapter Review, pp. 340–341
2. Blackline Masters, R85 and R86
3. Test 7-2, p. T44
4. Source Reading S24.

CHAPTER 3   American and French
Revolutions

Overview   A cry for representation in
Parliament led colonial Americans to fight for
their independence from Britain. America's
revolution created a new democratic society
that changed the way people thought about
government. In France, the people organized
themselves against their king, formed a new
government, took away the special rights of
their aristocracy, and declared all people free
and equal. Soon after, radical leaders ended
the monarchy, executed the king, and made
France a republic. Anyone suspected of
working against the radical government was
treated harshly.

Objectives

1. To explain why and how the Americans
   fought a war for independence.
2. To identify the results of the American
   Revolution.
3. To explain why the French revolted against
   the monarchy.
4. To trace the course of the French
   Revolution to the death of Robespierre.

Developing the Chapter

1. **Motivation:** Ask students to describe how
   and why they celebrate on July 4th every year.
   Then ask them to examine the photograph on
   page 342 and read the caption. Have them
   describe what is being celebrated in the
   photograph. Tell the students that both July
   4th and July 14th are celebrated to
   commemorate the outcomes of revolutions
   that took place over 200 years ago.

2. **Introduction:**
a. Direct the students to read the chapter title
   and the objective question. To find out how
   America changed as a result of its
   revolution, tell students to read the
   subheads titles that cover the American
   Revolution. **Ask:** How did the revolution
   change America? (from colony to
   independent nation)
b. Have the students look up the chapter's
   vocabulary words in the Glossary on pages
   728–738.

Ask: Which of these words describes
France before the revolution? (Old Regime)
Which of these words describes one way
France might have changed as a result of
the revolution? (constitutional monarchy).

3. **Review and Recall:** After the students
   have read the chapter:
a. List the following years on the chalkboard:
   1763, 1764, 1765, 1774, 1775, 1776, 1777,
   1778, 1779, 1781, 1783, 1789. Ask individual
   students to write an event important to the
   American Revolution or the forming of a
   new nation next to each of these years.
   Have the students determine where on the
   time line on page 342 the events would be
   placed. Then ask students to name the
   events on the time line that are related to
   the French Revolution and to recall why
   each was significant.

4. **Building Social Studies Skills:** Ask
   students to look up the French Revolution in
   the index on pages 739–749. Have them cite
   the pages on which the Revolution is
   mentioned. Instruct them to write a
   paragraph about the French Revolution using
   the information on these pages.

5. **Extension:**
a. Have students look up the full texts of the
   Declaration of Independence and the
   *Declaration of the Rights of Man and
   Citizen*. Ask them to compare the two.
b. Have the students read about the life of
   Marie Antionette. Based on what they
   learn, ask them to write a letter that she
   might have written to the people of France
   the night before she was guillotined in
   Paris.

Support Materials

Assignments can include:

1. Chapter Review, pp. 350–351
2. Workbook, pp. 52–53
3. Blackline Masters R87 and R88
4. Test 7-3, p. T45
5. Source reading S21.

CHAPTER 4   Napoleon's Empire

Overview   1n 1799, Napoleon overturned the Directory government in a coup d'etat. Three years later, he made himself emperor of France. Among the changes Napoleon made was a set laws that reflected many of the revolution's ideas. From 1807 to 1812, Napoleon ruled most of Europe. In 1813, the nations of Europe joined forces to defeat Napoleon. He escaped from prison in 1815 and returned to France, only to be finally defeated to Waterloo.

Objectives

1. To explain how and why Napoleon overturned the Directory government
2. To identify the changes Napoleon made as emperor.
3. To describe how Napoleon won an empire.
4. To explain how and why the nations of Europe overthrew Napoleon.

Developing the Chapter

1. **Motivation:** Have the students listen to the first movement to Beethoven's Symphony No. 3, *Eroica*. Tell the students that Beethoven originally dedicated this symphony to Napoleon, but later tore up the page on which the dedication was written. Have the students speculate why the composer did this.

2. **Introduction:**
a. Tell the students that the clue to why Beethoven decided not to dedicate his symphony to Napoleon is in the chapter title. The answer is in the introduction. Have the students read the introduction to the chapter.
b. Have individual students write the definition of each boldfaced term in the chapter on the chalkboard. Then isolate the terms dealing with government in the list. Have the students place these terms in the order in which the students believe they occurred in France when Napoleon seized power. (Directory, coup d'etat, plebiscite)

3. **Review and Recall:** After the students have read the chapter:
a. Have the students prove or disprove the following generalization: Napoleon's only interest was in his own power. (Students should note that Napoleon also incorporated the ideas of the Revolution in his government and spread these ideas across his empire.)
b. Have the students evaluate Napoleon's leadership qualities. Using Napoleon as a model, ask the students to devise a composite of a successful leader. (Some characteristics students might mention are taking risks, instilling loyalty, working quickly.) Students should back up each characteristic with a reference to Napoleon's career.

4. **Building Social Studies Skills:** Reproduce the excerpt in SPOTLIGHT ON SOURCES without the bracketed meanings for unfamiliar words. Distribute this version of the excerpts to the students. Have the students use context clues to guess the meaning of each unfamiliar word. You might give the students a set of three possible meanings from which to choose.

5. **Extension:**
a. Have students compare Napoleon I to Alexander the Great. Instruct the students to study the early lives, personalities, method of rule, and achievements of the two men. Have them draw some conclusions abut conquerors based on this comparison.
b. Napoleon's popularity influenced styles in the early 1800s. Have students work in groups to research the paintings, dress, architecture, furniture, and the decorative arts of the early nineteenth century, often called the "Empire" period. Each group should focus on one topic and present a pictorial report based on their findings.

Support Materials
   Assignments can include:
1. Chapter Review, pp. 356–357
2. Workbook, pp 54–55
3. Blackline Masters R89 and R90
4. Test 7-4, p. T46
5. Map Transparency 16 and Activity Sheet A16
6. Source readings S22 and S23.

UNIT 7

CHAPTER 5   Freedom for Latin America

Overview: Many Latin American colonists resented the wealth and prestige enjoyed by the Spanish-born living in America. When Napoleon conquered Spain, the colonists felt the time was right for revolution. The independence movement started in Mexico and spread south to Central America and South America. The leaders of the revolutions were Creoles and the fighters were Indians and Mestizos. Great differences between classes still remained after independence.

Objectives

1. To explain why the colonists of Latin America wanted independence from Spain.
2. To trace the course of the revolutions in Mexico, Central America, and South America.
3. To compare the struggle for independence in the Spanish colonies to those of the French and Portuguese colonies in Latin America.

Developing the Chapter

1. **Motivation**: Open the lesson on Chapter 5 by asking the students why Latin American history might be of special interest to North Americans.
   Ask: Why might the American Revolution have captured the interest of people in Latin America? Have the students examine the photograph on page 358 and read the caption.
   Ask: What do you think the South-American born did about their feelings of resentment? (revolted)

2. **Introduction:**
   a. Have the students determine the subject of the chapter by reading its title.
   b. Have the class write the definitions of the chapters boldfaced terms found in the Glossary in their notebooks.
   Ask: How would you group four of these terms? (groups of people in colonial Latin America) Which term does not belong to this group? (viceroyalties)

3. **Review and Recall:** After the students have read the chapter:
   a. Have the students use the main ideas from the chapter to help them evaluate the validity of the following generalizations. (1) The revolution in Latin America was a class struggle. (2) The revolution in Latin America was a fight for equality for all. (3) The fight for independence in Latin America would have failed had it been led by anyone but Creoles.

4. **Building Social Studies Skills:** Have the students imagine they are writing a research paper on the independence of Latin America. Ask them to write an introduction and conclusion to this paper. An introduction states what the subject of the paper is and what the writer wants to prove. The conclusion summarizes the main points of the paper.

5. **Extension:**
   a. Have students suppose they were either Miguel Hidalgo or Simon Bolivar. Ask them to write a declaration of independence as Hidalgo or Bolivar might have written one for his cause. After some students have read their documents aloud, discuss with the class the similarities and differences between each declaration.
   b. Have students report on the living conditions of the Indian and Mestizo populations in Latin America today. Ask them to evaluate conditions in light of what was learned in this chapter abut the role these groups played in the struggle for independence.

Support Materials

Assignments can include:

1. Chapter Review, pp. 364–365
2. Workbook, pp. 56–58
3. Blackline Masters, R91 and R92
4. Test 7-5, p. T47
5. Map Transparency 17 and Activity Sheet A17

UNIT 8

Nationalism and Unification

Unit Overview   The nineteenth century was an age of nationalism throughout Europe, though it took different forms in different countries. Early in the century the Congress of Vienna drew European boundaries and established rulers with an eye more to achieving a balance of power than to national aspirations. France saw a series of revolutions ending, in 1870, with the permanent establishment of a republic. Britain, through a series of reform bills, moved toward democracy. Russia continued as an autocratic regime, although the Revolution of 1905 finally forced a few reforms. Nationalist movements led to the unification of Italy under the king of Sardinia and of Germany under the king of Prussia and his chancellor Bismarck. Nationalist movements among the various peoples of the Austrian Empire led in 1867 to the establishment of the dual monarchy of Austria-Hungary, satisfying to Hungarian aspirations but not to the empire's many other nationalities. The Balkan peninsula was in continual ferment as nationalities broke away from the Ottoman Empire and sought to bring their compatriots still under Austrian rule into their newly independent states.

Unit Objectives

1. To list the ways in which the governments of Europe became more democratic during the nineteenth century.
2. To identify why nationalism gained strength in Europe in the nineteenth century.
3. To explain how nationalism affected the boundaries of Europe in the nineteenth century.

Unit Introduction

1. **Motivation:** Have students look through current newspapers and magazines to locate articles on political unrest. Tell students to read these articles and write a brief summary of the causes of the political unrest. Tell them that the many of the these causes (economic problems, political oppression, and nationalism) have also been around for a long time. In nineteenth century Europe, political

unrest erupted in many countries. This unrest led to important changes in the governments as well as the map of Europe.

2. **Visual:**
Ask: What is this man doing? (waving a flag) Why is he doing this? (He is a patriot.) Discuss the meaning of the expression "flag-waving." Was this a more respectable activity in the middle of the last century than it is now? If there is a difference, how do you explain it? Lead students to the idea that fervent patriotism was the leading form of idealism in the nineteenth century.

3. **Time line:** Ask students to count the number of countries mentioned on the time line. What does this suggest abut the importance of nationalism in the years 1815–1915? (Nationalism was widespread.) Besides the names of countries, find three words that appear at least twice. (revolt, uprising, war) What does this suggest about nineteenth-century nationalism?

Unit Activities:

1. **Cooperative Learning:** Divide the class into six groups. Assign one group to become class experts on the art, literature, and music of each of the following nineteenth century European nations: Great Britain, France, Russia, Germany, Italy, and the Austrian Empire. Students should use library resources to locate information about their nation's culture. Students should also ask the school's art teachers, music teachers, and English teachers for help in locating information.

2. **Compare and Contrast:** Have students compare and contrast the political changes that Britain experienced in the nineteenth century with the changes that went on in Russia during the same period. Put student answers into the form of a chart on the chalkboard. Then have students speculate as to why the experiences of these two nations were so different.

Support Materials

Assignments can include:

1. Unit Review, pp. 432–433
2. Unit 8 Test, pp. UT15–UT16
3. Unit 8 ESL/LEP Worksheet 1, p. ESL 15
4. Unit 8 ESL/LEP Worksheet 2, p. ESL 16

CHAPTER 1   Restoration of Europe

Overview   After Napoleon's defeat in 1814, European nations met at the Congress of Vienna, under the leadership of Metternich, to redraw national boundaries and restore the balance of power. Many of Europe's royal governments were brought back. To control the growth of nationalism and liberalism, the Quadruple Alliance was formed and censorship was encouraged. However, popular discontent in many nations grew and uprisings broke out in 1830 and 1848. Although most were crushed, they did spell the end of the Age of Metternich.

Objectives

1. To identify the purpose of and agreements reached at the Congress of Vienna.
2. To explain how Metternich proposed to stop the spread of nationalism and liberalism in Europe.
3. To list the events that brought the Metternich System to an end.

Developing the Chapter

1. **Motivation:** Ask students to explain why meetings or conferences are held at the end of a war. Students may mention issues including as the need to decide how the loser or losers should be treated, what to do with disputed territory, and what to do with prisoners of war.
Ask: After Napoleon's defeat, why did the nations of Europe need to hold a conference? Tell students they will explore the answer to this question in the following lesson.

2. **Introduction:**
a. Write the chapter's vocabulary words on the chalkboard. Have students look up their meanings in the glossary. Then check student understanding of the words by asking questions such as: With which nations does the United States try to maintain a balance of power?
b. Have students read the chapter title and Objective question. Have them make an inference based on the chapter title and Objective question.
c. Have students read the chapter.

3. **Review and Recall:** After the students have read the chapter:
a. Tell students that Metternich called the French Revolution "a disease which must be cured." What was the disease and how did he plan to cure it? Students should mention that the French Revolution spread ideas of nationalism and democracy among the people of Europe. Metternich hoped to cure it by restoring monarchies, encouraging censorship, and creating a balance of power.
b. Place a chart on the chalkboard entitled "The Congress of Vienna, 1814–1815," with these headings: Participants; Ideals of the French Revolution; Ideas of the Congress of Vienna; Outcome of the Congress. Ask students to fill in the appropriate information under each heading. Write in students responses as they are given.
c. Discuss with students why the Metternich System did not last. Discuss which countries were successful in achieving greater democracy and nationalist recognition by 1848.

4. **Building Social Studies Skills:** Have students practice their map and reading skills by studying the map on page 372 and using their text to answer the following questions: What parts of Napoleon's empire were removed from French control and made independent nations? What parts of Napoleon's empire were removed from French control and given to the other nations of Europe?

5. **Extension**
a. Have a group of students prepare a dramatization of one of the meetings of the Congress of Vienna. Students should represent different delegates and present their ideas and territorial demands.

Support Materials

Assignments can include:

1. Chapter Review, pp. 374–375
2. Blackline Masters, R93 and R94
3. Test 8-1, p. T48
4. Source Reading, p S25.

CHAPTER 2   The Growth of Democracy in Britain

Overview   Popular pressure forced Parliament to begin enacting democratic reforms in Britain in the 1830's. By the 1880's, all men could vote and serve in Parliament regardless of their wealth, property, or occupation, and the secret ballot had become law. Government leaders, such as Benjamin Disraeli and William Gladstone, and Queen Victoria helped make the era a period of democratic growth.

Objectives

1. To identify the ways in which British government was undemocratic prior to the 1830's.
2. To list the democratic reforms that were implemented between the 1830's and the 1880's.
3. To identify the British leaders who helped democracy to grow.

Developing the Chapter

1. Motivation: Ask students whether their families would be able to vote in the next presidential election if the government decided that only those who owned at least two acres of land could vote.

Ask: Whose interests and concerns would elected officials represent? Students should recognize that elected officials represent the interests of those who elect them. If their constituents are all landowners, then they will represent the interests of landowners.

2. Introduction:

a. Write the chapter's vocabulary words on the chalkboard. Have students write each word and its glossary meaning in their vocabulary notebooks.

b. Have students read the chapter title and Objective question.

   Ask: What are some ways in which people can gain a greater voice in government? Ask students if they can think of a nation in the news today that is experiencing demands by its people for a greater voice in government. Discuss what actions are being taken by the people and how the nation's government is responding to them.

c. Have students read the chapter.

3. Review and Recall: After the students have read the chapter:

a. Ask students to describe those aspects of nineteenth-century English life that were undemocratic. Students should mention unfair representation, the existence of property qualifications for voting, the system of "rotten boroughs," and the absence of a secret ballot. List student answers on the chalkboard.

b. Now ask students to name the laws that were passed during the 1800's to correct each of these problems. List these next to the problem they corrected. Which reform law do you think was the most important? Why? Which group of British citizens continued to be denied its political rights even after all these laws were passed? (Women)

4. Building Social Studies Skills: Write a series of generalizations on the chalkboard based on the material presented in this chapter. Have students locate statements in the text that support or refute your generalizations. For example, "Britain was a more democratic country by the end of the nineteenth century than it was at the beginning of the century." Students should cite statements regarding the reform laws passed during the nineteenth century to support this generalization.

5. Extension:

a. Have a group of students prepare a dramatization of the enactment of the Reform Bill of 1832. Appoint a prime minister and a leader of the opposition. Let the sides debate the proposed bill and have the class, acting as Parliament, vote on it.

b. Have students draw political cartoons that illustrate the impact of one of the reform laws of the 1800's on British society and government.

Support Materials

Assignments can include:

1. Chapter Review, pp. 380–381
2. Workbook, p. 59
3. Blackline Masters R95 and R96
4. Test 8-2, p. T49.

CHAPTER 3   France, a Republic

Overview   Throughout the first half of the nineteenth century, the French government changed often as the people revolted in 1830 and 1848 against unpopular kings. Democratic reforms were short-lived, however, as Louis Napoleon increased his power and turned the Second Republic into the Second Empire. When Louis Napoleon abdicated in 1870, the Third Republic was organized. It became France's most stable government in almost 100 years.

Objectives

1. To identify the causes of the Revolutions of 1830 and 1848.
2. To list the reasons why the Second Empire of Louis Napoleon fell.
3. To compare the government reforms of the Second Republic with those of the Third Republic.

Developing the Chapter

1. Motivation: Present the class with the following information: The Constitution of the United States was adopted in 1789. In over two centuries, only one type of government, a representative democracy, has ruled our nation. During the same period of time, France has had eleven complete changes in government in which absolute monarchies, limited monarchies, and republican types of government have held power. Tell students that this lesson will describe why France's government changed so often and how it finally developed into a more stable republic.

2. Introduction:
a. Write the chapter's vocabulary words on the chalkboard. Have students use each word in an original sentence to make sure they understand its meaning.
b. Have students read the chapter title and Objective question.
   Ask: Under what kind of circumstances would a government undergo a change? Possible answers include the death of a leader, popular discontent with current leaders, the loss of a war. List students' answers on the chalkboard. Tell students that many of these circumstances

contributed to frequent changes in the government of France during the nineteenth century.
c. Have students read the chapter.

3. Review and Recall: After the students have read the chapter:
a. Discuss with students why the French government changed frequently during the nineteenth century. Students should mention that rulers refused to grant democratic reforms, rulers followed economic policies that hurt consumers, and rulers got France involved in a war it could not win.
b. Have students construct a time line of the major changes in French government from 1814 to 1870. Let students use their textbooks to locate this information and have them put the time line into their notebooks.

4. Building Social Studies Skills: Have students re-read the Spotlight on Sources. **Ask:** What part do you think General Mercier and General Gense played in the Dreyfus affair? What evidence did the government use to get Dreyfus convicted? Why were the French people unable to get an unbiased account of the affair and the trial? Why does Zola accuse the War Office of a crime against the people of France?

5. Extension:
a. Have students prepare reports in which they compare the careers of Napoleon I and Napoleon III with respect to (a) how they became emperor, (b) their ambitions for France, (c) what they accomplished, and (d) how they fell from power.
b. Tell students to imagine they are newspaper reporters living in France during the Revolution of 1830 or 1848. Have them write an article describing the events of the revolution and the outcome.

Support Materials

Assignments can include:

1. Chapter Review pp. 386–387
2. Workbook p.
3. Blackline Masters
4. Test 8-2.

CHAPTER 4   Czarist Russia

Overview   During the nineteenth century, the czars kept tight control over life in Russia. The Decembrist Revolt of 1825 only made czarist rule more oppressive. Reforms finally came during the reign of Alexander II, but for many Russians it was too little too late. A radical movement was formed. By 1905 growing numbers of Russians had lost faith in their leaders. Rioting forced Nicholas II to set up the first parliament. Radicals, however, remained dissatisfied.

Objectives

1. To list the ways in which the czars maintained complete control of Russian society.
2. To identify the effects of the Decembrist Revolt on the Russian government.
3. To compare the reign of Alexander II with that of Nicholas II

Developing the Chapter

1. Motivation: Read the following poem by Alexander Pushkin, or duplicate copies and distribute them to the class. Ask students what the poem tells them about life in czarist Russia in the nineteenth century.

> Deep in the Siberian mines
> Keep your patience proud;
> The bitter toil shall not be lost,
> The rebel thought unbowed.
>
> The heavy-hanging chains will fall,
> The walls will crumble at a word;
> And freedom greet you in the light,
> And brother give you back the sword.

2. Introduction:

a. Write the chapter's vocabulary words on the chalkboard. Have students use the glossary to help them write a paragraph about czarist Russia in which they use all of the vocabulary words.

b. Have students read the chapter title and Objective question. Ask students if they can think of a recent issue over which a large group of Americans opposed a change in the law.
   Ask: Why would a government leader want to block change in his or her nation? Students should mention that a leader might want to block change when he or she is happy with the status quo and fears things might get worse if change is permitted. Tell students a similar situation existed among Russian leaders in the nineteenth century.

c. Have students read the chapter.

3. Review and Recall: After the students have read the chapter:

a. Ask students to list the ways in which the czars exercised absolute control over the people during the nineteenth century. Students should mention the following: czars made all the laws; the czarist secret police arrested those who spoke out against the government or proposed new ideas; censors banned writing critical of the government; minority groups had to adopt the Russian culture.

b. Why did the Decembrist Revolt fail to change Russia's government? Students should recognize that the czar saw the revolt as a threat to his power.

c. What made Alexander II willing to enact reforms? Students should recall that he believed the reforms would help modernize Russia and make her competitive with the nations of Europe.

4. Building Social Studies Skills: Have students make a time line of important events in czarist Russia. When they are done, ask them questions based on their time line to reinforce chronology skills.

5. Extension:

a. Have students write a diary entry in which they describe their reaction to life in nineteenth-century Russia from the viewpoint of an American visitor.

b. Interested students may want to research the reign of Alexander III and contrast it with the reign of his predecessor, Alexander II. Have students report their findings to the class, explaining why Alexander III was so opposed to reform.

Support Materials

Assignments can include:

1. Chapter Review, pp. 394–395
2. Blackline Masters R97 and R98
3. Test 8-4, p. T50
4. Source Reading, p. S26.

Overview   While the growth of nationalism in Europe was fueled primarily by the French Revolution and the spreading influence of Napoleon's rule, it was also inspired by the writers, poets, and composers of Europe. These followers of romanticism placed great value on the stories, language, and culture of the past. They encouraged a cultural revival among many of Europe's ethnic groups, and they served as a constant reminder of the desire to belong to one nation.

Objectives

1. To identify how the French Revolution encouraged the growth of nationalism in Europe.
2. To explain how the Romantic writers, poets, and composers helped nationalism to spread.
3. To list Romantic writers and composers of the nineteenth century.

Developing the Chapter

1. Motivation: Locate an art history book with a reproduction of Francisco Goya's *The Third of May* or Eugène Delacroix's *Greece Expiring on the Ruins of Missolonghi*. Show the paintings to the class and tell students that in the nineteenth century a movement began in European art, literature, and music that reflected the growing spirit of nationalism. The Goya painting illustrates the massacre of Spanish martyrs who died trying to resist Napoleon's invasion. The Delacroix illustrates the Greek struggle for independence. Discuss with students how these paintings differ from earlier European art.

2. Introduction

a. Write the chapter's vocabulary words on the chalkboard. Ask students to give you examples of each of the words.
b. Have students read the chapter title and Objective question. Discuss with students what it means to have school spirit. Ask them to describe what a school would be like where the entire student body was bursting with school spirit. Tell them that when the spirit of nationalism spread among Europeans in the nineteenth century, it had a similar effect. Europeans wrote poems and stories, painted pictures, and created music that glorified their nations.
c. Have students read the chapter.

3. Review and Recall: After the students have read the chapter:

a. Ask students to explain how the spirit of nationalism developed in Europe. Students should mention the effects of the rise of national monarchs, the effects of the French Revolution, and the effects of Napoleon's rule on the nations he conquered.
b. Discuss with students the effect that nationalism had on European writers and poets. Read the class one of Grimm's Fairy Tales and discuss with the class what the tale reveals about the German people and their culture.
c. Discuss with students how music can inspire feelings of nationalism. Ask them to name songs that have made them feel happy, sad, proud to be an American.

4. Building Social Studies Skills: Have students practice their skills at locating the main idea by having them find the main idea in paragraphs 2, 4, 6, 8, and 10. Tell students to write these main ideas in their notebooks. Then have them write down one supporting detail for each main idea.

5. Extension:

a. Have a group of students prepare a report on the history and words of the French national anthem, the "Marseillaise." Students should analyze how the words reflect the spirit of nationalism that existed in France.
b. France's greatest romantic novelist was Victor Hugo, whose *The Hunchback of Notre Dame* and *Les Miserables* tell stories of deep human suffering. Have interested students read one of these novels and present an oral book report to the class.

Support Materials

Assignments can include:

1. Chapter Review, pp. 400–401
2. Blackline Masters R101 and R102
3. Test 8-5, p. T51
4. Source Reading, p. S27.

CHAPTER 6   Germany Is United

Overview   During the nineteenth century Germany changed from a land of many independent states to a united nation. Napoleon consolidated the nation by reducing the number of states and joining them into a confederation. The Congress of Vienna cut the number of states further. However, the confederation lacked unity, and Austria continued to dominate the government. Under the leadership of Otto von Bismarck, Prussia took on Austria and then France in wars that led to a victorious and united Germany by 1871.

Objectives

1. To identify how Napoleon and the Congress of Vienna helped to bring the German states together.
2. To explain why early efforts to unify Germany failed.
3. To identify how Bismarck achieved German unification.
4. To list the steps Bismarck took to gain German unity.

Developing the Chapter

1. **Motivation:** Tell the class Germany never sent an ambassador to the United States before the Civil war.
Ask: Why not? Students should know that Germany did not exist at that time. This lesson will describe how the German states united under Prussia.

2. **Introduction:**
a. Write the chapter's vocabulary words on the chalkboard. Have students use each of the words in a sentence.
b. Have students read the chapter title and Objective question.
Ask: If someone wanted to unite the members of you history class for some purpose, how would they go about doing it? Students may mention persuasion, rewards, and threats. Tell students that some of these methods were employed in achieving the unification of Germany.
c. Have students read the chapter.

3. **Review and Recall:** After the students have read the chapter:

a. Ask students to explain how Napoleon and the Congress of Vienna helped unite German states. Students should mention that both reduced the number of German states and supported a confederation government for them.
Ask: Who are the strongest members of the German Confederation? (Austria and Prussia)
b. Discuss with students why the plan worked out at the Frankfurt Assembly failed to unite Germany. Students should recognize that terms of the plan were unacceptable to enough people that it could not be put in place.
c. Have students prepare a chronological table listing Bismarck's steps in unifying Germany, beginning with the war against Denmark in 1864. As students respond, place their comments on the chalkboard under the table heading "Bismarck's Blood and Iron Policy."

4. **Building Social Studies Skills:** Put the generalizations below on the chalkboard. Tell students to find facts in the chapter text to determine whether the generalizations are correct or incorrect.
a. France played an important role in German progress toward unification.
b. German unification was achieved peacefully.
c. Bismarck was an admirer of representative forms of government.
d. Bismarck united Germany politically, socially, and economically.

5. **Extension:**
a. Have students prepare an editorial written on the death of Bismarck in 1898. The editorial should assess the man and his achievements.
b. Have students draw political cartoons that might have appeared in newspapers in Denmark, Austria, or France in the 1860's.

Support Materials
Assignments can include:
1. Chapter Review, pp. 408–409
2. Workbook, p. 60
3. Blackline Masters R103 and R104
4. Test 8-6, p. T53.

CHAPTER 7   Italy is United

Unit Overview   At the beginning of the nineteenth century, Italy was divided into small states and provinces, many of which were ruled by foreigners. A nationalist movement began to gain strength among the Italian people, but most early attempts to revolt and overthrow the foreign leaders failed. Under the leadership of Camillo di Cavour, Giuseppe Mazzini, and Giuseppe Garibaldi, the unification of Italy was finally accomplished by 1870.

Objectives

1. To identify the sections Italy was divided into by the Congress of Vienna.
2. To identify the leaders of the unification movement and the roles they played in achieving unification.
3. To list the problems Italy faced after unification.

Developing the Chapter

1. **Motivation:** Have students look at the map of Italy on page 413. Locate the various states that made up the Italian "jigsaw puzzle." Discuss with students why it might be hard to unite a nation that was divided like this.

2. **Introduction:**
a. Write the chapter's vocabulary words on the chalkboard. Have students write each word and its glossary meaning in their vocabulary notebooks.
b. Have students read the chapter title and Objective question. Ask students to name current or past American leaders whom they would describe as being "strong." Put these names on the chalkboard. Then ask students to explain what it is that makes these leaders strong. Put their responses on the chalkboard, making a list of qualities strong leaders possess.
c. Have student read the chapter.

3. **Review and Recall:** After the students have read the chapter:
a. Have students review the obstacles to Italian unification. Students should mention the large number of foreign countries that controlled parts of Italy.

b. Put a chart on the chalkboard with the headings "Cavour," "Mazzini," and "Garibaldi." Tell students that Cavour is called the "mind," Mazzini the "soul," and Garibaldi the "sword" of Italian unification. Ask students to keep these descriptions in mind as they complete the chart by filling in the ways in which each man helped Italy achieve unification.
c. Have students prepare a chronological table in which they note the dates and events that led to Italian unification.
d. Have students make a list of the problems Italy faced after unification. Put the list on the chalkboard.
   Ask: How did Italy's situation after unification compare to Germany's? Students should recognize that Germany had a very strong leader in Bismarck while the Italians lacked strong leadership.

4. **Building Social Studies Skills:** Have students re-read the Spotlight on Sources. Help them interpret this primary source excerpt by asking them the following questions: What does Garibaldi mean when he says, "It is not a question of a republic now"? Why does Garibaldi fell that unification can only be achieved by appealing to the masses?

5. **Extension:**
a. Have students prepare newspaper headlines written for the events described in this chapter. Events may include the establishment of the Young Italy Society, the 1860 plebiscite, and Garibaldi's invasion of southern Italy.
b. Have a group of students create a bulletin board mural that illustrates the important events and battles that led to Italy's unification. You may prefer to have the student mural illustrate the headlines developed in the preceding activity.

Support Materials
   Assignments can include:
1. Chapter Review, pp. 414–415
2. Blackline Masters R105 and R106
3. Test 8-7, p. T54
4. Source Reading, p. S28.

CHAPTER 8   The Austrian Empire

Overview   Throughout the nineteenth century the Austrian empire was weakened by ethnic unrest. Nationalist feelings ran high among the empire's many ethnic groups. In 1867 Austria was forced to accept the separation of Hungary. The new nation was renamed Austria-Hungary. Other minority groups felt ignored and dissatisfaction continued to grow. The annexation of Bosnia and Herzegovina in 1908 only increased the Slavic minority and ethnic tension in the empire.

Objective

1. To list the reasons for ethnic unrest in the Austrian Empire in the nineteenth century.
2. To identify why the Hungarian revolution of 1848 ended in failure.
3. To identify why Austria finally agreed to the separation of Hungary in 1867.
4. To explain why ethnic unrest continued to grow in the empire into the twentieth century.

Developing the Chapter

1. **Motivation:** Turn to the map "Change Along the Danube River" on page 420, and have students study it.
Ask: What happened to the Austro-Hungarian Empire between 1867 and today? Students should recognize that a once-vast empire has disappeared and is now part of eight independent nations.

2. **Introduction:**
a. Write the chapter's vocabulary words on the chalkboard. Have students write each word and its glossary meaning in their vocabulary notebooks.
b. Have students read the chapter title and Objective question. Have students turn once again to the map "Change Along the Danube" on page 420. Review with students the meaning of ethnic group. Discuss with students why the presence of so many different ethnic groups might cause problems in governing the empire.
c. Have students read the chapter.

3. **Review and Recall:** After the students have read the chapter:

a. Have students name the different ethnic groups living in the Austrian Empire.
b. Discuss with students why the Hungarians were so successful in winning a greater degree of independence. (Their sheer numbers, inspirational leaders such as Széchenyi and Kossuth)
c. Ask students to identify the events that made Austria change its policy of stamping out ethnic differences. (Austrian defeat in the Seven Week's War in 1866)
Ask: What were the terms of the Compromise of 1867? Students should mention that Austria and Hungary were made equal but united countries.
Ask: Why was this compromise unable to solve the empire's ethnic problems? Students should recognize that the compromise was beneficial to the Hungarian minority but did nothing for the empire's other minorities.

4. **Building Social Studies Skills:** Have students practice finding the main idea by asking them to find the main idea in paragraphs 2, 5, 9 and 11. Write these main ideas on the chalkboard. Then ask students to locate supporting details in each of the paragraphs.

5. **Extension:**
a. Divide students into five cooperative groups. Assign each group to research one of the ethnic groups discussed in this chapter. Have each group present a report to the class describing the ethnic group's language, customs, dress, traditions, religious beliefs, and so on.
b. Divide the class into two groups and hold a debate between the supports of Istvan Széchenyi and Lajos Kossuth over the best way to achieve greater Hungarian independence.

Support Materials

Assignments can include:
1. Chapter Review, pp. 422–423
2. Workbook, pp. 62–63
3. Blackline Masters R107 and R108
4. Test 8-8, p. T54
5. Map Transparency 18 and Activity Sheet A18.

CHAPTER 9   Decline of the Ottoman Empire

Overview: A lessening of the sultan's influence and the rise of nationalism weakened the Ottoman Empire in the nineteenth century. Several Ottoman sultans thought that reforms and modernization would hold the empire together, but the empire continued to decline. After losing the Russian-Turkish War, the Ottomans were forced to give up most of their Balkan empire. The rest of the Balkan lands were lost during the Balkan Wars. By 1913, the Ottoman empire had almost disappeared from Europe.

Objective

1. To identify the causes of the decline of the Ottoman empire.
2. To compare the reforms and modernization programs implemented by Mahmud II and Abdul-Medjid I.
3. To identify how the Ottomans lost their empire in Europe.

Developing the Chapter

1. **Motivation:** Have students turn to the map "The Balkans, 1870–1914" on page 426. Students should locate the boundaries of the Ottoman Empire in 1870 and in 1913.
Ask: What happened to the area in Europe once controlled by Turkey? Students should note that these lands became either independent or part of other empires.

2. **Introduction:**
a. Write the chapter's vocabulary words on the chalkboard. Have students use each word in a sentence.
b. Have students read the chapter title and Objective question. Have students turn to the map on page 426 once again. Ask students to name the various nationalities that made up the Ottoman Empire at the beginning of the nineteenth century. Students should mention Greeks, Albanians, Bosnians, Serbians, Montenegrins, Macedonians, Bulgarians, and Romanians.
Ask: Based on what happened to the Austrian empire and your study of this map, what was a likely cause of the break-up of the Ottoman Empire? Students

should mention ethnic unrest and nationalism.
c. Have students read the chapter.

3. **Review and Recall:** After the students have read the chapter:
a. Have students explain the problems that weakened the Ottoman Empire in the 1800's. Students should mention the lessening influence of the sultan and the rise of nationalism in the Balkans. Discuss the reasons why the sultan's influence was declining and why Balkan peoples resented Ottoman rule.
b. Put a chart on the chalkboard with the headings "Reforms of Mahmud II" and "Reforms of Abdul-Medjid I." Have students compare the reforms implemented by these two sultans by completing the chart.
Ask: Why did the changes made by Mahmud and Abdul-Medjid fail to hold the empire together? Students should recognize that the changes went too far for some, such as traditional Muslims, and not far enough for others, such as the people of the Balkans.

4. **Building Social Studies Skills:** Have students prepare a time line of dates and events in the decline of the Ottoman Empire, beginning with the date 1829 and ending with 1913.

5. **Extension:**
a. Have students prepare an oral or written report on the changing role of women from the nineteenth-century Ottoman Empire to the modern Turkey.
b. Have students draw political cartoons about the last century of the Ottoman Empire based. Students might want to illustrate the causes of resentment among the peoples of the Balkans or the government's attempts at reform.

Support Materials

Assignments can include:
1. Chapter Review pp. 430–431
2. Workbook, pp. 64–65
3. Blackline Masters R109 and R110
4. Test 8-9, p. T55
5. Map Transparency 19 and Activity Sheet A19.

THE INDUSTRIAL REVOLUTION

Overview   The inventions in English textile manufacturing ushered in the Industrial Revolution. The factory system and its mass production of goods changed England's economy. Developments of railroads, steamships, and highway networks led to the rise of urban industrial centers. The Industrial Revolution spread to Western Europe, the United States, and Japan. Workers' lives were difficult but improved as the Industrial Revolution continued. Scientific and medical improvements helped increase life expectancy and improve public health. Social reforms also helped to spur improvements in industrial cities.

Objectives

1. To explain how changes in industry and agriculture led to the Industrial Revolution, first in England and then throughout the world.
2. To explain how new forms of transportation and communication allowed trade to expand and helped develop a worldwide economy.
3. To identify the problems that resulted from the rapid growth of cities and to explain the terms ubanism, socialism, and women's rights.
4. To identify some of the scientific and medical discoveries that happened as a response to conditions that developed during the Industrial Revolution.

Introduction:

1. Motivation: Discuss the health care in the United States today. Then have students consider what life today would be like without the health care that is available to them. Tell them that in this unit they will learn about a time of invention and discovery that improvements in industry, communication, health and social conditions, and the world's economy—and changed peoples lives forever.

2. Visual: Call the class's attention to the unit opener picture of English textile mill workers. Have them contrast this textile mill scene with its successor, the modern factory. What features remained the same? What features changed? Focus the discussion on the advent of mass production with the arrival of the factory system.

3. Time line: Establish the chronology of the Industrial Revolution as a long, ongoing process. Ask students how a revolution can be peaceful and last for so long a time. Discuss the word "revolution" as used to describe the basic economic and social changes brought about by the great changes in technology and business.

Unit Activities

1. Cooperative Learning: Divide the class into four cooperative groups. Have each group plan a TV special in which they will interview key people from the Industrial Revolution. Assign each group a set of key people to choose from: industrialists and/or socialists; political activists (as for women's rights); inventors; or scientists. Beside the guests, each group will need a moderator and one or two interviewers. Suggest that students go to the library while studying this unit and do some additional research on the set of key people their group will interview. (The audience of students listening to the interview may also ask questions of the "guests.")

2. Compare and Contrast: Compare conditions in cities during the Industrial Revolution with conditions in cities today. Which problems still exist (e.g., overcrowding, health care, education)? Do these problems today exist for the same reasons? What might be some solutions?

3. Making Judgements: What new forms of transportation and communication have been developed since the Industrial Revolution? What effect have these had on worldwide economy?

Support Materials

Assignments can include:
1. Unit Review, pp. 472–473
2. Unit 9 Test, pp. UT17–UT18
3. Unit 9 ESL/LEP Worksheet 1, p. ESL 17
4. Unit 9 ESL/LEP Worksheet 2, p. ESL 18

CHAPTER 1   Industry and Agriculture

Overview   Beginning in Great Britain in the early 1700s and lasting about 200 years, the Industrial Revolution changed the Western world from a rural, agricultural society to an urban, industrial society. New inventions, new industries, and changes in agriculture dramatically affected workers' lives and changed Great Britain's economic system.

Objectives

1. To describe the changes in industry in England that lead to the Industrial Revolution.
2. To list the changes in agriculture that helped spread the Industrial Revolution.
3. To explain how the Industrial Revolution changed the lives of workers in Great Britain.
4. To explain how the Industrial Revolution changed the economic system in Great Britain.

Developing the Chapter

1. Motivation: Turn to the Unit 9 visual of children in the coal mine on pages 434–435. While students are looking at the picture, tell them that children of all ages worked in the mines. Some five- and six-year-old boys worked as long as 12 hours a day.
Ask: Why do you think young children would work so hard in the mines? Tell students of some of the dangers of working in coal mines (cave-ins, the inhalation of coal gases, working alone, etc.)

2. Introduction:
a. Have students turn to the Vocabulary Review on page 442. Tell them to write each word and its glossary meaning in their vocabulary notebook.
b. Have students read the chapter title and Objective question.
c. Have students read the chapter.

3. Review and Recall: After the students have read the chapter:
a. Have them reread each heading question and answer it.
b. Have them reread and answer the Objective question.
c. Have them reread the OUTLOOK. Ask them to write down their answers to the questions. Answers may then be discussed as a class or in small groups.

4. Building Social Studies Skills: Explain to students that summarizing is a skill that can help them understand chapter content. Help students work through a summary of the section of this chapter on agriculture. Then assign the Skill Builder: Summarizing on page 443 of the Chapter Review.

5. Extension:
a. Cooperative Learning: Divide students into groups of four to eight depending on class size. Refer students to the time line for Unit 9, Chapter 1, on page 436. Have each student in a group choose one marker on the time line and write or discuss the importance of that invention to the Industrial Revolution. Have each group summarize the importance of new inventions to the Industrial Revolution.
b. Divide students into small groups. Have each group choose a business they might start as a class (recycling, car wash, bake sale, etc). Tell each group to draw up a plan of action that explains how to get started, how to raise capital, if partners will be necessary, how profits will be used, how partners will be paid back. After each group has presented its plan, have the class vote on one business they would like to try. You may want to assign this project over an extended period of time and, with the permission of your principal, have the class carry out their plans.

Support Materials

Assignments can include:
1. Chapter Review, pp. 442–443
2. Workbook, pp. 67–69
3. Blackline Masters R111 and R112
4. Test 9-1, p. T56
5. Source reading S29.

UNIT 9

CHAPTER 2   The Industrial Revolution
Spreads

Overview   The Industrial Revolution spread
throughout the world. As industrial nations
took control of new colonies they used them
as new markets and as suppliers of raw
materials. By the late 1800s the balance of
wealth and power favored the industrial
nations. Western Europe, the United States,
and Japan became the most powerful
countries in the world.

Objectives

1. To explain Great Britain's role in the
   development of new industries in other
   countries in the 1800s.
2. To explain how the cottage industry of
   weaving woolen goods led to large-scale
   textile production in Belgium.
3. To identify some of the obstacles France
   faced in its development as an
   industrialized nation.
4. To trace the industrialization of Germany
   before and after unification in 1871.
5. To identify the role of New England,
   Pennsylvania, and the South in the rise of
   industry in the United States.

Developing the Chapter

1. **Motivation:** Have students look at the map
"Leading Industrial Regions Today" on p. 448.
Discuss the location of these regions and
some reasons why the growth of industry
occurred there.

2. **Introduction:**
a. Write the chapter vocabulary words on the
   chalkboard. Have students write each word
   in an original sentence in their vocabulary
   notebook. Tell them to look in the glossary
   for the definition of any word of whose
   meaning they are not sure.
b. Have students read the chapter title and
   Objective question. Then have them read
   each subhead question.
c. Have students read the chapter.

3. **Review and Recall:** After the students
have read the chapter:
a. Have them ask each other questions about
   the chapter's content.

b. Ask each subhead question and discuss the
   answers.
c. Have students reread the Objective
   question. Tell them to use the time line on
   p. 444 to help them answer the Objective
   question. Then have students share their
   answers.
d. Have students reread the feature "A
   Geographic View of History" on page 448
   and answer the feature's questions.

4. **Building Social Studies Skills:** Have
students use the map "Early Industrialization
of Europe" on page 439 to answer the
following questions:
a. What were the industrial nations of the
   United Kingdom?
b. Which countries had industrialized areas
   in the Rhur Valley?
c. Where was the Sambre-Meuse Valley?

5. **Extension:**
a. Divide students into several groups. Assign
   each group one of the world's seven largest
   industrial powers to research. Have each
   group make a chart on their region. The
   chart should include the name of the
   region, the location of the region, the
   region's major industry or industries, and
   the total value of its goods and services.
   Each group should share its findings with
   the rest of the class.
b. Unemployment among young people in
   England today is high. Have interested
   students research unemployment in some
   of England's major cities—London,
   Birmingham, and Liverpool—and compare
   it with unemployment in American cities
   such as New York, Chicago, and San
   Francisco. Have students write a report on
   their findings.

Support Materials
   Assignments can include:
1. Chapter Review, pp. 450–451
2. Workbook, p. 70
3. Blackline Masters R113 and R114
4. Test 9-2, p. T57
5. Map Transparencies 20 and 21 and Activity
   Sheets A20 and A21
6. Source reading S30.

CHAPTER 3 Revolution in Transportation and Communication

Overview New forms of transportation and communication facilitated the rapid expansion of trade during the Industrial Revolution. This growing trade among nations helped develop a worldwide economy. This emerging world economy also was stimulated by improvements in communication. Inventions such as the telegraph and telephone brought the people of the world closer together than ever before.

Objectives

1. To explain how growing trade among nations helped develop a worldwide economy.
2. To list the inventions that brought about improvements in transportation.
3. To list the inventions that helped improve communication.

Developing the Chapter

1. **Motivation:** Turn to the People in History feature on page 455 and have students read about Guglielmo Marconi. Tell them that by the early 1900s home wireless sets had become a major form of entertainment in Europe and the United States.
Ask: What has taken the place of the home wireless set as today's major media of popular entertainment?

2. **Introduction:**
a. List the chapter vocabulary words on the chalkboard. Have students write each word in an original sentence in their vocabulary notebook. Have them look up the glossary definition of any word of whose meaning they are not sure.
b. Have students read the chapter title and Objective question. Brainstorm answers to the question. Then have students read the chapter.

3. **Review and Recall:** After the students have read the chapter:
a. Have them discuss the cause for the rapid expansion of trade; how it helped spread the Industrial Revolution; the effect it had on the world's economy.
b. Have them name the inventions that brought about improvements in transportation.
c. Ask them to name the inventions that helped improve communication.
d. Have students reread the Outlook paragraph on page 455. Then have the class answer and discuss the Outlook's questions.

4. **Building Social Studies Skills:** Explain to students that books contain statements of fact and statements of opinion, and that it is important in your reading that you recognize the difference between statements of fact and statements of opinion. Assign Skill Builder: Fact *versus* Opinion on page 457 of the Chapter Review.

5. **Extension:**
a. Have students explain the phrase "It's a small world" and tell how the phrase is as true today as it was in the later years of the Industrial Revolution.
b. Have each student prepare a biographical report on one of the following inventors: Robert Fulton, George Stephenson, Samuel F. B. Morse, Alexander Graham Bell, John L. McAdam.
c. The invention of the telephone changed the world forever. Remind students that use of the telephone is now part of our everyday lives. Have them use their local telephone directories to look up information on: types of home telephone service, how to obtain service in their home, special services provided by their local phone company, how to call local directory assistance and long distance directory assistance. Have students report this information to the class.

Support Materials

Assignments can include:

1. Chapter Review, pp 456–457
2. Workbook p. 71
3. Blackline Master R115 and R116
4. Test 9-3, p. T58
5. Source reading S32.

CHAPTER 4   Urbanism, Socialism, and
Reform

Overview   The Industrial Revolution
encouraged the growth of cities. But with this
growth the problems of housing, water supply,
and sewers also grew. Crime and disease
increased, and factory workers worked long
hours for low pay at uninteresting and often
unsafe jobs. Poor living and working
conditions led to socialism and communism,
but these lost out to nationalism in the West
as advances in education, science, technology,
and medicine improved the lives workers in
cities. In the last half of the 19th century
women were demanding equal rights.

Objectives

1. To list three problems that resulted from
   the rapid growth of cities.
2. To identify problems of factory workers.
3. To define socialism and communism and
   explain why a Communist revolution never
   took place in Western Europe.
4. To identify the role of education, science,
   and technology in improving people's lives.
5. To list some of the accomplishments of the
   struggle for women's rights.

Developing the Chapter

1. **Motivation:** Invite a local official to speak
   to the class about major problems in your city
   or town. Have the official explain the
   measures being taken to solve the problems.
   Allow time for concerned students to ask
   questions.
2. **Introduction:**
   a. Write the chapter vocabulary words on the
      chalkboard. Have students write each word
      and its glossary meaning in their
      vocabulary notebook.
   b. Have students read the chapter title and
      Objective question.
   c. Have students read the chapter.
3. **Review and Recall:** After the students
   have read the chapter:
   a. Ask volunteers to summarize each section
      and share their summaries with the class.
   b. Discuss suggested answers to each chapter
      subhead question provided by student
      volunteers.

c. Have students reread and answer the
   Objective question.
d. Have students read the Art and Artifacts
   feature aloud. Ask them to carefully
   observe and discuss the painting, noting
   the artist's use of light. The feature
   questions may be discussed orally or
   assigned as a writing exercise.
4. **Building Social Studies Skills:** Have
   students study the map "Early
   Industrialization of Europe" on page 439.
   Have them choose three of the ten regions and
   explain why cities grew in these areas.
5. **Extension:**
   a. Divide student into four or five groups.
      Have each group reread the section on
      utopian societies on page 460 and Karl
      Marx's ideal society on pages 460–461.
      Then ask them to decide if it is possible to
      have a utopian society. If it is, what would
      it be like? If it is not, explain why not. Have
      each group share their conclusions with
      the class.
   b. Women such as Mary Woolstonecraft,
      Lucretia Mott, and Elizabeth Cady Stanton
      led the movement for women's rights in the
      19th century. Women fought long and hard
      for their rights and continue to do so. Ask
      students to find newspaper articles about
      women who are leaders today in
      education, science, medicine, and
      business. Have students compare the
      opportunities women have today with the
      opportunities they had in the 1800s.
   c. Have interested students do research on
      labor unions. Ask them to make a chart,
      based on their research, showing the
      advantages and disadvantages of labor
      unions. The chart should be shared with
      the class.

Support Materials
   Assignments can include:
1. Chapter Review, pp. 464–465
2. Workbook, pp. 72–73
3. Blackline Masters R117 and R118
4. Test 9-4, p. T59

UNIT 9

CHAPTER 5   Science and Medicine

Overview   During the Industrial Revolution scientists such as Louis Pasteur and Joseph Lister made important discoveries that helped control the spread of disease and facilitated modern medicine. Other scientists' discoveries led to the development of new sources of power and energy that accelerated the growth of industry. Albert Einstein's theory of relativity changed people's understanding of the universe, while Charles Darwin's theory of evolution changed the way people viewed the world.

Objectives

1. To identify the scientists and their research that led to major advances in medicine.
2. To list the scientific discoveries that made possible new sources of power for industry.
3. To explain the impact of the scientific ideas of Einstein and Darwin.

Developing the Chapter

1. Motivation: Bring to class several articles on medical and scientific research today. Include such topics as drug rehabilitation, organ transplants, and AIDS. Read excerpts from one or two articles and have students discuss the importance of scientific research in their own lives.

2. Introduction:
a. Have students locate the new chapter vocabulary words in the text. Ask them to write each word and its glossary definition in their vocabulary notebook.
b. Read the chapter title and Objective question aloud.
c. Have students read the chapter.

3. Review and Recall: After the students have read the chapter:
a. Have them state what each of the following persons contributed to medical science: Louis Pasteur, Robert Koch, Alexander Fleming, Walter Reed, Carlos Juan Finlay.
b. Have them name several scientific discoveries that increased the use of electricity in the industrial age.
c. Have them reread the section on Charles Darwin on pages 468–469. Ask them to explain Darwin's theory of evolution and the term *natural selection*. Discuss how Darwin's theory of evolution has been used by scientists, economists, and politicians to explain their theories of science, business, and society. **Ask:** Has Darwin's theory ever been misused?

4. Building Social Studies Skills: Charts present useful information in ways that are clear and easy to understand. Divide students into small groups. Suggest that each group make a chart showing the facts presented in this chapter. Charts should include the name of major scientists, their nationality, and their contribution to the Industrial Revolution. When charts are completed have students share them and compare their findings.

5. Extension:
a. Have students do research on the Nobel Prize. Ask them to write a report that includes the following information: Who was Alfred B. Nobel? How did he create his fortune? How much of his fortune did he leave for the peace prize? In which fields is the Nobel Prize awarded? In what year was the first Nobel Peace Prize given? When and in what fields did Marie Curie win the Nobel Prize? To whom would you give the Nobel Prize for peace today and why?
b. In 1865, the year that Pasteur succeeded in curing silkworm disease and Joseph Lister introduced antiseptic surgery, many other important events were taking place throughout the world. Have interested students discover what events took place in the following areas in 1865: history and politics, literature, theater, music and art. Ask them to share this information with the class.

Support Materials

Assignments can include:
1. Chapter Review pp. 470–471
2. Workbook p. 74
3. Blackline Masters R119 and R120
4. Test 9-5, p. T60.

UNIT 10

Imperialism Leads To War

Overview   During the nineteen century the industrialized nations established colonial empires in Africa and Asia. Western European nations, Japan, and the United States took control of other nations to acquire resources and markets for their growing economies. Rule by the imperialist nations differed, but all were alike in ignoring the aspirations of the people they governed. In time, nationalist movements among the colonial peoples would lead to the break-up of these empires. In the same way, economic and political rivalry among the imperialist nations would eventually plunge the world into wars.

Unit Objectives

1. To explain why imperialism developed in the late nineteenth century.
2. To show how imperialism effected countries in Africa, Asia, and Latin America.
3. To identify the causes of World War I and the territorial changes that resulted.

Unit Introduction

1. Motivation: Lead a class discussion about competition and rivalry (in sports, to get a good grade, etc.) to introduce the topics of imperialism and World War I.

2. Visual: Direct the class's attention to the painting in the Unit opener (p. 475). Ask students to hypothesize how the ruler of a small nation became the empress of a large country thousands of miles away. In fact, Victoria's reign as Empress of India was symbolic. It symbolized British control of India as a colony—the jewel in Britain's colonial crown. Her reign also coincided with the years of Britain's worldwide empire.

3. Time line: Have the class examine the Unit time line to survey the time frame of the chapters on imperialism.

Unit Activities

1. Cooperative Learning: Have students work together to create a bulletin board time line on imperialism from 1850 to 1918. Divide the class into six groups, with each group assigned to either Africa, China, India, Southeast Asia, Japan, or Latin America.

Students in each group are to read outside material on imperialist rule in the area assigned to them. To facilitate the search, individual students in each group should be given a block of years from 1850 to 1918 to investigate. As students read about their assigned areas, instruct them to take notes about any important event and the date it occurred. Have them form a final list of events with the members of their group. As a text chapter is completed on a specific area, have a representative from the relevant group write the final list of events on the bulletin board time line. When the unit is completed, have students describe how certain events in one part of an imperialist empire might have influenced the events in some other area.

2. Compare and Contrast: Have students compare and contrast the style of rule of two imperialist nations. They might choose among the following powers to research: Britain, France, Germany, the United States, Japan. Or they can compare the style of rule in two areas of the imperialist power's empire and give reasons for these different types of control or techniques of governing.

3. Cause and Effect: Have students create a map of colonial empires and spheres of influence in the world in 1900. Distribute the outline map of the world (on blackline master) at the beginning of the unit. Instruct students to fill in the map as they complete a chapter. After they have read the final chapter on World War I, ask them to make a map of the colonial empires after the peace settlement. Then have them compare the two maps and discuss the causes and results of World War I.

Support Materials

Assignments can include:

1. Unit Review, pp. 530–531
2. Unit 10 Test, pp. UT19–UT20
3. Unit 10 ESL/LEP Worksheet 1, p. ESL 19
4. Unit 10 ESL/LEP Worksheet 2, p. ESL 20

CHAPTER 1   Imperialism and Africa

Overview   Between 1870 and 1914 European countries took control of nearly all of Africa. Many factors motivated these nations to take over the continent, including economic needs, nationalism, political rivalry, and religions. These forces, plus the industrial might and technology of these countries, led them to carve up Africa and subjugate its people. Imperialism in Africa created conflict and rivalries among the European countries. It also brought hardships and foreign dominance to Africa.

Objectives

1. To identify the imperialist nations and the areas of Africa in which they established colonies.
2. To explain why and how European nations built colonial empires in Africa.
3. To describe some of the ways Africans were affected by European imperialism.

Developing the Chapter

1. **Motivation:** Ask students if they might like to relocate to a new country. Then ask students how their feelings might be affected if they were forced to move to this country and change their whole way of life against their will. Conclude the discussion by drawing a parallel with imperialism and the imposition of European culture on the African way of life.

2. **Introduction:**
a. Write the word *imperialism* on the chalkboard. Ask students to look up its definition in the Glossary on pages 728–738 and to write it in their notebooks.
b. Have students write the definitions of the other vocabulary words in their notebooks. **Ask:** How are *colony, sphere of influence,* and *protectorate* related to imperialism? (They are methods of imperialist takeover.)

3. **Review and Recall:** After the students have read the chapter:
a. Conduct an informal debate on whether European imperialism helped or hindered Africa from 1870 to 1914. On the chalkboard, write the headings PRO-IMPERIALISM and ANTI-IMPERIALISM.

As students debate the issue, write the reasons they give for each side under the appropriate headings. PRO examples might be economic development and growth of nationalism; ANTI examples might be the uprooting of traditional African economies, the disregard of tribal loyalties, and the loss of African peoples' freedom. After students have given their reasons, have them draw conclusions about the effect of imperialism on Africa.
b. Write the following generalization on the chalkboard: European countries used Africa as a means to increase their own political and economic power. Ask students to find facts from the chapter to support or disprove this generalization.

4. **Building Social Studies Skills:** Have students compare the map of Africa in 1914 on page 479 with a map of Africa today. What major change has occurred in Africa since 1914? Have students name the countries that achieved independence since 1914. You might have one group of students create questions about the two maps and have another group of students answer the questions.

5. **Extension:** Have students review a daily newspaper for examples of imperialism in the world today. Instruct them to underline the words of phrases in the news article that describe an imperialist action or viewpoint. Ask them to cut out the articles and bring them to class.

Support Materials

Assignments can include:

1. Chapter Review, pp. 482–483
2. Workbook, pp 75–77
3. Blackline Masters R121 and R122
4. Test 10-1, p. T61
5. Map Transparency 22 and Activity Sheet A22
6. Source reading S32.

Overview   By the 1800s China under the Manchu dynasty was becoming increasingly weak. Taking advantage of this weakness, the British forced the Chinese to open trade with them and to cede them much Chinese land. Other imperialist powers soon followed Britain's example. Peasant uprisings also increased political instability in China. Some Chinese formed secret groups to drive out foreigners. In 1911, nationalism led to the overthrow of the Manchu dynasty and the creation of a republic.

Objectives

1. To describe the conditions that made China a target for European imperialism.
2. To identify the causes and results of the Boxer Rebellion.
3. To explain the roles of Sun Yat-sen and nationalism in the struggle to end foreign rule.

Developing the Chapter

1. Motivation: Have students look at the illustration of the Taiping Rebellion on page 484. Ask students to describe what they see happening in the photograph. List student responses on the chalkboard. Tell students that one result of political instability in China in the late 1800s was domination of China by the West.

2. Introduction:

a. Have students read the chapter title and Objective question.

   b. Ask students to look up the meaning of the two vocabulary terms: Boxers and Open Door Policy. What do these terms have in common? (Both describe responses to the policies of imperialist countries in China.)

3. Review and Recall: After the students have read the chapter:

a. Read to them the message from a Chinese official to Queen Victoria that discusses the trade in opium, quoted on page 485, paragraph 4. Have them identify the subject matter of the quote and explain the circumstances surrounding it.

b. Read the "Spotlight on Sources" to them.

Have them identify what was being protested. Ask them to explain why the Boxers felt this way about the Europeans.

c. In 1899, American Secretary of State John Hays said that a certain agreement would "safeguard for the world the principle of equal and impartial trade with all parts of the Chinese Empire." Have the students identify this proposed agreement as the Open Door Policy. (Explain to the class that it failed to achieve its purpose, however.)

d. Have the students read the statement made by Sun Yat-sen quoted in the Outlook on page 487. Ask them to explain the symbolism used by Sun Yat-sen.

Ask: Who are the other men? (European imperialists) Why are they the carving knife and the serving dish and the Chinese the meat and fish? (The Europeans cut up China for their own use without regard for the people whose land they were dividing.)

4. Building Social Studies Skills: Have students analyze the time line on page 484 to explain how seeing events in time order can help illuminate cause and effect. For example, while the Taiping Rebellion was in progress (1851–1864), China in its weakened condition was forced to open additional ports of foreign nations. (1860–1880).

5. Extension: Have students research photographs of the interiors of upper-class British homes at the turn of the century to find evidence of the use of imported goods from China (for example, silk, and porcelain).

Support Materials

Assignments can include:

1. Chapter review, pp. 482–483
2. Workbook, pp 78–79
3. Blackline Masters R123 and R124
4. Test 10-2, p. T62
5. Map Transparency 23 and Activity Sheet A23.

CHAPTER 3   Japan's Power Grows

Overview   To keep foreign nations from taking control, Japan began to modernize while preserving its own culture and traditions. In 1868, the Meiji government established strong rule in Japan. It ended feudalism, began to industrialize the nation, and set up a new education system. It also built up Japan's military strength and annexed territory. By 1900 Japan had become the most powerful nation in Asia.

Objective

1. To explain why the decision was made to make Japan a modern nation.
2. To explain how Japan became industrialized.
3. To describe how Japan became an imperialist power.

Developing the Chapter

1. **Motivation:** Bring to class photographs that show how tradition exists alongside modern-day technology in Japan today. (An example might be a photograph showing Japanese women in traditional dress walking through a shopping mall in Tokyo. You can find such photographs in travel brochures or magazines.) Once you have shown the students the photographs,

Ask: What do these photographs tell you about Japanese life? (Students should note that Japan has become a modern nation without giving up its traditions.) Tell students that growth by adopting Western methods but without sacrificing its traditional culture is what made Japan a powerful modern nation beginning in the late 1800s.

2. **Introduction:**
a. Have students look at the chapter title, subheads, and visuals to get clues as to how Japan's power grew. List these clues on the chalkboard.
b. Have students read the Objective question. Tell them to take notes on information in the chapter that answers the Objective question.

3. **Review and Recall:** After the students have read the chapter:
a. Have them compare what was happening in Japan between 1868 and 1910 with what

was happening in China during this same period. You might have them compare the time lines at the beginning of Chapters 2 and 3. Ask them to give the reason behind the differences. (Students should note that China and Japan differed markedly in their response to Western powers. Unlike China, which tried to resist the ideas and economic power of foreign nations, Japan chose to adopt Western ideas while retaining its culture and way of life.)
b. Have them summarize how Japan became a world power. To do this, instruct students to write a separate summary sentence for paragraphs 17, 18, 19 and 20.

4. **Building Social Studies Skills:** Students can practice finding direction on a historical map by answering these questions about the map on page 493. (a) In which direction was Korea from Japan? (west) (b) In which direction from Kyoto on the Japanese island of Honshu was Japan's sphere of influence in China? (northwest)(c) What island is southwest of Japan? (Taiwan) When did this island become part of the Japanese Empire? (1875–1910)

5. **Extension:**
a. Have students imagine they are Japanese students visiting the United States in 1900. Tell them to write a letter to the editor of an American newspaper commenting on the Boxer Rebellion in China.
b. Ask students to go to the library to find some samples of Japanese art in the late 1800s. Instruct them to examine the art for evidence of the new attitude toward women the Japanese adopted in the late 1800s.

Support Materials

Assignments can include:
1. Chapter Review, pp 496–497
2. Workbook, pp. 80
3. Blackline Masters R125 and R126
4. Test 10-3, p. T63

CHAPTER 4   Great Britain in India

Overview   In the late 18th century, the British East India Company took control of trade in India. The Company's influence became so great that it stirred nationalist feelings in some Indians. However, the British put down early revolts against their rule. By the 1860s, Britain ran most of India directly or through local officials. It ruled India for the benefit British business, with little regard for the economic well-being of the people of India. However, India did benefit in some ways through the modernization of its economy.

Objectives

1. To explain how the British came to rule India.
2. To describe the political, economic, and cultural effects of British rule in India.
3. To show how religious division in India helped Britain maintain power.

Developing the Chapter

1. **Motivation:** (Preview tape and use your discretion.) Show students a scene from the movie *A Passage to India*, which was nominated for several Academy Awards in 1984. This film shows the relationship between the resident British and the people of India at the turn of the century. Choose a scene that you think best summarizes the effect the British had on the Indian way of life. After students have viewed the clip, tell them that in Chapter 4 they will learn why the British were in India and how their rule affected the Indian people.

2. **Introduction:**
a. Have students read the chapter title and Objective question. Ask them to describe the method that the British used to build an empire in India. (The term *colonization* in the Objective question should give students a clue that the British set up a colony in India and that they completely controlled and governed India.)
b. Write these vocabulary words on the chalkboard: rajahs, sepoys, reforms, suttee, mutiny, resident commissioner. Have the students read the definitions of these words as they appear in the Glossary on pages 728–738.
Ask: Which words identify something or someone who was Indian? (rajahs, sutee) Which words stem from British rule in India? (sepoys, resident commissioner)

3. **Review and Recall:** After the students have read the chapter:
a. Have them predict what happened in India when British rule later came to an end. (This activity will require students to review how British rule affected India's ability to feed its people as well as to govern itself. Students also should note the effect religious division may have had in an independent India.)
b. Ask them to imagine that the British still rule India today. Have them discuss what the global reaction might be to such a political arrangement. (This activity will require students to make judgments about the ethics of imperialist rule.)

4. **Building Social Studies Skills:** Have students practice using the card catalog in the library by having them develop a bibliography on one of these people: Ram Mohan Roy, Mohandas Gandhi, or Rudyard Kipling.

5. **Extension:**
a. Ask students to write a report on the life of Ram Mohan Roy, Rudyard Kipling, or Gandi. Instruct them to use the bibliography they developed in activity 4, above, in conducting their research.
b. Have students reread the poem by Rudyard Kipling quoted in the Spotlight on Sources. Instruct the students to rewrite the poem to express the Indian people's view of British rule.

Support Materials

Assignments can include:

1. Chapter Review, pp. 502–503
2. Blackline Masters R127 and R128
3. Test 10-4, p. T64
4. Source reading S33.

UNIT 10

Overview   By the 1700s Europeans were setting up trading settlements in Southeast Asia. In most cases, they reshaped the economies of their colonies to benefit their own business interests. As imperialist nations of the 1800s developed trade routes in the Pacific, they took control of many islands as refueling stations and naval bases. Again, Britain led the way, establishing colonies in Australia and New Zealand.

Objectives

1. To explain why the Dutch, British, and French set up colonies in Southeast Asia.
2. To describe how the United States gained control of the Philippines and Hawaii.
3. To list the reasons why imperialist nations needed islands in the Pacific.
4. To describe how Australia and New Zealand became colonies and later part of the British Empire.

Developing the Chapter

1. **Motivation:** Read aloud the excerpted McKinley speech on page 506. Tell students that the imperialist attitude evident in this excerpt was shared by most leaders of the major industrial countries by the end of the 1800s. (This chapter tells how and why.)

2. **Introduction:**

a. Have students read the title and Objective question to find out the parts of the world to which imperialism spread.

b. Write the vocabulary words on the chalkboard: Filipinos, coaling stations, Malay Peninsula. Ask students to find the definitions of these words in the Glossary on pages 728-738. Have them locate the Malay Peninsula on the map on page 508; the Philippines, where the Filipinos live; and Australia, the home of the aborigines.

3. **Review and Recall:** After the students have read the chapter:

a. Draw a chart on the chalkboard that shows how imperialist powers developed their colonies in Southeast Asia and in the Pacific. (You might want to use the sample chart, following.)

Dutch	building plantations to grow crops for export
British	set up trading posts; build railroads, schools, dams, and canals; developed plantations to grow rubber and tea
French	build roads, railroads and canals to increase rice production for export; opened mines; started plantations
Americans	expanded American trade; developed new business opportunities

Ask: Which parts of Southeast Asia and the Pacific did the British, French, and Americans colonize?

b. Direct the students to study the chart. Then ask: Why were the imperialist nations interested in Southeast Asia and the Pacific?

4. **Using Social Studies Skills:** Have students practice the skill of note-taking by dividing them into four groups, assigning each group a section to take notes on in Chapter 5. Write the subhead question for each section on the chalkboard. Have each group skim the section for words or phrases that directly answer the subhead question and list them under the appropriate subhead on the chalkboard.

5. **Extension:**

a. Have students write a report on the Pacific islands today. Instruct them to show in their report how foreign control has affected the economy, culture, and way of life of these islands.

b. Have students report on the influence the United States has had on the Philippines since that country's independence in 1946. Ask them to include in their report examples of this influence.

Support Materials

Assignments can include:

1. Chapter Review, pp. 508–509
2. Blackline Masters R129 and R130
3. Test 10-5, p. T65

CHAPTER 6   Economic Imperialism in
            Latin America

Overview   After the nations of Latin America
gained their independence in the 1820s they
borrowed huge sums from foreign nations to
develop their economies. Since many Latin
American nations were politically unstable,
they were not able to repay these debts.
Lendor nations threatened action. To protect
its economic and political interests and to
secure its borders, the United States began to
intervene in Latin American affairs. This
policy eventually alienated the Latin
American countries, causing them to distrust
the United States.

Objectives

1. To define economic imperialism and show
   how it affected Latin America's relations
   with foreign nations.
2. To trace the events which led to a United
   States policy of intervention in Latin
   America.

Developing the Chapter

1. **Motivation:** Gather newspaper clippings
   that show headlines abut the economic and
   political condition of some nations in Latin
   America today. After students have reviewed
   the headlines, ask them to summarize the
   problems facing these Latin American
   nations. Tell students that some of these
   problems may stem from the pattern of
   relationships with foreign nations that began
   soon after Latin America gained its
   independence.

2. **Introduction:** Ask students to read the
   chapter title. Have them deduce the meaning
   of the term *economic imperialism* by first
   looking up the meanings of these important
   terms in the Glossary on pages 728–738:
   Monroe Doctrine, Platt Amendment,
   Roosevelt Corollary. Students should
   understand that economic imperialism has to
   do with foreign interference to protect
   business interests. Then ask them to look up
   economic imperialism in the Glossary to see
   how close they came to the correct definition.

3. **Review and Recall:** After the students
   have read the chapter:

a. Have them compare imperialism in Latin
   America with imperialism in Africa.
   (Students should note the similarities and
   differences between colonization [in
   Africa] and economic and political
   interference to protect business interests
   [in Latin America].)
b. Have them show their understanding of
   cause and effect by asking them to discuss
   how economic imperialism might have
   been prevented in Latin America. (Sample
   answer: The Latin American countries
   might have developed strong economies by
   exporting their valuable resources to
   supply the vast funds needed for economic
   development. In this way, they would not
   have been so dependent on foreign loans.)
c. Have students judge Roosevelt's foreign
   policy:
   Ask: What would you have done to try to
   help Latin American nations and to
   maintain their trust?

4. **Building Social Studies Skills:** Have
students compare a climate map of the United
States with an economic map of the United
States to determine how climate affects the
way people earn their livings.

5. **Extension:**
a. Have students do library research on the
   occasions in American history when
   various Presidents have invoked the
   Monroe Doctrine. Ask them to place this
   information on a time line from 1829 to
   the present.
b. Assign a different Latin American country
   to each student or group of students. Have
   them report on the geography, history,
   economy, and current problems facing that
   country and offer possible solutions to the
   country's current problems.

Support Materials

Assignments can include:
1. Chapter Review, pp. 514–515
2. Blackline Masters R131 and R132
3. Test 10-6, p. T66

UNIT 10

CHAPTER 7   The World At War

Overview   The chief causes of World War I were the growth of nationalism, the arms race, and the rivalry among European imperialist powers. A source of great tension centered in the Balkans. The alliances between nations caused the conflict to spread quickly once war started. The United States was the last major power to ally itself and to join the struggle against Germany and Austria-Hungary. The strength of the German army and the introduction of new and deadly weapons made this the first global war in modern history. The arrival of American troops strengthened the Allies and enabled them to defeat Germany and win the war.

Objectives

1. To identify major causes of World War I.
2. To describe how World War I was waged.
3. To explain how the entry of the United States was decisive in winning the war.

Developing the Chapter

1. Motivation: Have students discuss how they feel about this statement: By supporting the buildup of our nation's military strength we can help to keep peace in the world. Lead the discussion to the arms race in Europe in the early years of this century. Tell students that this arms race did not keep the peace; in fact, it led to the first global conflict in world history.

2. Introduction

a. Have students read the chapter title and Objective question.
b. List these vocabulary words on the chalkboard: Central Powers, Allied Powers, neutral, Western Front, Eastern Front. Have students suggest the meaning of these terms by studying the map on page 518.
d. List the remaining vocabulary words on the chalkboard: Triple Entente, Triple Alliance, mobilized, and stalemate. Have the students look up the definitions of these terms in the Glossary on pages 000–000. Ask them to locate the nations that formed each of the two alliances. Have the students write sentences using the words mobilized and stalemate.

3. Review and Recall: After the students have read the chapter, ask them to cite evidence to prove or disprove these conclusions.

a. World War I would never have happened if Archbishop Francis Ferdinand of Austria and his wife had not been killed by a Serbian nationalist. (Students should note the underlying causes of the war and understand that some other event also could have sparked the conflict.)
b. Had Russia stayed in the war, the Allies would have won the war without American military aid. (In evaluating this conclusion, students should consider the weak state of Russia's army, the great military strength of the German army, and the use of deadly weapons on both sides.)

4. Building Social Studies Skills: Have students draw conclusions from the account of a young Belgian civilian in the "Daily Life in…" feature (p. 517). Ask them to: (1) List ways in which civilians were affected by the war; (2) Explain why there wasn't any gas for heat or lighting; (3) Determine when this account was written, 1914 or 1918 (Probably 1918, since the last sentence indicates "four long years" were to go by and the writer could not have know this in 1914).

5. Extension:

a. Have students decide whether they would have favored or opposed America's entry into World War I. Then ask them to create a flyer that they might have circulated in their neighborhood, to try to rally people to support their view point.
b. Have students create a pictorial account of World War I by collecting copies of photographs taken during the war of soldiers, battle scenes, and wartime civilian life; or have them draw pictures based on accounts they have read about the war.

Support Materials

Assignments can include:

1. Chapter Review, pp. 522–523
2. Workbook, p. 81
3. Blackline Masters R133 and R134
4. Test 10-7, p. T67
5. Map Transparency 24 and Activity Sheet A24.

CHAPTER 8   After World War I

Overview   In January 1919, leaders of the Big Four met to draft the postwar peaceterms. President Woodrow Wilson presented his Fourteen Points for a lasting peace. However, the other world leaders disagreed with many of these points and forced Wilson to accept terms that were much harsher on Germany. New postwar boundaries in Central and Eastern Europe were also established. The peace terms caused deep bitterness in defeated Germany and soon created problems in the new countries of Eastern Europe.

Objectives

1. To identify the peace treaties that ended the war, and the terms that the Central Powers were forced to accept.
2. To identify key provision in Wilson's Fourteen Points.
3. To compare the map of Europe before and after the signing of the Versailles treaty.

Developing the Chapter

1. **Motivation:** Write the following figure on the chalkboard: 30,000,000 casualties. Ask students if they can guess what this figure represents. Explain that it is the total number of soldiers who were killed or wounded in World War I on both sides of the conflict. After students have reacted to the terrible human cost of the war, ask them to read the introduction to Chapter 8.

2. **Introduction:**
a. Have students read the chapter title and Objective question
   Ask: What provisions would you include in a peace treaty to end a war?
b. Ask students to look up the vocabulary words in the Glossary on pages 728–738 and write the definitions in their notebooks.

3. **Review and Recall:** After the students have read the chapter:
a. Have them practice making judgments by having them decide whether the peace achieved after World War I was a "peace without victory."
b. Have them decide if the following is a generalization: Germany suffered more than any other nation as a result of World

War I. (Students should note that the generalization is not valid. Separate treaties made with the other Central Powers treated Austria-Hungary just as harshly. Russia also was treated like a defeated power by its former allies. France suffered tremendous damage during the war from the stalemated trench warfare occurring along its western border. Finally, some of the nationality groups who now lived in the nations created by the treaty still lacked a homeland.)

4. **Building Social Studies Skills:** Have the students study the time line on page 524.
Ask: How long did it take from the truce till the peace treaty? (about nine months) Then have students write the time line events in the order in which they occurred...1. Treaty of Versailles is signed by Germany; 2. Austria, Czechoslovakia, and Yugoslavia become new nations; 3. The Allies threaten to invade Germany; 4. The Paris Peace Conference begins; 5. German officials refuse to sign "war-guilt" clause.

5. **Extension:**
a. Conduct a mock peace conference at Versailles. Assign groups of students to represent each of the major powers at the meeting—France, Britain, the United States. Have students research beforehand the position their nation took at the conference.
b. Have students research the history of one of the countries in Eastern Europe since its creation after World War I. Ask them to determine how the settlement made after World War I affected the problems that that nation has had since that time.

Support Materials

Assignments can include:
1. Chapter Review, pp. 528–529
2. Workbook, p. 82
3. Blackline Masters R135 and R136
4. Test 10-8, p. T68
5. Map Transparency 25 and Activity Sheet A25
6. Source reading S34.

UNIT 11

THE WORLD TORN APART

Unit Overview   Men and women looked forward to peace and prosperity in the years following World War I. But nationalist movements, a worldwide economic depression, and bitterness among the defeated nations led to world-wide unrest. In Germany, Italy, and Japan, tough new leaders who stressed military strength came to power. In the democracies, the Great Depression and war weariness left Britain, France, and the United States unprepared for the Second World War. The Second World War brought these nations together in victory. Their victory paved the way of the creation of the United Nations, a new organization for world peace.

Unit Objectives

1. To list reasons for the failure of peace after World War I.
2. To identify economic causes of aggression by Germany, Japan, and Italy that led to World War II
3. To name instances of nationalism in the 1920s and 1930s and to describe the results of such movements.
4. To define fascism and communism and to describe their growth between the wars.
5. To chronicle the sequence of the major events of World War II.

Unit Introduction

1. Motivation: Bring in a glass of water. Drop a pebble into it for the class to see.
Ask: What happens when you drop a pebble into a lake or a pond? Elicit comments about a ripple effect. Tell students that events occurring in a distant part of the world also have a ripple effect that reaches us. Ask for specific examples of historic events that had wide-ranging consequences. You can give an example connected with World War I, the assassination of Archduke Francis Ferdinand, as a starter. Ask volunteers to come up to the chalkboard to write examples of events that contributed to World War II.

2. Visual: Have the class look at the unit opener photograph.
Ask: Why are all of these workers women? In wartime, why would there be a shortage of men as workers? Explain how this marked a shift in the status of women and their role in American society.

3. Time line: Have students look at the time line for the unit. Remind them that it provides a good overview of the key events and people in the chapters that follow. They will find it helpful to refer to it as they read the chapters.

Unit Activities

1. Cooperative Learning: Write three topics on the board (or make three handout sheets):
—"War and aggression occur when people are denied their human dignity."
—"Economic imbalance is the main reason for political unrest and war."
—"The only way to stop aggression is by aggression."
   Assign the topics to different groups of students. Have each group first decide how it wants to approach the topic, pro or con. Then have the group compile supporting data from the text. Finally, have each student write a short essay on the topic.

2. Making a Mural: Have a group of students create a mural depicting the years up to and including World War II. As preparation, require them to submit tentative lists of people, places, and events they may want to include.

3. Making an Illustrative Chart: Have individuals or a group create a chart of weapons or aircraft used in World War II. This activity can go beyond classifying by comparing to weapons of World War I or by comparing to current weapons systems.

4. Hypothesizing: Observe the map on page 584, "Taking Sides in World War II." Name the countries that were considered neutral. Have students suggest reasons why each nation decided to remain neutral.

Support Materials

Assignments can include:
1. Unit Review, pp. 584–585
2. Unit 11 Test, pp. UT21–UT22
3. Unit 11 ESL/LEP Worksheet 1, p. ESL 21
4. Unit 11 ESL/LEP Worksheet 2, p. ESL 22

CHAPTER 1   The World, 1920 to 1939

Overview   Hopes of peace and prosperity gave way to war and depression in the years between World War I and World War II. Beginning in 1929, the Great Depression caused economic ruin around the world. By 1939, totalitarian regimes in Germany, Italy, and Japan were on a path of war and conquest.

Objectives

1. To list underlying causes of the Great Depression.
2. To identify conditions that led to fascism and the outbreak of World War II.
3. To explain economic concepts such as inflation, unemployment, and depression.
4. To identify actions nations took in an effort to recover from the Great Depression.

Developing the Chapter

1. Motivation: Hand out a ditto sheet or blackline master with the headline UTOPIAN TIMES. Date: January 1, 1920. Tell each student to jot down people's hopes for a better world right after the war. Encourage students to personalize their answers, such as "brother home from the army" or "a new car" or "repair roof." Share these lists with the class. Begin discussion of the aspirations of the postwar generation. Students should be encouraged to invent and personalize. Then the class can share these contributions and use them to make generalizations about the postwar era.

2. Introduction:

a. Call on the individual students. Have each write a chapter vocabulary word on the board and define it in his or her own words. Then amend the definitions until all are correct enough to record in their vocabulary notebooks.
b. Read the chapter title and Objective question aloud to the class. Tell the students that their task will be to come up with alternate titles and an Objective in their own words after they read the chapter.
c. Have students read the chapter aloud in class. Refrain from making any comments as they read the chapter for the first time.

d. Have each student write a new chapter title and an originally worded Objective.

3. Review and Recall: After the students have read the chapter aloud in class:

a. Have them summarize it concisely in their own words (100 words or less).
b. Have individual students or small groups compile FACT LISTS from the chapter. This can be done as a contest.
c. Have students write an original paragraph describing the information found in the graph on page 540.
d. Have students write an outline from memory on the main points of the chapter. Then have them compare it to the actual chapter headings and subheadings.

4. Building Social Studies Skills: Review the graph on unemployment on p. 540. Have students prepare the groundwork for an Extension activity creating their own graphs. This can be done as a class exercise or a bulletin board project. For now, have students:

a. Select five possible topics for a graph.
b. Narrow the list to one topic, based on practicality and research considerations.
c. Decide what type of graph will be used: bar, line, pie, etc.

(Note: Teacher may want to guide special-need students to make an alternate version of the graph in the book, using different years, a different nation, or a different type of graph format.)

5. Extension:

a. Construct the graph prepared in the previous activity.
b. Have each student write a paragraph interpreting the data listed in the graph. Cite at least three examples of specific years or number displayed in the graph.

Support Materials

Assignments can include:

1. Chapter Review, pp 540–541
2. Workbook, pp. 83–85
3. Blackline Masters R137 and R138
4. Test 11-1, p. T69.

UNIT 11

CHAPTER 2   Russia Turns to Communism

Overview   After the overthrow of Czar Nicholas II in 1917, the Bolsheviks set up Communist rule in Russia. After a bloody civil war, Lenin consolidated his power in 1921 and rebuilt the economy under the New Economic Policy (NEP). Starting in 1928, Joseph Stalin instituted a series of Five-Year Plans to expand the Soviet economy. Stalin executed millions of farmers and party workers during his years as dictator.

Objectives

1. To describe when and how the Communist party gained power in Russia.
2. To list the steps that Lenin took to strengthen the country.
3. To define Stalin's policies and their effect on the Soviet people.

Developing the Chapter

1. Motivation: Bring a cassette tape recorder to class. Write WHAT COMMUNISM HAS MEANT TO RUSSIA on the chalkboard. Set up the tape recorder in the front of the class. Have each student come up to the recorder and recite one sentence about what he or she thinks communism has meant to Russia. These speculations will be compared with the content of the text chapter. Tell students that they will now explore further by reading. They can compare their ideas with the facts presented in the book by playing back the tape after the chapter has been read.

2. Introduction:

a. Call on students to read each vocabulary word and glossary definition aloud. Then have the class record the words and definitions in their vocabulary notebooks.
b. Have students copy the chapter title and Objective question into their notebooks.
c. Have students read the chapter silently on their own.

3. Review and Recall: After the students have read the chapter:

a. Have them compile a list of NAMES AND DATES cited in the chapter. This can be a class project, and results shared on a ditto or blackline.
b. Have students make notes toward answering the Objective question. Tell them that they will use these notes later to write a short essay.
c. Have students re-read the PEOPLE IN HISTORY section of Lenin. Then have them summarize it by writing an UP CLOSE AND PERSONAL AUTOBIOGRAPHY on Lenin, imagining Lenin's own words.

4. Building Social Studies Skills: Being such a vast country, the Soviet Union's problems have often revolved around agriculture. To explore cause/effect relationships and to compare and contrast Soviet agriculture with American farm policies, have students fill out a chart with the following headings: ownership of land, productivity, marketing of crops/products, economic growth.

5. Extension:

a. Have students write and perform a skit depicting the life of kulaks exiled to Siberia for opposing Stalin's force collectivization.
b. As a cooperative learning project, have students write and "deliver" a series of speeches on Soviet agricultural policy. Assign the following roles: general party secretary, chief agricultural minister, a typical farmer, a military leader, a consumer, a factory worker. Topic: the scarcity of quality meat. Forum: a regional party meeting.
c. Have students study the map of the Soviet Union on page 690. Ask individual students to describe why Russia has traditionally been fearful of invasion. Students must cite specific countries.
d. Have students write an essay that answers the Objective question. Tell them to rely on the notes taken for the Review and Recall exercise.

Support Materials

Assignments can include:

1. Chapter Review, pp. 546–547
2. Blackline Masters R139 and R140
3. Test 11-2, p. T70
4. Source Reading, p. S35.

CHAPTER 3   Fascism in Italy and Spain

Overview   As a reaction to dire economic conditions after World War I, Italy and Spain turned to fascism. Benito Mussolini became dictator of Italy and Francisco Franco became dictator of Spain. The Spanish Civil War served as a bloody preview of World War II, as leftists battled rightists.

Objectives

1. To describe the conditions in Italy and Spain that led to fascism.
2. To define fascism and cite examples of its application in Italy and Spain.
3. To chronicle the rise of power of Mussolini and Franco.
4. To explain how the Spanish Civil War was prelude to World War II.

Developing the Chapter

1. **Motivation:** Create a ditto sheet or blackline master with the heading: WHY THERE ARE DICTATORS. Place the numbers 1–10 along the left margin, with ample blank spaces to the right. Allow 20 minutes to fill out the sheet. This is an ungraded exercise; students do not even have to write their names on the sheet. Collect student responses and read them to the class. Call on one or two individuals to take notes. Then, with the class, arrive at a consensus on ten reasons why dictators assume power. Tell the class: Let's see if these reasons prove true as we look at Italy and Spain before World War II."

2. **Introduction:**
a. Read the chapter title and Objective question.
b. Ask students to predict answers to the Objective question.
c. Write the chapter's vocabulary words on the chalkboard. Then, as you recite random glossary definitions of the vocabulary words, ask students to identify the word whose definition you are reading. Then have students write each word and definition in their notebooks.

3. **Review and Recall:** After the students have read the chapter:
a. Have them compose a TRUE or FALSE quiz on its contents (minimum: 10 questions).

b. Have students make a table of contents for the chapter. Tell students that this is similar to an outline, with page numbers added for reference.
c. Have students write a list of things they do not understand in the chapter. Again, these can be submitted anonymously. Providing answers can be an open-book, class exercise.

4. **Building Social Studies Skills:** Bring in the front page of a local or national newspaper. Show it to the class. Read aloud two or three quotations, either from a local or national source. Remind students that the newspaper in your hand is a primary source. Tell them that books, magazines, letters, and videotapes can also be considered primary sources.
Ask: How are our views influenced by the time and place we live in? Elicit that current popular notions, our race, our set, our economic status—all these and more might influence how we interpret the primary sources that we study.

5. **Extension:**
a. Study the primary source quoted in the chapter. Have students tell why people today might respond to the quotation differently than people did when it was first written. Have them suggest why some might respond in the same way.
b. Have students pretend they are newspaper editors. Have them write an editorial opposing Mussolini's or Hitler's ideas.
c. Have a small group of students bring in a copy of Picasso's rendering of the atrocities at Guernica. Have them give a brief history of the painting, include the controversy over displaying it.
d. Ask individuals or groups to draw their own depictions of the horrors of war or people's sufferings under totalitarianism.

Support Materials

Assignments can include:
1. Chapter Review, pp. 552–553
2. Blackline Masters R141 and R142
3. Test 11-3, p. T71.

CHAPTER 4   The Nazis in Germany

Overview   After World War I, Germany's democratic Weimar Republic encountered staggering inflation. Seizing on the people's discontent and low national morale, Adolf Hitler built his Nazi party. After sizable election victories, Hitler was named chancellor in 1933 and embarked on a course of aggression and of brutality against the Jews.

Objectives

1. To list the actions that led to Hitler's rise to power as dictator of Germany.
2. To define inflation and its consequences for postwar Germany.
3. To define propaganda and its role in Nazi Germany.
4. To explain how both aggression and appeasement led to German expansion and finally to war.
5. To describe Hitler's policies toward the Jews and the consequences of these policies.

Developing the Chapter

1. **Motivation:** Have students look at the map of Nazi Aggression in the 1930s on page 556. **Ask:** Which lands were next? Which nations do you think Nazi Germany would have tried to conquer next? Then tell the students to imagine you are a student in Czechoslovakia in 1939. Hitler's armies are stationed in your town. Describe how you would feel living in the shadow of enemy soldiers.

2. **Introduction:**
a. Distribute a small strip of paper to each student. Write the chapter's vocabulary words on the chalkboard. Assign each row or class section a word, making sure all words are assigned. Tell each student to write a telegram definition of 10 words or less for his or her assigned word. After collecting the telegram definitions, post them on a bulletin board. As a follow-up activity, discuss the definitions and amend as needed before having students write them in their notebooks.
b. Call on a student to write the Objective question on the chalkboard. Tell the class

that the Objective question is the goal of this chapter.
c. Read *selected* portions of the chapter aloud. Have students read selected portions. Ask how these selections help to answer the Objective question.

3. **Review and Recall:** After the students have read the chapter:
a. Have them review the map on p. 556 of Nazi Aggression in the 1930s. Tell them to find the page numbers and sentences that describe these map items: the remilitarizing of the Rhineland, the occupation of Austria, the annexation of the Sudetenland, the occupation of the rest of Czechoslovakia. Write the information on a separate piece of paper.
b. Have each student rewrite a paragraph of the text in his or her own words.

4. **Building Social Studies Skills:** Explain to students that a research report requires thought and preparation. Tell them that before they can locate source materials, they must narrow their topics. As groundwork for an Extension activity, have students narrow the topic "Nazi Germany" three times. Use the following model: Nazi Germany narrowed to use of propaganda; narrowed to use of propaganda against the Jews; narrowed to propaganda against the Jews in newspapers and speeches.

5. **Extension:**
a. Using library resources, have students list at least three sources for finding out more information about the narrowed topic.
b. Have students write notes on the topic from the three or more sources.
c. Have students write a rough draft of a report that explores the topic just cited.
d. As an alternative exercise: Have students trace the map on p. 556 and name the rivers shown on the map.

Support Materials
Assignments can include:

1. Chapter Review, pp. 558–559
2. Workbook, pp. 86–87
3. Blackline Masters R143 and R144
4. Test 11-4, p. T72.

CHAPTER 5   Militarism in Japan

Overview   After a brief democratic era, military leaders took control of Japan in the early 1930s. To increase its power, markets, and sources of raw materials, Japan embarked on the conquest of East Asia. Japan's victims were Manchuria, south and central China, and then Indochina on this path to World War II.

Objectives

1. To explain the sequence of events and conditions that allowed the military to take power in Japan.
2. To describe the economic conditions leading to Japan's aggression in the 1920s and 1930s.
3. To name the countries and territories Japan invaded in its quest for an empire in the 1930s.
4. To compare and contrast Japan's militarism with Italy's and Germany's.

Developing the Chapter

1. Motivation: By prior arrangement with several students, have them bow deeply to you before they take their seats. Return the bow to each student who bows. Have these same students respond with exaggerated politeness during roll call or during review of homework. Then ask the entire class: Why do we view the Japanese as obedient to authority? Is this based on fact? Would such obedience make it easy or hard for military leaders to rule?

2. Introduction:
a. Hand out a ditto sheet or black line with the Objective question written at the top. Draw a vertical line down the center. Leave the rest of the sheet blank.
b. Tell students: Before you read the chapter, take 10 minutes to predict how the text will answer the Objective question. Write your predictions in notes on the left side of the sheet.
c. Tell students to read the chapter. As they read, in the right column they should write phrases and facts that help to answer the Objective question. Tell them to put a check in the left column for any predictions that also were included in the right column.

c. While reading, have students list any vocabulary words they do not understand.

3. Review and Recall: After the students have read the chapter:
a. Have students review the map on p. 563 on Japanese aggression. Have each student compose a quiz (with answers) about information related to the map.
b. Have students review the index of their textbook. Show students how to cite page references for a specific topic. Then have students select or invent two additional categories not already in the index. Have them provide page references. (The entire exercise can be done as a class project for those who find it difficult.)

4. Building Social Studies Skills: Allow students to research and to hypothesize by creating "what-if" newspaper front pages for the following:
a. December 6, 1941—The U.S. learns of an impending attack and declares war on Japan.
b. 1931—Japan begins to invade Manchuria. But after threats from the Soviet Union, the United States, and Britain, Japan withdraws.
c. September 1940—Resistance to the Japanese invasion of French Indochina is so fierce the Japanese withdraw.

5. Extension:
a. Conduct a class debate on the following: "Resolved, Japan's aggression was caused by its geographical isolation."
b. Have students write an essay on the topic "Why the League of Nations Failed to Halt Japanese Aggression."
c. Have students present a dramatic reading of selections from Franklin D. Roosevelt's "Day of Infamy" speech.

Support Materials

Assignments can include:

1. Chapter Review, pp. 566–567
2. Blackline Masters R145 and R146
3. Test 11-5, p. T73
4. Map Transparency 26 and Activity Sheet A26.

CHAPTER 6   Other Nationalist Struggles

Overview   During the 1920s and 1930s, nationalist movements inspired many peoples. Under Gandhi, India embarked on a course that would eventually lead to its independence from Great Britain. Egypt reached an agreement with Britain for some measure of self-rule. Led by Kemal Ataturk, Turkey became a modern nation after the break-up of the Ottoman Empire. Jews began a struggle to set up a nation in Palestine, a land also claimed by the Arabs.

Objectives

1. To describe nationalist independence movements in India, Turkey, Egypt, and Palestine.
2. To define civil disobedience and its role in India's independence.
3. To describe the break-up of the Ottoman Empire and the effects of this break-up.

Developing the Chapter

1. Motivation: Hand out several ditto sheets or blackline masters for students to complete creatively as an ungraded exercise. Each sheet will be blank, except for these heading:

a. The Saddest Day of My Life…by the Sultan of Turkey
2. My Greatest Hope…by an Arab in Palestine
c. My Greatest Hope…by a Jew in Palestine
d. The Happiest Day of My Life…by a Turkish peasant

Make sure students consult the map on p. 574, the Break-up of the Ottoman Empire, for help in composing these writings.

2. Introduction

a. Call on a student to read the chapter title and Objective question.
b. Ask students what nationalism is. Elicit responses about America's war for independence.
c. Discuss the terms *civil disobedience* and *Zionism*. Have students copy glossary definitions into their notebooks.
d. Have students read the chapter. Assign each student a nation to focus on while reading the chapter. Tell them: You will be an expert on this country's drive for independence, so take notes about it.

3. Review and Recall: After the students have read the chapter:

a. Tell students to review their notes about their assigned country. Have students gather in groups to pool their findings.
b. Conduct a PATH TO INDEPENDENCE project. Groups will present text-based summaries on India, Turkey, Egypt, and Israel. Each group must distribute to the rest of the class a FACT SHEET with text page references.
c. Have all students read and observe the visual in the Arts and Artifacts section. As a writing exercise, have the students write three more questions related to the visuals. Use the question as the basis of a follow-up discussion.

4. Building Social Studies Skills: Have the class publish a class book based on their just-completed PATH TO INDEPENDENCE project. Assign editors, proofreaders, and rewrite people. Make sure that FACT SHEETS avoid errors and duplication. Encourage students to make a cover, table of contents, and index for their books.

5. Extension:

a. Modeled on the PATH TO INDEPENDENCE project, have groups or individuals conduct research on Iraq, Jordan, Syria, and Lebanon and these countries' efforts at self-rule during this period.
b. Have groups make displays of flags of the nations cited in the chapter.
c. Have students review the map on page 574, the Break-up of the Ottoman Empire. Have students choose one of the countries created in 1920. Then, using library resources, have them draw a detailed map of that country. Maps must include the capital, major rivers, mountains, three major cities and a key.

Support Materials

Assignments can include:

1. Chapter Review, pp. 574–575
2. Blackline Masters R147 and R148
3. Test 11-6, p. T74.

UNIT 11

CHAPTER 7   World War II

Overview   German and Japanese aggression eventually engulfed much of the world in war again. Turning points in the early fighting including the fall of France and the fall of the Scandinavian countries in 1940, the Battle of Britain, and the German invasion of the Soviet Union. Germany's losses in Africa, the Soviet campaign, the Normandy invasion, and the attack on Europe insured Hitler's downfall. Defeats in the Pacific and atomic bombing brought about Japan's surrender.

Objectives

1. To identify major battles in the Pacific, Europe, and Africa.
2. To explain why the United States shifted from neutrality to involvement.
3. To chronicle the events leading to the Allied victory and the defeat of the Axis.

Developing the Chapter

1. **Motivation:** After roll has been taken, turn the lights off. Ask students to put their heads on the desk, with their hands covering their heads. Ask them to close their eyes. Then tell them: Imagine enemy bombers are flying overhead. Air-raid sirens are blaring. They must quickly go into the hallway or down into basement. This was what it was like for British students in the 1940s. Now open your eyes. You're about to discover exactly what led to these terrible events.

2. **Introduction:**
   a. Write the chapter's vocabulary words on the board. Ask students to find them within the chapter and recite the entire paragraph where each word was found.
   b. Ask students to define the words and to tell what other words give context clues about their meaning.
   c. Explain to students the concept of a theme. Tell them they might want to express a theme as a moral, or conclusion. Then have each student write two themes related to this chapter. To get students started, you can offer suggestions such as "Unchecked aggression leads to war" or "War is inhuman."
   d. As a follow-up activity, have students cite references in the chapter to back up their theme statements.

3. **Review and Recall:** After the students have read the chapter:
   a. Have students consult the map on p. 578 and describe the farthest Axis advance in Europe by naming the countries that came under Axis control.
   b. Have students consult the map on p. 579 and describe the farthest Japanese advances. Have students name the islands and countries Japan occupied.
   c. Divide the class into cooperative groups. Have students construct time lines for the war in the Pacific, the war in Africa, and the war in Europe.

4. **Building Social Studies Skills:** Explain to students that people often think in stereotypes, or false pictures, of Japan or Germany during World War II. Ask students to choose one of the following, and in the students own words, write an imaginary diary: a German student who despises Hitler's policies; a Japanese student who is a pacifist; a German or Japanese soldier who wants the war to end so he can return to his family.

5. **Extension:**
   a. Have individuals or groups of students use library resources to find examples of American journalism during World War II. Students are especially encouraged to find newspaper accounts of major battles. As students report to the class, have them discuss language and prejudice, bias and objectivity, and appeals to emotions.
   b. Find some photos of particular battles or events: D-Day, the bombing of Dresden or Hiroshima or Nagasaki, Pearl Harbor. Have student write poems or songs, or paint posters related to the events.

Support Materials

Assignments can include:

1. Chapter Review, pp. 582–583
2. Workbook, pp. 88–90
3. Blackline Masters R149 and R150
4. Test 11-7, p. T75
5. Map Transparencies 27–28 and Activity Sheets A27-A28
6. Source readings, pp. 536–537.

UNIT 12

THE POST-WAR WORLD

Overview   International relations after World War II were dominated by the competition between the superpowers. While nations were recovering from the devastation of the war, a Cold War developed which pitted East against West in such places as Greece, Berlin, and Cuba. In Korea this tension erupted into a shooting war. Meanwhile, the two communist nations of China and the Soviet Union became rivals instead of allies.

Objectives

1. To discuss changes that occurred in Europe, Japan, and China after World War II.
2. To give examples of East-West competition in the years after World War II.
3. To describe "battles" in the Cold War.

Developing the Chapter

1. Motivation: Read aloud the following excerpt from a speech delivered by President Truman in 1947. "The seeds of totalitarian regimes [dictatorships] are nurtured in misery and want. They spread and grow into the evil soil of poverty and strife. They reach their full growth when the hope of a people for a better life had died.
We must keep that hope alive.
The free people of the world look to us for support in maintaining their freedoms. If we falter in our leadership, we may endanger the peace of the world—and we shall surely endanger the welfare of our own Nation."
Ask: (a) according to Truman, what conditions allow dictatorships to take hold in a country? (b) What responsibility does the United states have to other countries? (c) Do you think the United States should take the responsibility to maintain the freedom of other countries? Why or why not?

2. Visual: Direct students' attention to the unit opening visual (p. 675). Ask students if they know who Mao was. Explain that his goals were to make China a modern industrial nation and to set up a classless society.
Ask: Why do you think students and peasants supported Mao's leadership? Is a "classless society" desirable? Why or why not?

3. Time line: Encourage students to survey the unit by reading the events on the unit time line (pp. 274–275).

Unit Activities

1. Cooperative Learning: Divide the class into groups of four or five students, each of which is responsible for preparing an article for a special-edition newspaper written and published in the U.S.S.R. about the Cold War. Assign topics based on events covered in the chapter (sample topics include: the Chinese Civil War, the Berlin Blockade, the formation of NATO and the Warsaw Pact). Members of a group are to share the job of library research. They may choose to appoint one student to write a draft of the editorial, but they must work together as a group to edit the draft. After the article is researched and written, the group should generate a headline for the article. Stress that when writing and editing their articles, students should keep in mind how the Cold War looked from a Soviet perspective.

2. Point of View: Ask students to write a short essay about the Korean War from one of these points of view: American, Soviet, Chinese, Korean. Have volunteers share their essays with the class.

3. Summarizing: Have the class or groups of students prepare a bulletin board display on the state of international affairs after World War II. This display should include a world map on which they locate and identify by means of brief captions places where important postwar events took place. The captions should serve as summary statements of postwar events.

Support Materials

Assignments can include:
1. Unit Review, pp. 720–721
2. Unit 12 Test, pp. UT23–UT24
3. Unit 12 ESL/LEP Worksheet 1, p. ESL 23
4. Unit 12 ESL/LEP Worksheet 2, p. ESL 24

CHAPTER 1   Effects of World War II

Overview   After World War II the Allies took command in Japan and Germany. Japan embarked on a remarkable economic recovery as an ally of the United States. Germany became a country divided between East and West. European nations recovered rapidly and moved toward economic cooperation. The United Nations was formed as an organization to help keep peace throughout the world.

Objectives

1. To describe the changes that took place in Japan after World War II.
2. To explain how Germany became two countries.
3. To recount the main arguments made at the Nuremburg war crimes trials.
4. To list ways that European countries and countries throughout the world worked together for peace and economic growth.

Developing the Chapter

1. Motivation: Lead a discussion on how the victorious countries in a war ought to treat the defeated countries. Ask students to brainstorm possible approaches to this problem. (Have them review the treatment of Germany after World War I.) Then ask them to consider the advantages and disadvantages of each approach.

2. Introduction

a. Write the chapter vocabulary words on the chalkboard. Have them choose the approach they prefer. Finally, have them compare their approach to the one actually taken after World War II.

b. Have students read the chapter title and Objective question.

c. Have students read the chapter.

3. Review and Recall: After the students have read the chapter:

a. Ask them questions about the chapter content.

b. Have them reread and answer the Objective question.

c. Have them read The Arts and Artifacts feature aloud. Ask them to observe the picture carefully. Then use the feature questions to generate a discussion.

4. Building Social Studies Skills: Below are some statistics about the diet of Europeans after World War II. First have students use the information to make bar graphs. Then ask these questions: (a) How much meat did a person in Britain eat per year between 1947 and 1950? How did that changed by 1956–1958? (b) How many pounds of potatoes did an average German eat per year between 1947 and 1950? Between 1956 and 1958? (c) Write a sentence describing the diet of Europeans between 1947 and 1958.

	Potatoes	Fresh fruit	Cheese	Meat
Britain				
1947–50	253	83	9	100
1956–58	209	94	9	145
France				
1947–50	326	72	10	117
1957–58	266	92	10	117
Germany				
1947–50	416	65	7	52
1956–58	339	128	15	114

Average pounds per person per year.
Source: P. Lamartine Yates, *Food, Land and Manpower in Western Europe,* as quoted in *World History,* Burton F. Beers (Prentice-Hall, 1986), p. 639.

5. Extension

a. Have students read and take notes on current articles about the European Economics Community. Then lead a discussion about the issues facing the Community today and the advantages of the organization for its members.

b. Have students learn more about what the United Nations does. Then ask them to write a brief report on this topic: Is the United Nations an effective organization for keeping world peace?

Support Materials

Assignments can include:

1. Chapter Review, pp. 594–595
2. Workbook, pp. 92–93
3. Blackline Masters R151 and R152
4. Test 12-1, p. T76
5. Map Transparency 29 and Activity Sheet A29
6. Source Reading S38

CHAPTER 2   The New Superpowers

Overview   After World War II the United States and the Soviet Union were the world's strongest nations. These former Allies had developed contrasting ways of life and ideologies. They had become the leaders of groups of competing nations. The two superpowers engaged in races to build arms and to conquer space.

Objectives

1. To contrast the economies of the United States and the Soviet Union after World War II.
2. To identity the goals and programs of Joseph Stalin as the leader of the Soviet Union.
3. To describe the rivalry between the United States and the Soviet Union in arms and in space exploration.

Developing the Chapter

1. Motivation: Read aloud this excerpt from a speech delivered by Winston Churchill in 1946: "From Stettin in the Baltic to Trieste in the Adriatic, an iron curtain has descended across the Continent." Then have students look closely at the map on page 599. Have them name the countries that lie east of the Iron Curtain.

Ask: How do you think Churchill felt about the presence of an iron curtain in Europe?

2. Introduction

a. Write the chapter vocabulary words on the chalkboard. Have students write each word and its glossary meaning in their vocabulary notebooks.

b. Have students read the chapter title and Objective question.

c. Have students read the chapter.

3. Review and Recall: After the students have read the chapter:

a. Have them ask each other questions about the chapter.

b. Have them identify the main idea of each section.

c. Have students reread and answer the Objective question.

4. Building Social Studies Skills: Refer students to the map of Eastern Europe after World War II on page 600. Then have students (a) name three boundaries that changed after World War II; (b) Identify three lands taken over by the Soviet Union after the war; (c) Locate four satellite nations; (d) Locate two communist countries that were not satellite nations.

5. Extension

a. Divide the class into two groups. Direct the students in group A to find out more about the space program in the United States from 1955 to the present via library research. Students in group B will find out about the space program in the Soviet Union from 1955 to the present. Have each group prepare a time line of the important events and achievements of each space program. Then have them report to each other about what they have learned.

b. Have students prepare and act out a skit in which young people from the United States and the Soviet Union in 1955 meet each other and try to learn more about each other countries. (Students should assume that their audience is a group of junior high school students who have no background in the subject.)

c. One result of the arms race is that Russia and the United States have developed missiles that can travel thousands of miles and can carry atomic or hydrogen bombs to any place on earth. Nations with such weapons have the ability to destroy each other within minutes. Ask students to prepare an essay on one of these two statements: If a nation want peace, it must prepare for war. War can only be avoided if nations agree to disarm.

Support Materials

Assignments can include:

1. Chapter Review, pp 602–603
2. Workbook, p 91 and p. 94
3. Blackline Masters R153 and R154
4. Test 12-2, p. T77
5. Source Reading S39

CHAPTER 3   A Cold War

Overview   The rivalry between the United States and the Soviet Union became a Cold War of threats and words. The Cold War erupted in Turkey and Greece, in Berlin, in Cuba, and elsewhere. After the Cuban Missile Crisis, during which the superpowers stood on the brink of nuclear war, tensions eased, and the United States and the Soviet Union began to seek peaceful ways of settling their differences.

Objectives

1. To define the Truman Doctrine and describe the events that led to it.
2. To give examples of "hot spots" during the Cold War.
3. To describe the events leading to the Berlin Airlift, the building of the Berlin Wall, the creation of NATO, the Warsaw Pact, and the Cuban Missile Crisis.

Developing the Chapter

1. Motivation: Ask students to brainstorm about events that take place during a war (bombings, shooting, fires, and so on). Tell them that these are examples of a "hot war." **Ask:** What might take place during a "cold" war? How would two nations fight each other without violence? Save their list of suggestions for review after they have read the chapter.

2. Introduction

a. Write the chapter vocabulary words on the chalkboard. Have students write each word and its glossary definition in their vocabulary notebooks.
b. Have students read the chapter title and Objective question.
c. Have students read the chapter.

3. Review and Recall: After the students have read the chapter:

a. Have them reread each subhead question and answer it.
b. Have them review the chapter time line and describe the events on it.
c. Have them reread and answer the Objective question.

4. Building Social Studies Skills: Have students reread the quotation about the

Marshall Plan in the Spotlight on Sources on text page 000.
Ask: (a) Why did the United States begin the Marshall Plan? (b) To whom was the Marshall Plan directed? (c) Did the United States offer Marshall Plan fund to the Soviet Union? (d) How did the United States benefit from the Marshall Plan?

5. Extension

a. Refer students to the suggestions they made in the Motivation activity about the events that might take place during a cold war. Have them compare their suggestions to the actual events discussed in the chapter.
b. Ask students to make up a crossword puzzle about the Cold War. They should write clues for all the *across* words and *down* words. Then have them exchange completed puzzles with a partner and try to solve the partner's puzzle.
c. Have students imagine they lived in West Berlin in 1948. Have them write a journal entry about life during the Berlin Airlift. They should use facts but can also use their imaginations to make the journal entry more interesting.
d. Tell students that during the 1950s the Cold War and the threat of its exploding into a nuclear war was so frightening that many people in the United States built fall-out shelters, which were supposed to be capable of protecting their occupants from the effects of a nuclear bomb blast. Have students discuss these questions in small groups: Were fall-out shelters a realistic response to the Cold War? Were they an understandable response? Why or why not?

Support Materials
Assignments can include:

1. Chapter Review, pp. 610–611
2. Workbook, p. 95
3. Blackline Masters R155 and R156
4. Test 12-3, p. T78
5. Source Reading S40

UNIT 12

CHAPTER 4 Crisis and Change in Europe

Overview   Great changes took place in Europe during the 1950s and 1960s. The Soviet Union, though under the more moderate leadership of Nikita Khrushchev, crushed popular uprisings in its satellite nations. West Germany showed remarkable economic growth, while Britain's and France's economies were somewhat weaker. Gradually the Cold War began to thaw.

Objectives

1. To explain the significance of Khrushchev's coming to power in the Soviet Union.
2. To describe the causes and results of popular uprisings in Eastern Europe during the 1950s and 1960s.
3. To identify changes in the situations in West Germany, Great Britain, and France during the 1950s and 1960s.
4. To list examples of the thaw in relations between the superpowers.

Developing the Chapter

1. **Motivation:** Review what students have read about he satellite nations in Eastern Europe. Lead a discussion about how these nations might have felt about being Soviet satellites.

Ask: If such nations did not like the situation, what might they have done about it? How would the Soviet government have reacted? Do students think the United States should have acted to "liberate" these satellite nations? Why or why not?

2. **Introduction**
a. Write the chapter vocabulary words on the chalkboard. Have students write each word and its glossary definition in their vocabulary notebooks.
b. Have student read the chapter title and Objective questions.
c. Have students read the chapter.

3. **Review and Recall:** After the students have read the chapter:
a. Ask them questions about the chapter's content.
b. Have them reread and answer the Objective question.

c. Divide them into teams to play a game of 20 questions based on important events, people, and places from the chapter.

4. **Building Social Studies Skills:** Remind students that note-taking is an important skill that can help them learn a chapter's content as well as to study for a test. Help students take notes on the first section of this chapter. Then assign separate groups of students to take notes on different sections of the chapter.

5. **Extension**
a. Have students find out more about one of the uprisings in Eastern Europe against Soviet domination. Suggest they write a newspaper article recapping the main events and including "eyewitness" accounts of the situation (the latter as a creative writing exercise). Have them include a headline for the story.
b. Lead a class discussion based on these questions: (a) Why was it significant that Khrushchev let the Soviet people and the world know that Stalin has oppressed the Soviet people? (b) Why do you think that in the Soviet Union the government controls the press, deciding what articles may be published in newspapers and what books may be published (c) Why was it significant when the Soviet Union began letting writers and artists take trips out of the country?
c. Have students make a chart showing developments in West Germany, Great Britain, and France in the 1950s and 1960s. The chart should include names of leaders, the major economic policies carried out, and other important features of these countries post war development.

Support Materials

Assignments can include:
1. Chapter Review, pp. 618–619
2. Blackline Masters R157 and R158
3. Test 12-4, p. T79

CHAPTER 5   Communism in China and Korea

Overview   In 1949 the civil war in China resulted in the creation of two Chinas. At first the communist People's Republic of China allied with the Soviet Union, but soon ideological differences split the two powers. At the time, the United States recognized only Nationalist China. In 1950 the Cold War erupted into a shooting war in Korea; when the war was over, North and South Korea were still divided. In the 1970s the People's Republic of China and the United States established diplomatic relations.

Objectives

1. To describe the events leading to the creation of the People's Republic of China and Nationalist China.
2. To list the reasons for the split between Communist China and the Soviet Union.
3. To describe the main events of the Korean War.

Developing the Chapter

1. Motivation: Tell students that they will be reading about events that led to great changes in people's lives in China after 1949. Then have students read the Spotlight on Sources on page 621. Ask students to list facts about life in China after 1949 on the basis of their reading. Then ask them to identify advantages and disadvantages of peasant life in China at that time.

2. Introduction

a. Write the chapter vocabulary words on the chalkboard. Use each word in a sentence and have students try to define the words from the content. Then ask them to confirm their definitions by looking up the words in the glossary.
b. Have student read the chapter title and Objective questions.
c. Have students read the chapter time line.
d. Have students read the chapter.

3. Review and Recall: After the students have read the chapter:

a. Have them ask each other questions about the chapter content.
b. Have them reread and answer each subhead question.

c. Have them study the chapter maps and locate places mentioned in the chapter. Let them take turns telling what happened in each place.

4. Building Social Studies Skills: Divide the class into groups of four or five students. Ask each group to write five statements of fact and three statements of opinion based on information in the chapter. Then have the groups alternate reading one of their statements. The rest of the class must decide whether the statement is an opinion or a fact. You might want to make it a contest in which the group that answers the most questions correctly wins.

5. Extension

a. Have students research the life of Mao Zedong. Then ask them to write a character sketch of the man focusing on his chief personality traits.
b. Have students review the material on the Korean War and study the map on page 625. Then lead a discussion about the progress of the war.
   Ask: (a) Who seemed to be winning the war in 1950? (b) Who seemed to be winning the war in 1951? Why had the tide turned? (c) When the war was over, what seemed to have been gained by each side?
c. Have students imagine that they are Chinese leaders in 1964. Their country has just successfully tested a nuclear bomb. Relations with the Soviet Union are strained. Have students draw a political cartoon about the situation.
d. As the price of friendship, trade, and cultural exchange, the People's Republic of China insisted that the United States stop giving military equipment to Taiwan. Should the United States have stopped military aid to Nationalist China? Have students prepare an essay that addresses this issue.

Support Materials

Assignments can include:

1. Chapter Review, pp. 626–627
2. Workbook, pp. 96–98
3. Blackline Masters R159 and R160
4. Test 12-5, p. T80

MODERN NATIONALISM

Unit Overview   Many of the nations in Asia, the Middle East, and Africa achieved independence after World War II. Latin American countries won independence a number of years before, but have faced many of the same problems as developing nations in other regions. The countries in these regions have made some progress toward solving political, economic, and social problems. However, deep-seated religious, ethnic, and political differences have continued to cause conflict. Political upheaval and debt have ruined the economies of many of these countries. Since the fall of communism in the Soviet Union and Eastern Europe, there has been a growing trend toward democratic and free-market reform.

Unit Objectives

1. To compare and contrast the factors that influenced the political development of South Asia, the Middle East, Southeast Asia, Africa, and Latin America.
2. To identify the contributions of political leaders in those areas of the world.
3. To identify the problems facing the developing countries of Asia, Africa, the Middle East, and Latin America.
4. To trace the political influence and involvement of the United States in Latin America, Asia, Africa, and the Middle East.

Unit Introduction

1. **Motivation:** On a world map, point to the nations of South Asia, the Middle East, Southeast Asia, Africa, and Latin America or instruct students to preview the maps of these regions in their textbooks on page 636 (South Asia), pages 644 and 672 (Middle East), page 654 (Southeast Asia), page 659 (Africa), and page 668 (Latin America). Ask students to think about the many ways their own lives have been influenced by the diverse cultures of these world regions. (Influences include food, clothing, music, art, theater, and language.) Explain that students will learn more about the political development of countries in these regions as they read Unit 13.
2. **Visual:** Direct students' attention to the unit opening visual (p. 631). Point out the contrast between the oil derrick/modern machinery and the camels and tents. Tell students that as they study Unit 13. they will learn how in many areas of the world, older ways of life exist side by side with modern technology. **Ask:** Can you think of reasons why people might not want to change their older ways?
3. **Time Line:** Ask students how many countries of the world are represented on the unit time line (pp. 630–631). As they give their answers, list the countries on the board. **Ask:** How many years does the time line cover? (55) Ask students if they can think of reasons why so many areas of the world would be engaged in political conflict during such a relatively short period of time. After their study of Unit 13 is completed, refer to this question again and ask students to predict whether the political situation in any of these areas is likely to change soon.

Activities

1. **Cooperative Learning:** Divide students into five cooperative learning groups. Assign each group one of the following themes to be developed in each chapter of the unit: Important Political Leaders; Daily Life; Colonialism and the Struggle for Independence; Economic Life; Social Change. The goal for each group is to produce a chart that sums up key facts about the assigned topic pertaining to each region studied in the Unit. The students must work as a group to decide how best to organize the materials in chart form and what visuals should be used to illustrate the chart.
2. **Cause and Effect:** Have students make a chart in which they summarize the causes and effects of major political upheaval in each of the five regions studied in this Unit.

Support Materials

Assignments can include:

1. Unit Review, pp. 672–673
2. Unit 13 Test, pp. UT25–UT26
3. Unit 13 ESL/LEP Worksheet 1, p. ESL 25
4. Unit 13 ESL/LEP Worksheet 2, p. ESL 26

CHAPTER 1   South Asia

Overview   The political changes in some South Asian countries are related to ethnic and religious conflicts. The Sinhalese and Tamil factions of Sri Lanka (formerly Ceylon) have been at war since 1958. The Muslim state of Pakistan was created after India's independence to reduce the conflict between the Hindu majority and the Muslim minority. India has developed its agriculture and industries but has been plagued by violence resulting from religious and ethnic conflicts.

Objectives

1. To identify the effects of ethnic conflicts in South Asian countries.
2. To compare and contrast the recent political histories of Sri Lanka, India, and Pakistan.
3. To name the current leaders of the countries of South Asia..

Developing the Chapter

1. Motivation: Remind students that America is a melting pot in which different ethnic and religious groups peacefully coexist. Help students to understand the ethnic diversity of their own community by listing the different ethnic restaurants near their school and identifying the country or ethnic group each restaurant represents.

Ask: What do you think happens when people from various religious or ethnic backgrounds live together in one country but do not get along? Point out that the countries they are going to read about all faced problems resulting from religious and ethnic conflicts. Have students discuss the probable effects of such conflicts on the political life of a country.

2. Introduction

a. Write the chapter vocabulary words on the chalkboard. Have students look up each word in the and glossary and use it in an original sentence.
b. Have student read the chapter title and Objective question.
c. Have students read the chapter.

3. Review and Recall: After the students have read the chapter:

a. Have them reread and answer the Objective question and subhead questions.
b. Ask them to look at the map on page 636. Have them identify the countries that were former British-ruled lands and those that were never colonies. Then ask them to identify the date when each of the former colonies gained independence.

4. Building Social Studies Skills: Explain that using the scale of distance on a map is an important skill that will help them to determine the distance between specific locations, such as cities or geographical features. Have students turn to the map on page 636 and locate the scale of miles. Using this scale, ask students to determine the approximate number of miles and kilometers between the following cities: new Delhi and Calcutta (800 miles; 1280 kilometers); Karachi and New Delhi (600 miles; 960 kilometers); Dhaka and New Delhi (800 miles; 1280 kilometers).

5. Extension

a. Have students work in groups to research the community development programs that have taken place in India since 1951. Each group should choose one topic to research, such as agriculture, industry, education, or public health. Students should look in encyclopedias and other reference books to find out what has been achieved and what problems still need to be solved. They should present their findings in oral reports to the class.
b. Ask students to write diary entries about imaginary visits to Bombay, one of the most densely populated cities in the world. Suggest that they supplement their knowledge about the city by additional library research.

Support Materials

Assignments can include:

1. Chapter Review, pp. 638–639
2. Workbook, p.99
3. Blackline Masters R161 and R162
4. Test 13-1, p. T81
5. Source Reading, S41

Overview The Middle East has been a region of almost constant turmoil for a number of years. In 1956, a dispute over the Suez Canal led to war. Arabs and Israelis have fought two wars since the 1960s. Islamic fundamentalism has also contributed to conflict in the region. Some Arab countries have used their oil reserves to gain political power. Iraq's invasion of Kuwait led to the Persian Gulf War in 1991. After coalition forces defeated Iraq, peace talks between Israel and its Arab neighbors began.

Objectives

1. To identify how the goals of nationalism and religion have influenced today's Middle East countries.
2. To explain the reasons for the conflict between Israel and the Arab nations.
3. To identify the influence of oil production on Middle East countries.
4. To discuss the causes and effects of the Persian Gulf War.

Developing the Chapter

1. Motivation: Ask students to study the map of the Middle East Today on page 672 of their textbooks. Call on volunteers to explain what they know about the conflicts in the Middle East today. Ask them to locate Israel, Egypt, and Iraq on the map. Explain that students will learn more about the conflicts that involve these nations as they read the chapter.

2. Introduction:

a. Write the chapter vocabulary words on the chalkboard. Have students write each word and its glossary definition in their vocabulary notebooks.

b. Have students read the chapter title and Objective question. Then have them skim the chapter headings and write their personal objectives for reading the chapter.

c. Have students read the chapter.

3. Review and Recall: After the students have read the chapter:

a. Have them summarize the content of each subhead section.

b. Have them read each subhead question aloud and answer it.

c. Have them reread and answer the Objective question.

d. Have them use the map on page 644 to answer the following questions: What countries in the Middle East are not members of OPEC? Where are three oil refineries located?

4. Building Social Studies Skills: Remind students that note-taking can be helpful when reviewing for a test, studying, or preparing a research report. Ask students to take notes on the first section of the chapter (New Arab Nations) by listing the main ideas in each paragraph.

5. Extension:

a. Ask students to do additional research on oil, focusing on the importance of this resource in our world today. Then have students list the many ways their lives would change if the supply of oil was suddenly cut off. As an alternative, students could write a short story or essay describing one day in their lives without oil.

b. Ask students to do additional research on the events surrounding the seizure of the Suez Canal and the subsequent U.N.intervention. Then have the class stage a mock U.N. debate involving representatives from the United States, Great Britain, France, and Egypt, as well as a U.N. moderator. The question to be debated is: Should the U.N. army be sent into Egypt to keep the Suez Canal open? The other students in the class should be prepared to ask the debate participants questions.

Support Materials

Assignments can include:

1. Chapter Review, pp. 646–647
2. Workbook, pp. 100–102
3. Blackline Masters R163 and R164
4. Test 13-2, p. T82
5. Map Transparency 30 and Activity Sheet A30
6. Source Reading S44

CHAPTER 3 Conflict in Southeast Asia

Overview   The newly independent countries of Southeast Asia had a difficult time setting up democratic governments. In the Philippines, the corrupt government of Ferdinand Marcos was overthrown in 1986 and Corazon Aquino became president. In 1992, Aquino was succeeded by Fidel Ramos. After President Sukarno nearly drove Indonesia into bankruptcy, he was replaced by General Suharto, who rules the country today. Prolonged conflict plagued the nations of Vietnam, Laos, and Cambodia. U.S. involvement did not stop Communist governments from seizing control in these countries. During the early 1990s, these countries, as well as Thailand, began to show signs of political and economic reform.

Objectives

1. To identify the reasons why Ferdinand Marcos was forced out of office.
2. To compare and contrast the recent political history of the Philippines, Indonesia, and Thailand.
3. To identify the events leading to the Vietnam War.
4. To trace the history of the Vietnam War.

Developing the Chapter

1. Motivation: Ask how many students are familiar with the monument in Washington, D.C., dedicated to the memory of the men and women who died in the Vietnam War. Encourage students to volunteer information about this war memorial. Explain that in the following chapter they will read about the history of the Vietnam War and other conflicts that took place in Southeast Asia.

2. Introduction

a. Write the chapter vocabulary words on the chalkboard. Have students look up each words in the glossary and use four of the word in an original paragraph.

b. Have students read the chapter title and Objective question. Then have them preview the rest of the chapter by reading each subhead question. Finally, have students make up their own objectives for reading the chapter.

3. Review and Recall: After the students have read the chapter:

a. Have them reread each subhead question and answer it.

b. Have them reread and answer the Objective question.

c. Have them read and answer their own Objective questions.

d. Have them read aloud the People in History feature and then summarize the life and achievements of Corazon Aquino.

e. Have them read the Outlook feature and answer the questions at the end of the paragraph.

4. Building Social Studies Skills: Explain that outlining is an important skill that helps students master chapter content, study for tests, and write research reports. Guide students through preparing an outline of paragraphs 2, 3, and 4. Briefly review the outline format with the class on the chalkboard. Remind them to use capital letters for the main ideas and Arabic numbers for supporting information.

5. Extension

a. Remind students that during the Vietnam War, many U.S. citizens protested the conflict by attending huge demonstrations in Washington, D.C., and throughout the country. Have students create posters either supporting or protesting the Vietnam War. The posters should incorporate appropriate visuals, such as pictures from magazines and newspapers. Students can work together in cooperative groups to make the posters.

b. Briefly review the concept of martial law with the students. Then ask them to think about what it would be like to live in a country where martial law had been imposed. Have students write letters to friends or relatives describing their feelings and experiences. Call on volunteers to read their letters aloud to the rest of the class.

Support Materials

Assignments can include:

1. Chapter Review, pp. 654–655
2. Blackline Masters R165 and R166
3. Test 13-3, p. T83

CHAPTER 4   Movements in Africa

Overview   After World War II, most African nations won independence. In countries such as Nigeria, the transition was peaceful. In nations such as Kenya and Southern Rhodesia, violence erupted. After years of restricting blacks and other non-whites through apart-heid, South Africa has shown signs of change. In 1990, Nelson Mandela was released from prison and Namibia achieved independence. However, poverty and political uncertainty continue to hinder progress throughout Africa. In 1992, international forces entered Somalia to distribute food in a country torn by political strife.

Objectives

1. To list the reasons why many African countries became independent after World War II.
2. To compare and contrast the achievements of black African leaders, such as Nelson Mandela and Jomo Kenyatta.
3. To explain both the problems and benefits that independence has brought to African countries.

Developing the Chapter

1. Motivation: Have students turn to the map on page 659 and locate South Africa. **Ask:** When did South Africa gain independence? (1910) Next, have students discuss recent political developments in South Africa that they have read or heard about in the news media. Encourage students to volunteer information about apartheid and the struggle of Nelson Mandela. Tell them they are going to read about South Africa and other African nations that have achieved independence since World War II. Encourage students to suggest what problems these newly emerging nations might face.

2. Introduction
a. Write the chapter vocabulary words on the chalkboard. Have students write each word and its glossary meaning in their vocabulary notebooks. Then have them use each word in original sentences.
b. Have student read the chapter title and Objective question.
c. Have students read the chapter.

3. Review and Recall: After the students have read the chapter:
a. Have them summarize three main ideas from each section of the chapter.
b. Have students turn to the map on page 659. Ask them to identify five African nations that achieved independence before 1960 and five countries that achieved independence after 1960.

4. Building Social Studies Skills: Remind students that understanding the difference between facts and opinions is especially important in evaluating current events. Ask students to reread the Spotlight on Sources on page 658. Have them identify the statements that are facts (paragraph 11) and those that are opinions (excerpt from *Cry, the Beloved Country*.) Ask how a person can form sound opinions. (By studying a situation carefully before making a judgment)

5. Extension:
a. Divide students into five cooperative groups. Assign each group one of the African countries studied in this chapter. Each group is to create a bulletin board with recent news articles relating to political and social events in the country.
b. Have students read Alan Paton's *Cry, the Beloved Country*. Then have students write diary entries in which they describe one day in the life of either a black or a white citizen of South Africa.

Support Materials

Assignments can include:
1. Chapter Review, pp. 662–663
2. Workbook, pp. 103–105
3. Blackline Masters R167 and R168
4. Test 13-4, p. T84
5. Map Transparency 31 and Activity Sheet A31
6. Source Reading S45

CHAPTER 5 Latin America's Role

Overview The countries of Latin America have undergone a great deal of political turmoil—much of it due to a lack of democratic traditions. Countries such as Brazil and Argentina have been ruled by a series of dictators, military leaders, and leaders chosen in free elections. In addition, huge national debts, high inflation, and recession have hurt the economies of many Latin American countries. The United States has fought against communism in Latin America. Although the threat of communism has receded somewhat since the fall of the Soviet Union, Castro has remained leader of Cuba.

Objectives

1. To explain why Latin America has experienced so much political turmoil.
2. To compare and contrast the recent political history of Argentina, Brazil, and Mexico.
3. To trace the involvement of the United States in Latin American affairs.

Developing the Chapter

1. **Motivation:** Have students turn to the map on page 668 of their textbooks. Call on volunteers to read the names of the Latin American countries aloud. Then ask students whether they or anyone they know emigrated to the United States from any of these countries. Call on volunteers to cite examples of Hispanic music, food, and social customs that have enriched the cultural life of the students' community. Explain that in this chapter students will read about the political situation of some of these Latin American countries. Suggest that each student set a personal goal to define what he or she hopes to learn about Latin America.

2. **Introduction**
a. Write the chapter vocabulary words on the chalkboard. Have students write each word and its Glossary meanings in their vocabulary notebooks.
b. Have students read the chapter title and Objective question.
c. Have students skim the subhead questions.
d. Have students read the chapter.

3. **Review and Recall:** After the students have read the chapter:
a. Have them reread and answer the Objective question and subhead questions.
b. Have them skim each section and write three main ideas from each one.
c. Have them reread the Outlook feature and answer the question.

4. **Building Social Studies Skills:** Explain to students that using a map legend is an important skill that will enable them to make better use of the maps in their textbooks. Ask them to identify the capitals of the following countries: Bahamas (Nassau); Cuba (Havana); Costa Rica (San Jose); Nicaragua (Managua); and El Salvador (San Salvador). Then have them find the distance in both miles and kilometers between the following cities: Port-au-prince and Kingston (300 miles; 480 kilometers); Belize and Havana (500 miles; 800 kilometers); Guatemala City and San Jose (500 miles; 800 kilometers)

5. **Extension**
a. Have students do additional research on the Bay of Pigs invasion. Then have them stage a mock press conference at which President Kennedy answers reporters' questions about the invasion. Each student reporter should be prepared to ask at least five questions based on his or her research.
b. Divide students into four or five cooperative learning groups. Have each group design a poster protesting the changes in the rain forests of the Amazon brought about by Brazil's attempts to modernize. Suggest that they use either original illustrations or pictures from magazines and newspapers to illustrate their posters.

Support Materials

Assignments can include:
1. Chapter Review, pp. 670–671
2. Blackline Masters R169 and R170
3. Test 13-5, p. T85

GLOBAL CHALLENGES IN THE
TECHNOLOGICAL AGE

Unit Overview   After World War II, many
nations began to build relations based on interdependence and mutual cooperation. For
example, 12 European nations joined the European Community to encourage economic and
political interdependence. The Cold War
between Communist countries and the democratic countries had a great impact on foreign
policy and world events from the 1950s to the
1980s. By the late 1980s and early 1990s,
however, communism in Eastern Europe and
the Soviet Union had failed. But ethnic and
religious violence threatened to destroy the
hope for a new era of peace and prosperity.

Unit Objectives

1. To list the nations discussed in Unit 14 and
   cite distinguishing political and
   economical features of each of the nations.
2. To cite examples of the growing economic
   interdependence of the nations of the
   world.
3. To compare and contrast the political
   system of the nations discussed in Unit 14.
4. To explain the contributions by key figures
   to political, economic, and scientific
   achievements of today's world.

Unit Introduction

1. **Motivation:** Distribute copies of a
   blackline master map of the world to students.
   From the table of contents for Unit 14, have
   them locate the areas of the world to be
   studied in this unit.
   Ask: What are some possible major themes of
   Unit 14 in relation to the present-day world?
   Write class answers on the board. Have
   students copy these answers in their
   notebooks. Tell the class they will have a
   chance to reread and discuss these themes
   when they have completed the unit.
2. **Visual:** Direct students' attention to the
   opener picture. Have one student read the
   photo caption aloud. Ask the class to explain
   why the Olympics symbolize the ideal of
   cooperation as well as competition among
   nations.
3. **Time line:** Have the class study the unit
   time line. Look at the earliest date and latest

date shown. Focus the discussion on the
concept of recent history.

Unit Activities

1. **Contrasting and Comparing:** Mount a
   large sheet of oaktag on the bulletin board. As
   the study of each nation is completed, have
   the students excerpt the material needed to
   complete the following chart.
   **(Place names of countries across the top of
   the chart)**
   Geographic location:
   Form of government:
   Government:
   Economic Policy:
   Standard of living:
2. **Cooperative Learning:** Divide the class
   into four groups and pose the following
   hypothesis: As the twentieth century draws to
   a close, the nations of the world are becoming
   a global community. Assign each group one of
   the following examples. Ask the students to
   prove this hypothesis by citing examples of:
   a. Economic interdependence
   b. International cooperation
   c. Cultural Diffusion
   d. Science and Technology

Support Materials
Assignments can include:

1. Unit Review, pp. 720–721
2. Unit 14 Test pp. UT27–UT28
3. Unit 14 ESL/LEP Worksheet 1, p. ESL 27
4. Unit 14 ESL/LEP Worksheet 2, p. ESL 28

Overview Since World War II, many Western European nations have formed organizations that allow them to cooperate on economic and political issues. Some nations are eager to unify Europe through these organizations. Others are concerned about giving up power to a central organization. During this period, Great Britain and France have tried to improve their economies. In 1989, the fall of communism in Europe led to the unification of East and West Germany.

Objectives

1. To locate nations of Europe on a map.
2. To identify the leaders of the major nations of Western Europe.
3. To list and explain the steps in the development of the European Community.
4. To compare the economic policies of Great Britain, France, and Germany.
5. To describe the unification of East and West Germany.

Developing the Chapter

1. Motivation: Have students read the opening paragraphs on the Channel tunnel. Pose this problem: Throughout history, Great Britain has been an island nation separated from the continent of Europe by the English Channel. How has this separation affected the history of England and the history of Europe? Suggest areas to consider: defense; trade; economy. How may the trans-Channel tunnel change this relationship?

2. Introduction

a. Write vocabulary words related to the chapter on the chalkboard: free trade; currency; standard of living. Have students write each word and its glossary definition in their notebooks. Develop a lesson that includes using each word or term in a sentence that shows understanding.

b. Use the section heading questions as the basis of developing homework assignments.

3. Review and Recall: After the students have read the chapter:

a. Class reading: People in History; Thatcher. How did her policies change the British economy? How did her policies compare with earlier governments' economic policies in Great Britain?

b. Define socialism. How did socialism work in France in the 1980s?

c. Describe West Germany's economic recovery after World War II. What circumstances led to the reunification of Germany? How will reunification affect Germany's economy?

d. Why is it important for the Western European nations to work together for economic reasons? For political reasons?

4. Building Social Studies Skills:

a. Explain to students the importance of note taking while reading a chapter.

b. Select a section of the chapter and write a paragraph omitting key words and ideas.Have students work in teams to complete the reading in class. Have teams report to the class as a whole.

c. On a map of Europe, have students label members and nonmembers of the European Community. Review possible reasons for nations joining or not joining the common markets.

5. Extension

a. Prepare a chart outline for students to complete that compares the economies of the three major Western European nations in the 1980s.

b. Have teams of two or three students compose a list of places they would like to visit in Europe. Have students bring in pictures and brochures and give reports to the class about the historical background of each place. Pictures may be mounted on a class bulletin board.

Support Materials

Assignments can include:

1. Chapter Review, pp. 682–683
2. Workbook, p. 106
3. Blackline Masters R171 and R172
4. Test 14-1, p. T86
5. Source Readings, p. S46

CHAPTER 2   The Soviet Union Dissolves

Overview   From 1917 to 1991, the Soviet Union was run by a Communist government that controlled its citizens' political, economic, and personal lives. The inefficiencies and inequalities created by communism, coupled with new freedoms introduced by Gorbachev, led to the decline of communism during the 1980s. In addition, the satellite countries of Eastern Europe began renouncing communism. A 1991 coup marked the end of communism in the Soviet Union and the breakup of the country into 15 independent nations.

Objectives

1. To understand how the failings of the Communist system led to its downfall.
2. To identify the policies of Mikhail Gorbachev.
3. To describe the downfall of communism in Eastern Europe.
4. To explain the events leading to the breakup of the Soviet Union.

Developing the Chapter

1. **Motivation:** Have the class read the opening section of the chapter on the hard-line coup of August 1991. Ask students to imagine that they were in Moscow during the coup and that they witnessed Boris Yeltsin's actions. Have them write a diary entry about their experiences on this day. Ask volunteers to read their diary entries aloud.

2. **Introduction**
a. Write these vocabulary words on the chalkboard:

Solidarity   Politburo
perestroika   quota

Have students copy each word with its Glossary definition into their notebooks.
b. Have students read the chapter, noting the question in each section heading. Students should be instructed to take notes while reading.

3. **Review and Recall:** After the students have read the chapter:
a. Define perestroika and explain the main features of this economic policy in comparison with the Five-Year plans of Stalin.

b. Define communism and capitalism. What are the main features of each economic system?
c. Read People in History: Gorbachev. Why were his policies revolutionary in the Soviet Union?
d. Define Solidarity and have students give examples of how this movement changed life in Poland in the 1980s.

4. **Building Social Studies Skills:**
a. Distribute copies of an outline map of the newly independent nations. Have students locate and label each country and its capital city.
b. Divide the class into teams. Have each team summarize a section of the chapter for presentation to the class.
c. Review the events that led to the breakup of the Soviet Union. Create a time line that shows the major events.

5. **Extension**
a. Assign research papers that compare the history students studied in this chapter with Chapter 2 in Unit 11 on the Lenin-Stalin years in Russian history. Show differences and similarities in political and economic strategies.
b. Have students discuss the basic rights guaranteed U.S. citizens by the Bill of Rights. List these rights on the chalkboard. Then, have students prepare a bill of rights for one of the newly independent nations. How would this bill of rights be similar to the U.S. Bill of Rights? How would it be different?
c. Tell students that since most of the new nations are introducing elements of capitalism, they will need advice on how to operate privately owned businesses. Have students list things they would tell people in these countries about opening new businesses.

Support Materials
Assignments can include:
1. Chapter Review, pp. 690–691
2. Workbook, pp. 107–109
3. Blackline Masters R173 and R174
4. Test 14-2, p. T87
5. Map Transparency 32 and Activity Sheet A32
6. Source Readings, p. S47

Overview During the 1980s, Deng Xiaoping attempted new solutions to economic, political, and social problems. Deng's Four Modernizations aimed at bringing a primarily agrarian society into the age of technology. In agriculture and industry the profit motive was introduced to increase incentives for production. In addition, China opened its doors to foreign capital and joint ventures. Although economic reform was encouraged, attempts to reform the political system were suppressed.

Objectives

1. To list the social and economic problems facing Communist China today.
2. To compare the leadership of Deng Xiaoping with that of Mao Zedong.
3. To identify the Four Modernizations.
4. To discuss China's resistance to democratic reform.

Developing the Chapter

1. **Motivation:** Have students read the Spotlight on Sources section of the chapter. On the chalkboard have them list the problems that have faced the Chinese nation through the centuries. Ask them to propose possible solutions to these problems.

2. **Introduction**
a. Write the chapter vocabulary words on the chalkboard: Joint Venture; Four Modernizations: profit motive. Have students write each term and its glossary definition in their notebooks for later use.
b. Introduce the chapter by a review of traditional Chinese culture and achievements.

3. **Review and Recall**
a. Review paragraphs 2–7 on page 693.
b. **Ask:** What are the problems of an agricultural society? How do these problems apply in China?
c. **Ask:** What were the Four Modernizations?
d. People in History: Deng Xiaoping: How did Deng's leadership change the role of the Chinese government in the life of the Chinese people?

e. Why did China need foreign help for joint ventures? How did China benefit? How did the world benefit?
f. Was Communism in China strengthened or weakened by the policies of Deng Xiaoping?

4. **Building Social Studies Skills:**
a. Utilize population charts to illustrate a comparison of China with other nations.
b. Have students prepare a chart on the Four Modernizations. The chart should have a left-to-right row for each area of modernization, and it should have three columns headed, respectively, "Area of Reform," "Plan," and "Significance". The students who prepare the chart should present it to the class, explaining its content and discussing its importance.
c. Use a topographical map of China to show geography, resources, land types, and centers of population.

5. **Extension**
a. Have students research the history of China under Mao Zedong. Compare the policies of that period with the policies of Deng Xiaoping.
b. Have students research developments in China since this chapter was written. Has Deng remained in power? Has China continued on the same path, or has it moved in a different direction? What has been the lasting effect of the events of June 1989?
c. Have students create a bulletin board of Chinese culture in the United States.
d. Have students consider themselves as citizens in a nation where all the art forms are determined by the government. What would they be missing in their everyday lives. How would they feel?

Support Materials

Assignments can include:
1. Chapter Review, pp. 696–697
2. Blackline Masters R175 and R176
3. Test 14-3, p. T88

Chapter 4 Japan Becomes an
           Economic Superpower

Overview After World War II, Japan rebuilt its industries and by the 1980s was one of the world's leading economic powers. During the 1990s, Japan worked to maintain a strong position by producing high-technology products. As an island nation, Japan's economy relies on trade and is therefore sensitive to world economic trends. Ruled by a democratic government, the Japanese enjoy a high standard of living. Japan has also become more active in world affairs.

Objectives

1. To explain how Japan became an economic superpower.
2. To describe Japan's reliance on trade.
3. To describe Japanese government.
4. To explain how Japan's relations with the world have changed in recent years.

Developing the Chapter

1. **Motivation:** Have the students read Spotlight on Sources.
Ask: How are our lives affected by computers? How might artificial intelligence computers impact on the way we work and the way we live in our homes?
2. **Introduction**
a. Have the students copy this vocabulary term from the chalkboard: Trade Deficit. Have students write the glossary definition of the term and then develop examples of how a trade deficit affects a nation. Cite the example of present-day United States.
b. Have students use the chapter headings as the basis for homework, writing a short essay including the main ideas of the chapter.
3. **Review and Recall**
a. Why is the emperor an important symbol to the Japanese people?
b. How did the United States assist Japan in rebuilding after World War II?
c. How did economic growth lead to Japan's status as a superpower in today's world?
d. What are the characteristics of the Japanese work ethic?
e. Describe Japanese family life today.
f. Define keiretsu. Why has this form of business organization been so successful?
g. Explain MITI and government policy toward private business in Japan.
h. What are the characteristics of Japan'smodern high-tech economy?
i. Explain Japan's changing role in world affairs.
4. **Building Social Studies Skills**
a. Have students draw a bar graph showing Japan's major exports. The information reported on the graph should be as up to date as possible. You can provide the information or have them look it up in a standard reference source.
b. Have students prepare a line graph showing the levels of Japanese exports from 1945 to the present.
c. Have students construct a tabletop topographical map of the island nation of Japan to illustrate some of the land-use and population-density problems of that nation.
d. Have students research the role of the emperor in earlier Japanese history and compare his power with that of the emperor today.
5. **Extension**
a. Have students list the appliances in their homes. How many are foreign-made? Have them read labels on their clothing. How many are foreign-made? Identify those items made in Japan.
b. Discovery lesson: Imagine living in an island nation. What resources does your nation have? What does it need for its survival? What does it need to compete with other nations?
c. Organize the class to present a traditional Japanese tea ceremony. Invite another class to participate.

Support Materials

Assignments can include:
1. Chapter Review, pp. 704-705
2. Workbook, p. 112
3. Blackline Masters R177 and R178
4. Test 14-4 p. T89

CHAPTER 5 The United States Moves Ahead

Overview Although the United States maintained a high standard of living during the 1980s and 1990s, foreign competition and a recession threatened the job security of U.S. workers. During this period, some economic and political gains were made by women, African Americans, and Hispanics. In 1992, voters elected Bill Clinton President of the United States, hoping that he would improve the economy. In world affairs, the fall of the Soviet Union left the United States the lone superpower. As such, the United States took an active role in initiating peace talks in the Middle East. In addition, the United States sent troops to Somalia during the early 1990s.

Objectives

1. To discuss the economic and political challenges the United States faces in the 1990s.
2. To list the gains made by women, African Americans, and Hispanics.
3. To explain the United States' growing role in world affairs.

Developing the Chapter

1. Motivation: Have the students read the introductory paragraph on the United States as a nation of immigrants. Distribute data on the major immigration groups during the past 100 years. Have the class form teams of two or three students and write generalizations about the American people based on their reading and the data.

2. Introduction

a. Write the following vocabulary terms on the chalkboard for students to copy into their notebooks: budget deficit; recession; social programs. Have them research the definitions in the Glossary and research the uses of these terms in the chapter.

b. Have students preview the chapter by outlining the chapter headings.
   Ask: How well do you think America has done in the last few years? What good things have happened? What bad things? What are the main problems the country faces? Have students keep these points in mind as they read the chapter.

3. Review and Recall

a. Describe the changes that took place in the U.S. economy in the 1980s and 1990s.

b. **Ask:** How has advanced technology affected the U.S. work force?

c. Explain the changing role of women in U.S. society.

d. How has technology affected U.S. agriculture?

e. In what ways did American society change in the 1980s and 1990s?

f. What is the role of the United States in the world?

4. Building Social Studies Skills

a. Have students compile a bar graph showing the major groups in the U.S. population, giving the numbers of each group in 1980 and 1990.

b. Using a map of the United States, show the main pattern of population movement from one area to another. What are the causes of this movement? What are the economic and political effects of this movement?

5. Extension:

a. Have students prepare a report on immigration to the United States in the 1990s. From which countries or areas have the largest numbers of people come? How have these numbers been affected by developments in other parts of the world? In which parts of the United States have most of these people settled?

b. Have students research the summit meetings between President Reagan and Secretary Gorbachev, using the chapter on the former Soviet Union plus library research. What comparisons in leadership style may be drawn between the two leaders? What programs did they both appear to favor? What are the prospects for peace in the future?

Support Materials

Assignments can include:

1. Chapter Review, pp. 710–711
2. Blackline Masters R179 and R180
3. Test 14-5, p. T90
4. Source Reading, p. S48

CHAPTER 6 The Challenge of the Future

Overview The last half of the twentieth century witnessed a revolution in science and technology that left an impact on every aspect of life. The technology of industrialism has moved from mass production to automation. In agriculture, new methods of farming and new forms of crops have increased the world's food supply. Yet with all this progress, problems of famine and poverty still abound in parts of the world. In space technology, the major powers compete to achieve new "firsts." The people of the world know more than they have ever known before, but they are in danger of destroying their world with pollution in many forms.

Objectives
1. To define the word "civilization" and to relate what it means to students as individuals.
2. To define technology and cite examples in the field of space exploration.
3. To list ways in which people can endanger the environment by their actions.
4. To explain the impact of the Industrial Revolution on the work force and on people's lifestyles.

Developing the Chapter
1. Motivation: Have the class read the Arts and Artifacts feature about the pyramid addition to the Louvre. Ask them to consider the elements of this reading. Have them contribute elements and record on the chalkboard for later summary and evaluation. Elements include: Historic Palace; Art Treasures; I.M. Pei; Canadian firm; French glassmakers; Architect's staff; Pyramid form; Reaction of people.
Ask: Why are these elements important or interesting? How did they reflect history? Why is the pyramid form significant?

2. Introduction
a. Write the chapter's vocabulary words on the chalkboard for students to copy. Have them scan the chapter for definitions and then check their definitions against those given in the glossary.

b. Have students scan the chapter in class after reading it at home. Have them note the major divisions of the material to facilitate outlining of the chapter. Record these divisions on the chalkboard and have students copy them into their notebooks to assist them in outlining.
3. Review and Recall: After the students have read the chapter:
a. Have students read People in History. How has science overcome international borders?
b. Have students make a 2-column list— Advantages of Technology/Problems related to Technology.
c. Ask students what they would be willing to give up for the sake of a cleaner environment. How might they help?

4. Building Social Studies Skills
a. Have students make a technology time line to visualize the rapid progress of technology from 1950 to the present.
b. Ask students to compose an outline of the chapter sections dealing with Industry/Agriculture. Use key words for students to define and explain.

5. Extension
a. Divide the class into teams. Each team is assigned one area of science or technology to research in the chapter and to collect visuals to bring to class. Have teams report to the class and share their information.
b. Have students research the technology of a particular area in the 20th century in comparison to some earlier century in history.
c. Have students construct a model space shuttle or pyramid.
d. Have students explain the causes and forms of pollution from people in their own community.
e. Have students set up a panel discussion to debate the advantages and disadvantages of nuclear energy.

Support Materials
Assignments can include:
1. Chapter Review, pp. 718–719
2. Workbook, pp. 110–111
3. Blackline Masters R181 and R182
4. Test 14-6, p. T91

ANSWER KEY TO CHAPTER AND UNIT REVIEWS

UNIT 1 ❧ CHAPTER 1

VOCABULARY REVIEW

1. prehistoric 2. archaeologists 3. anthropologists
4. Paleolithic 5. glacier 6. nomads

SKILL BUILDER: SOURCES OF INFORMATION

1. a 2. b 3. d
4. Answers might include: a person's location during the event can affect their ability to observe it accurately; individuals use different descriptive words to express their own reaction to or opinion of an event; some people have better powers of observation and recollection of details than others.

SKILL BUILDER: CRITICAL THINKING AND COMPREHENSION

1. **Main Idea b.** Human life was strongly affected by the discovery of fire 750,000 years ago.

ENRICHMENT

1. Suggest that students use an encyclopedia. Example: *Encyclopedia Britannica's* article, "Paleolithic Art." Report could include these facts: Paleolothic art was mostly small sculpture and work found in caves. Many of the artists were hunters. Their subjects were mostly animals, although many small figures of women have been found from this period (these are called Venus figures). The art was probably created because people of the Paleolithic period thought it gave them control over nature. The art was mostly symbolic, and not intended to tell a story.
2. Help students decide which medium they should use: drawing, painting, or diorama. Suggest they show such things as tools, foods, hunting, cave painting, gathering in groups around a fire.

SKILL BUILDER/MAPS

1. Africa 2. Asia, Europe, North and South America, Australia 3. During the Ice Age there was a land bridge across what is now the Bering Strait. Many people may have traveled from Asia to North America over this bridge. 4. The Philippines and Indonesia, and New Guinea and Australia were linked by land bridges during the Ice Age. This allowed early humans from Asia to travel through Indonesia by land, then across a short distance of open sea to New Guinea and Australia.

UNIT 1 ❧ CHAPTER 2

VOCABULARY REVIEW

1. domestication: d 2. irrigation: a 3. shards: e
4. alloy: b 5. civilization: f 6. merchants: g 7. barter economy: c 8. culture: h

SKILL BUILDER: PREVIEWING

1. Mesopotamia
2. How are the Mesopotamian civilizations and the civilizations of today similar?

3. **MESOPOTAMIA:** Why were different groups of people drawn to the valley of Mesopotamia?
THE SUMERIANS: How did the Sumerians create a civilization?
BABYLON: What have archaeologists learned about the Babylonians?
SPOTLIGHT ON SOURCES
THE ASSYRIANS: How were the Assyrians different from the Sumerians and Babylonians?
THE PERSIANS: How did the Persians unite and rule their vast empire in the Middle East?
OUTLOOK
4. Fertile Crescent, dates, cuneiform, city-states, ziggurat, Code of Hammurabi, satrapies, rites
5. Answers will vary.

SKILL BUILDER: CRITICAL THINKING AND COMPREHENSION

Main Idea
1. c. paragraph 9 2. a. paragraph 11 3. d. paragraph 13
4. e. paragraph 14
Main Idea
1. paragraph 5: The change from hunting and gathering to an agricultural way of life did not happen overnight.
2. paragraph 6: The domestication, or taming, of animals began at about the same time that farming first appeared.
3. paragraph 8: As more and more prehistoric people took to farming, new ways of living began to develop.
4. paragraph 10: Cloth-weaving and pottery-making were two other skills developed during the New Stone Age.
5. Daily life in. . .Catal Huyuk, a settlement in what is now Turkey, was one of the first towns in the world.

ENRICHMENT

1. Answers will vary, but might include things such as people could become better farmers or potters, etc., if they could do just that particular thing rather than having to do everything for themselves. Fewer people would need to learn each trade, leaving others free to develop in different fields. All people do not do the same things equally well. As for the barter economy, there would be opportunities to produce things that would be of value in obtaining other desirable things.
2. Answers will vary, but might include the ability to remain in one place, being in control of the food supply, domestication of animals, and a change from wearing animal skins to the weaving of cloth as possible aspects of change within their lives.
3. Answers will vary. Students' ideas should reflect a knowledge of what materials were generally available during the Stone Age.

A GEOGRAPHIC VIEW OF HISTORY

Suggest that students skim through other chapters in Unit 1 to find answers for some of these questions.
1. Tigris-Euphrates, Nile, Indus, Huang He (Yellow) River
2. Mesopotamia—Syrian Desert; Egypt—Sahara and Arabian deserts; Indus Valley—Great Indian Desert; Huang He Valley—Gobi Desert

3. In Mesopotamia early farmers had to build canals to irrigate the dry land. In Egypt, farmers dug ditches and canals to water their crops in the dry areas. The yearly flooding of the Nile left the land along the river fertile and moist enough for growing crops. The Indus Valley was also a desert region. Early settlers had to irrigate the land. They also built a sewage system. In China, settlers along the Huang He River learned how to control river floods by building dikes. They also built ditches and canals for irrigation.

UNIT 1 ❧ CHAPTER 3

VOCABULARY REVIEW

1. Fertile Crescent: i
2. date: b
3. scribe: a
4. cuneiform: e
5. city-state: g
6. ziggurat: d
7. Codes of Hammurabi: f
8. chariot: *distractor*
9. rite: c
10. satrapies: h

SKILL BUILDER: READING A TABLE

1. The Sumerians and the Elements of Civilization
2. **a.** Specialization of labor **b.** System of writing **c.** Organized government ruling from a central place **d.** A culture supported by a large population over a long period of time **3.** They had farmers and construction workers **4.** clay tables and a stylus **5.** kings and religious leaders **6.** 1,000 years

SKILL BUILDER: CRITICAL THINKING AND COMPREHENSION

1. **Main Idea a.** paragraph 3 **b.** paragraph 18 **c.** paragraph 8 **d.** paragraph 21 **e.** paragraph 12
2. a. paragraph 3: The Mesopotamian valley provided several important natural resources for survival of the Sumerians.
b. paragraph 13: The king who made the greatest impact on Babylon was Hammurabi, who came to power in 1792 B.C.
c. paragraph 17: From about 900 B.C. to about 630 B.C., Assyria's warlike people built a large empire.
d. paragraph 2: The Sumerian civilization began in the Middle East in a valley between the Tigris and Euphrates rivers.
e. paragraph 5: Among the key ingredients of a civilization is specialization of labor.

ENRICHMENT

1. Answers will vary.
2. Answers will vary. Table headings should include the four elements of a civilization which are: specialization of labor, system of writing, organized government ruling from a central place, a culture supported by a large population over a long period of time.

UNIT 1 ❧ CHAPTER 4

VOCABULARY REVIEW

1. desert: f **2.** mummy: e **3.** pyramid: c **4.** dynasty: d **5.** pharaoh: g **6.** papyrus: b **7.** hieroglyphics: a

SKILL BUILDER: READING A TIME LINE

1. b, d, c, e, a **2.** b **3.** c **4.** b

SKILL BUILDER: CRITICAL THINKING AND COMPREHENSION

Main Idea
1. c **2.** c **3.** c **4.** c

ENRICHMENT

1. Answers will vary, but should speak of these items as things that the deceased person will need on his journey to the underworld.
2. Answers will vary, but could mention the incredibly heavy stones and the labor involved in moving them. The elements of religious devotion and duty to the ruler might also be mentioned. This labor took many years; the same people could not have worked continuously on this. The laborers probably went home from time to time to see their families, and to plant and harvest crops. Students might mention how glad the laborers were to get home to their loved ones in the village.

SKILL BUILDER/MAPS

1. Mediterranean Sea **2.** It flows northward. You can tell by looking at the map's legend. The Nile flows from the mountains (high elevation) to the desert (lower elevation). **3.** The Blue Nile River and the White Nile River. **4.** The White Nile contributes a steadier flow of water because it originates in an area of Central Africa where it rains all year.

THE ARTS AND ARTIFACTS

1. 8 years old
2. gold-covered chariots, a solid gold throne, tables and chairs, jewelry, statues, stone animals, jewel-covered knives, a toy box, a board game, a paint set, the pharaoh's mummy, and a gold mask.
3. This tomb contained many artifacts that revealed details of Egyptian life and the life of the pharaohs never known before. Facts about Egyptian religious beliefs, art, architecture, government, language, and virtually every aspect of Egyptian society were discovered in the tombs and in the writings and wall paintings found in the tombs.

UNIT 1 ❧ CHAPTER 5

VOCABULARY REVIEW

1. **treaty:** A formal written agreement between nations about boundaries, trade, etc.
2. **colonies:** Settlements of people governed by a foreign nation.
3. **alphabet:** The letters of a written language arranged in their customary order.
4. **Judaism:** The Hebrew religion.
5. **monotheism:** The belief in one god.
6. **cedar:** A tall tree from the pine family known for its fragrance and durability.
Sentences will vary.

SKILL BUILDER: FOLLOWING DIRECTIONS

1. Answers will vary. **2.** c, b, d, e, a **3.** The Hittites, the Phoenicians, and the Hebrews were important people of the Middle East.

SKILL BUILDER: CRITICAL THINKING AND COMPREHENSION

1. Classifying

GROUP OF PEOPLE	MAJOR CONTRIBUTIONS
Hittites	horse-drawn chariots iron-working
Phoenicians	the alphabet trading colonies purple dye
Hebrews	belief in one god Old Testament

2. Main Idea
paragraph 3: One of the most important achievements of the Hittites was the discovery of how to make iron weapons and tools.
paragraph 6: The wars with the Egyptians had weakened the Hittite Empire.
paragraph 11: The Hebrews came from Mesopotamia into Palestine about 2000 B.C.

ENRICHMENT

1. Answers should include references to hunger, disease, enemy armies, and doubt in their faith in God's promise.
2. Examples could be the atom bomb, tanks, the machine gun, ironclad ships, and lasers.
3. Answers will vary. **4.** Answers will vary. **5.** Answers will vary.

UNIT 1 ❧ CHAPTER 6

VOCABULARY REVIEW

1. nirvana **2.** caste system **3.** rajah **4.** monsoons **5.** pariahs **6.** Buddhism **7.** Hinduism **8.** reincarnation

SKILL BUILDER: READING A TIME LINE

1. c. Aryans settle in Ganges Valley e. Caste system begun b. Carthage founded f. Assyrians sack Israel a. Buddha born d. Buddha founds new religion
2. a. 1000 B.C. b. 722 B.C. c. 35 years old d. 437 years e. ninth century B.C.

SKILL BUILDER: CRITICAL THINKING AND COMPREHENSION

1. Classifying

RIVERS	MOUNTAINS	SURROUNDING WATERS
Ganges	Hindu Kush	Arabian Sea
Indus	Himalayas	Indian Ocean
		Bay of Bengal

2. Main Idea a. Hindu beliefs strengthened the caste system b. paragraph 13 c. first d. Hinduism

ENRICHMENT

1. Answers will vary, but should include menial jobs such as streetsweeping, dishwashing, emptying outhouses, and performing hard labor, such as digging ditches.

2. List should include: India, Burma, Thailand, Vietnam, China, Laos, Tibet, Nepal, Cambodia, Indonesia, Korea, and Japan.

UNIT 1 ❧ CHAPTER 7

VOCABULARY REVIEW

1. ancestor worship: To honor or reverence as divine beings with super powers, an individual or group one is descended from.
2. filial piety: A central idea of Confucius' teachings; that children and young people must honor and love their parents and all older family members.
3. Mandate of Heaven: The belief that each of China's dynasties received its power from the gods. The dynasty could rule only as long as it kept the mandate.
4. extended family: A family that includes several generations of relatives living together or near one another.
5. calligraphy: Fancy or elegant style of handwriting.

SKILL BUILDER: READING A MAP

1. China, Korea **2.** Mesopotamia (Persia, or modern-day Iran) **3.** India **4.** Israel **5.** the Persian Gulf, the Mediterranean Sea **6.** India

SKILL BUILDER: CRITICAL THINKING AND COMPREHENSION

1. Classifying
Answers will vary, but might include some of the following:
Culture of China
a. Artisans and skilled crafts workers produced lovely jewelry and figures of animals carved in ivory and jade stone.
b. Bronze vases, often in the form of animals, were the greatest achievement of Shang art.
Trade of China
a. The chief goods traded were silk cloth, jade and ivory jewelry, wooden furniture, bronze vases, pottery, and iron tools.
b. During the Zhou Dynasty traders began to use coins as a way to trade for goods.
Leaders of China
a. China's first dynasty of rulers began in the Huang River valley, where early farming villages were governed by local leaders.
b. The Zhou rulers helped develop a view of China's government called the Mandate of Heaven.
Geography of China
a. China is a huge land that covers much of eastern Asia.
b. China's geography provides natural barriers against invasions.
Daily Life of China
a. During the Zhou Dynasty nearly all of China's people were farmers.
b. The use of oxen to plow fields increased China's wheat and millet crops.
Chinese Technology and Science
a. Like the Egyptians along the Nile River, the people in the Huang River Valley learned how to build dikes to control river floods.
b. The use of the iron plow and hoe helped increase the output of crops under the Zhou Dynasty.
Religion of China
a. One of the main beliefs of Chinese religion was ancestor worship.
b. The Mandate of Heaven became an important and lasting belief in Chinese thinking and religion.

2. Main Idea
paragraph 13: China's unity and strength in the Zhou Dynasty depended on the family, which was the backbone of Chinese society.
paragraph 15: The Chinese people made other important achievements during the Shang Dynasty.
paragraph 16: During the Zhou Dynasty, which followed the Shang, production of silk and other goods increased.
3. Summarizing
Mountains, deserts, and jungles make up a large part of China, and Chinese geography provided natural barriers which allowed Chinese civilization to endure for so long.

ENRICHMENT

1. Answers will vary.
2. Answers will vary, but might include some of the following:
a. Establish uniform weights, measures, and currency.
b. Build roads that would connect distant regions to the capital.
c. Establish a uniform code of laws.
d. Establish a uniform system of education.

UNIT 1 • CHAPTER 8

VOCABULARY REVIEW

1. Sahara: a 2. steppe: d 3. savanna: c 4. desertification: e 5. terra cotta: b 6. migration: f

SKILL BUILDER: MAKING A TIME LINE

Answers will vary, but could include birth; any awards or important sports events, arts activities, etc.; moving to a different place; family events such as births, weddings, reunions; travel and special vacations.

SKILL BUILDER: CRITICAL THINKING AND COMPREHENSION

1. Classifying

NOK	CUSH	AKSUM
1. sculpture	1. traders	1. strong, powerful ships
2. farmers	2. ironworker	2. Greek language and education
3. terra cotta	3. writing system	3. Christianity
4. mud huts	4. built pyramids, a temple, and a royal palace in Meroe	4. traders

2. Main Ideas
a. The land and climate of Africa are varied.
Most of north Africa is a hot dry desert called the Sahara.
South of the Sahara is a hot area called the steppes.
The steppes give way to savannas.
To the south of the savannas is a tropical rain forest.
South of the equator is another huge savanna and more steppes.
These steppes give way to the Kalahari and Namib deserts.
b. The Kingdom of Cush continued to grow as an important civilization after it was separated from Egypt.
About 540 B.C. Meroë was founded.
The people of Cush developed a writing system; built pyramids, a temple, and a royal palace; learned to make iron weapons.
There were large deposits of iron ore around Meroë.

c. Nok art has lasted until today.
Nok artisans made sculptures of terra cotta, iron, and bronze.
The figures, mostly of humans, had large heads, for they felt the head was the source of life's power.
Nok art probably influenced the art of Yoruba and Benin.
3. Summarizing:
3-1. b **3-2.** c **3-3.** b **3-4.** a

ENRICHMENT

Answers will vary.

UNIT 1 • CHAPTER 9

VOCABULARY REVIEW

isthmus: Narrow strip of land joining two larger bodies of land.
jaguar: A large cat of tropical America.

SKILL BUILDER: STUDYING FOR A TEST

1. Have students use the Table of Contents and chapter headings to help complete the outline.
2. Provide students with any references you may have used or suggest that they look through the class or school library. Students may want to use other parts of their book, such as the Atlas.
3. Suggest that students study in some systematic way. They might review one section, or one page a day. For each day of study they could choose to skim over the material, look for main ideas, write out important facts, or answer the chapter text questions.
4. Suggest that students prepare questions about the main topics and vocabulary words. Remind them to vary the types of questions (i.e., multiple choice, matching, etc.). They can use other chapter reviews as a guide.
5. and 6. Assign students a classmate to share tests with. Set aside class time for the sample tests and correction of the tests.
7. You might have students select the best question on their partner's test. The class could choose the best question(s) out of the finalists. Use the winning question(s) on the chapter or unit test for extra credit.

SKILL BUILDER: CRITICAL THINKING AND COMPREHENSION

1. Classifying
Olmec farming: b, e, g
Religion of the Olmecs: a, c, h
Major cities of the Olmecs: d, f
2. Main Idea
paragraph 3: c
paragraph 4: b
paragraph 5: c
paragraph 11: c
3. Summarizing
3-2. Because it includes all the main points of the two paragraphs, whereas the other does not. The other summary states that the people were cold and hungry most of the time. This statement is not in either paragraph.

ENRICHMENT

1. Models should depict a pyramid with a rounded base. A courtyard should be around this, with altars on the outside edges.
2. Answers will vary.
3. Answers will vary. The last part of the question should include references to the cold, winter weather, although an example such as winter wheat could be introduced.

UNIT 1 🐦 REVIEW

SKILL BUILDER: READING A MAP

1. The Mesopotamian civilization **2.** Asia **3.** The Indian and Chinese civilizations **4.** The Egyptian civilization **5.** The Olmec civilization **6.** North America **7.** All are located near 30 degrees north latitude. The climate was tropical.

SKILL BUILDER: CRITICAL THINKING AND COMPREHENSION

1. Main Idea
1-1. c: Smaller nations have introduced many important ideas to the world.
1-2. d: The belief in life after death was an important part of Egyptian civilization.

2. Classifying
Mesopotamia ziggurat cuneiform Code of Hammurabi
Egypt papyrus mummy pharoah hieroglyphics
India monsoon caste system city-state Hinduism rajah reincarnation
China Confucius filial piety ancestor worship calligrapy

ENRICHMENT

1. Answers will vary. **2.** Answers will vary.

UNIT 2 🐦 CHAPTER 1

VOCABULARY REVIEW

1. bureaucracy: h **2.** vaccines: c **3.** edicts: a **4.** missionaries: g **5.** murals: d **6.** Sanskrit: f **7.** astronomers: b **8.** universities: e

SKILL BUILDER: READING A TIME LINE

321 B.C.
Asoka becomes emperor 274 B.C. or Asoka dies; Maurya empire declines 232 B.C.
1. Magadha becomes powerful 400 B.C.
2. Height of Gupta Empire occurs A.D. 320–467
3. Asoka becomes emperor of the Maurya Empire
4. About 147 years

SKILL BUILDER: CRITICAL THINKING AND COMPREHENSION

1. Introduction to Generalizing
a. Asoka wanted to win the support of the Indian people through kindness.
b. Science and education flourished during the Gupta Empire.
c. Hindu society was based on the extended family.

2. Classifying
a. vaccines invented: M
b. the decimal system invented: G
c. a government bureaucracy set up: M
d. canals and roads built: M
e. astronomers studied the stars and planets: G

ENRICHMENT

1. Answers will vary.
2. Suggest that students use books on India and Indian History to research the Iron Pillar of Delhi. Their drawings of pillars should show monuments, historic events, important landmarks, etc.

UNIT 2 🐦 CHAPTER 2

VOCABULARY REVIEW

1. civil service: A group of workers hired to carry out the government's work.
2. alms: Something given to the poor, usually money.
3. Silk Road: Trading route from China to western Asia and the Roman Empire.
4. seismograph: An apparatus for measuring or recording the intensity, direction and duration of an earthquake.
5. prosperity: A state of economic well being.
6. dynastic cycle: The rise and fall of dynasties.
7. monochrome: Paintings done in only one color.
8. polo: A game which came from Persia where teams of players on horseback use longhandled sticks, to drive a ball across the playing field.
9. porcelain: A hard, fine-grained, nonporous, and usually translucent and white ceramic ware, such as: cups, bowls, dishes, etc.

SKILL BUILDER: USING CONTEXT CLUES

Possible definition: Acupuncture is a Chinese medical technique using needles inserted in the patient's body during surgery.

SKILL BUILDER: CRITICAL THINKING AND COMPREHENSION

1. Classifying
Answers will vary, but might include:
Shi Huang Di unified China:
a. The emperor made the country operate under just one system of laws.
b. Roads, canals, and bridges were built to connect the towns and states.
c. Standards, or common rules, were set for the written language; for weights, measures, and coins; even for the length of cart axles.
China prospered under early Tang rulers:
a. People from Syria, Persia, Central Asia, and South Asia traded in the two large marketplaces of Changan, Tang China's capital city.
b. Artists, writers, and entertainers from all over the world made life in the capital richer.
c. The rich of the city amused themselves with poetry, art, and sports.

2. Main Idea
paragraph 3: c   paragraph 10: a   paragraph 12: b

3. Summarizing
Possible summary: in the 700s and 800s the Tangs lost their hold on power and China once again fell apart into city-states. The Song Dynasty that began in 960 built up China's trade, industry, and farming. It brought good times for some. However, not all people enjoyed this period. There were many poor people in the cities and countryside.

4. Generalizing
a. Song emperors encouraged the development of industry.

ENRICHMENT

1. Answers will vary.
2. Answers will vary.
3. a. paper; China—A.D. 105; Europe—approx. A.D. 1100
b. movable type: China—approx. A.D. 1041–48; Europe—approx. A.D. 1375–1400
c. steelmaking methods: Asia Minor—1400 B.C.; China—approx. 1000 B.C.; Europe—by 300 B.C.

d. seismograph: China—first century A.D.; Europe—1785
e. crossbow: China—unknown; Europe—A.D. 851
4. Answers will vary.

THE ARTS AND ARTIFACTS

1. Possible answers: The realistic quality of the pieces shows that the Qins were concerned with the real world. They believed in some kind of spirit or soul that had to be protected in death.
2. Because it was uncovered near the tomb mound of Shi Huang Di.

UNIT 2 ❧ CHAPTER 3

VOCABULARY REVIEW

1. animism   2. batik   3. javelin   4. megaliths
5. scripts   6. deltas   7. terraces

SKILL BUILDER: INTERPRETING A MAP

1. Southeast Asia   2. Khmer Empire, Champa
3. Burma   4. South   5. Approximately 800 miles (1400 kilometers)

SKILL BUILDER: CRITICAL THINKING AND COMPREHENSION

1. Classifying
a. India b. China c. China d. India
2. Main Idea
b. In Thailand today monks still study in Buddhist monasteries.
3. Summarizing
c. Early cultures in mainland Southeast Asia grew up around river deltas because these areas were good for farming.
4. Generalizing
paragraph 12

ENRICHMENT

1. The how-to manual should include a list of supplies needed (i.e., fabric, dyes, utensils, wax, etc.), and the steps involved in the process in the correct order.
2. Answers will vary.

A GEOGRAPHIC VIEW OF HISTORY

1. In northern India, near Benares.   2. Third century B.C.; fourth century A.D.   3. Possible answer: When empires fell, old routes may have become dangerous and unprotected, so new routes were found.

UNIT 2 ❧ CHAPTER 4

VOCABULARY REVIEW

1. Ainu   2. paddies   3. kami   4. Shinto   5. clans
6. missionaries   7. shoguns   8. samurai

SKILL BUILDER: INTERPRETING A HISTORICAL TIME LINE

1. 552: Korean king sends Buddhist writings to Japan.
630 to 838: Japanese send cultural missions to China.
Buddhism came from China to Japan.
The purpose of the missions was to get more ideas from China.
2. The Japanese took up the Buddhist religion.

3. Check placement of event at approximately A.D. 710 on student answer sheets.
Answer: The Japanese followed the Chinese example of a central government at a capital city and modeled Nara after the Chinese capital at Changan.

SKILL BUILDER: CRITICAL THINKING AND COMPREHENSION

1. Summarizing
a. The loss of power by the emperor and the rise of clans in the government were part of a new age in Japan that began in A.D. 794.
2. Generalizing
c. Samurai lived by a hard set of rules that kept them prepared for battle.
3. Sequencing
d. The Ainu people came to Japan.
a. Early Japanese society divided itself into clans.
c. Buddhism was introduced to Japan by Koreans.
b. Shoguns became powerful leaders in Japan.

ENRICHMENT

1. Ainu are considered to be indigenous Caucasoid people who survive in limited numbers in Hokkaido, Sakhalin, and the Kuril Islands. Their language is almost extinct. Typically they were short statured and brunette, with the men having heavy beards. They were hunters, fishermen, and trappers. Their religion centered on the local forces of nature.
2. Answers will vary, but might include these characteristics: a. seated and standing b. facial expressions—smiling, otherworldly, etc. c. clothing variations from culture to culture d. materials used to make sculpture
3. Answers will vary.

SKILL BUILDER/MAPS

1. green   2. orange and red   3. Honshu

UNIT 2 ❧ CHAPTER 5

VOCABULARY REVIEW

1. **migrated:** One who has moved from one country or territory to another to live.
2. **navigate:** To direct one's course in a ship or aircraft.
3. **outrigger canoe:** A projecting frame on a float attached to the side of a canoe to prevent tipping over.
4. **ocean currents:** Swift-moving stream (or river) in the ocean.
5. **aborigines:** The original inhabitants of a country.

SKILL BUILDER: MAKING AN OUTLINE

Possible additions to student outline:
B. European settlers
  1. Explorers.
  2. British convicts.
  3. British founded new towns.

SKILL BUILDER: CRITICAL THINKING AND COMPREHENSION

1. Main Idea
paragraph 3: Historians believe that people originally came to Oceania from Southeast Asia during the Ice Age about 40,000 years ago.
paragraph 7: The people of Oceania learned to read the signs of nature to navigate, or steer a course, across the Pacific Ocean.

2. Summarizing
paragraph 6
3. Generalizing
It is a poor generalization. During the centuries leading up to that time, major new land discoveries had been made. Therefore, it is entirely understandable that Europeans would believe that there was a great southern continent. European explorers also spent many years trying to find a Northwest Passage through North America. It is basic to exploration that one keep an open mind.
4. Sequencing
Aborigines came to Australia.
The first people came to Micronesia.
Polynesians reached Hawaiian Islands about A.D. 500.
Captain James Cook mapped the east coast of Australia.

ENRICHMENT

1. You may elect to use a condensed version of *Kon Tiki,* or possibly assign it as a long-term project to several students.
2. Answers will vary.
3. Easter Island, also known as Rapanui, was discovered on Easter Day in 1722 by the Dutch admiral Jacob Roggeveen. Archaeological expeditions occurred in 1914, 1934, and 1955. Historians believe that the stone statues were used as religious symbols for several reasons. The statues were set on platforms (ahus) that were constructed according to the astronomical movements of the sun. Archaeologists feel that the statues represent important people who were deified after death. Another book that you might have your students research is *Aku Aku,* by Thor Heyerdahl. This is a fascinating story that could be assigned as a long-term project to several students.
4. The best source for the answer to this question is the February, 1988 issue of *National Geographic* magazine, pages 233–245. You may want to have one or two students research this and then have them present an oral report to the class.

SKILL BUILDER/MAP

1. N **2.** SW **3.** SE **4.** SE

UNIT 2 ❧ REVIEW

SKILL BUILDER: FINDING LONGITUDE ON A MAP

1. Between the Prime Meridian and 60 degrees east.
2. The Etruscans, Greeks, Phoenicians, and Persians.
3. The Indo Aryan and Zhou Chinese, in addition to all of the above.

SKILL BUILDER: CRITICAL THINKING AND COMPREHENSION

1. Compare and Contrast
Answers will vary, but should include some of the following comparisons. Both built their empires by conquest. Both rulers established strong central governments and created large systems of roads throughout their empires. Both built canals for irrigation. Shi Huang Di established one set of laws that applied throughout his empire and a common system of weights and measures and coinage. Both rulers recognized the need both to unify their empires and to govern them effectively.
2. Fact versus Opinion
a. Fact b. Fact c. Fact d. Fact
3. Classifying
a. China   b. India   c. China   d. Cambodia
e. Japan f. Vietnam g. Japan

ENRICHMENT

1. Answers will vary.
2. Answers will vary.

UNIT 3 ❧ CHAPTER 1

VOCABULARY REVIEW

1. e **2.** g **3.** i **4.** f **5.** a **6.** d **7.** b **8.** h **9.** c

SKILL BUILDER: USING CONTEXT CLUES

1. a **2.** c **3.** a **4.** b

SKILL BUILDER: CRITICAL THINKING AND COMPREHENSION

1. Classifying
a. Athens b. Sparta c. Sparta d. Sparta e. Sparta f. Athens   g. Sparta   h. Athens   i. Athens j. Athens
2. Drawing Conclusions
A direct democracy was at work in the government of Athens before the Council of Five Hundred. Athens had adopted a constitution that allowed citizens more involvement in the government. It was the duty of all male citizens over the age of 18 to take part in the passing of the laws. Laws were made and voted on by the General Assembly where anyone could stand up and express a viewpoint.
3. Generalizing
c.   Pericles was one of the most influential statesmen in the history of Greece.

ENRICHMENT

1. The court system was administered by magistrates called archons. There were the popular courts (dikasteria) and the Areopagus. A special archon presided over affairs involving metics. The Areopagus was a group of elder archons who judged severe cases, such as murder. Any male citizen over 30 years of age could be an archon. Juries were composed of 1,501 1,001, or 501 men, depending on the severity of the crime. Customarily a complaint was filed, the defendant summoned, and a preliminary examination was held to determine if further action was warranted. All decisions or awards could be appealed to a higher court.
2. Zeus: bearded, kingly, deep voice; Diana: bow and quiver of arrows, running; Athena: flowing dress with spear, shield, and helmet.

UNIT 3 ❧ CHAPTER 2

VOCABULARY REVIEW

1. **agora:** The market place or place of assembly in an ancient Greek city.
2. **Metics:** Foreigners who settled in Greece.
3. **rhetoric:** The art of speaking or writing effectively.
4. **Sophists:** Special Greek teachers who were trained in the art of teaching rhetoric, grammar, logic, and philosophy.
5. **philosophy:** The study of knowledge.
6. **dialogue:** An exchange of ideas and opinions between two or more persons.
7. **myth:** An unsupported belief that explains a natural phenomena.
8. **philosopher:** One that seeks wisdom or enlightenment.
9. **logic:** Thinking through reasoning.

SKILL BUILDER: OUTLINING

I. Work in ancient Greece
  A. Many Greeks were shopkeepers and farmers
    1. They sold their goods in the agoras
    2. They traded with foreign peoples
  B. Metics and slaves
    1. Slaves did a lot of the work
    2. Metics were shopkeepers
II. Homes in ancient Greece
  A. Most Greek citizens owned their own homes
    1. They were built close together in towns
    2. They were constructed of sun-dried bricks
    3. They were built around open-air courtyards
  B. Greek homes were simple inside
    1. Houses were sparsely furnished
    2. Houses had few windows
III. The family in ancient Greece
  A. The family was the most important unit in ancient Greece
    1. It was made up of a father, mother, sons, unmarried daughters, and slaves
    2. The men worked, met with friends, or exercised
  B. Women of ancient Greece worked at home
    1. They managed the household, including money
    2. They prepared the food
    3. They nursed the sick back to health
IV. Education in ancient Greece
  A. Girls were taught at home
    1. They learned reading, writing, and arithmetic
    2. They learned to spin and weave in addition to music
  B. Boys attended private school from the age of six to sixteen
    1. At school they were taught reading, writing, arithmetic, music, and gymnastics
    2. Gymnastics was the most important part of a boy's education
    3. At 18 they became soldiers
    4. At 21 they became citizens
V. Religion in ancient Greece
  A. The Greeks believed in many gods
    1. There were gods of love, art, music, and harvest
    2. Each city and family had its own god
  B. Festivals were held once a year to honor the gods
    1. There would be parades, feasting, and games
    2. Today's Olympics started as a celebration of the festival of Zeus

SKILL BUILDER: CRITICAL THINKING AND COMPREHENSION

1. Drawing Conclusions
Persian Empire, Egyptian Empire
2. Generalizing
Agree. The myths that surrounded the gods were the basis of much of the cultural life of ancient Greece. Not only did the towns have their own gods, but each family did as well. There would be an altar to the family god in the central courtyard of the family's home. Festivals to the gods were held regularly. The Greeks believed the gods were in all things.
3. Classifying
3-1. c. Religion in Ancient Greece
3-2. a. f b. T c. T
3-3. a. Slaves b. Sophists c. women
4. Fact versus Opinion
a. Fact b. Opinion c. Opinion d. Fact e. Fact

ENRICHMENT

1. Models should show a house built around an open courtyard.
2. The Olympic Games by tradition were first held in Olympia, Greece in 776 B.C. It was one of four Panhellenic festivals held in ancient Greece. The Games were held at measured intervals until Emperor Theodosius abolished them in A.D. 393. At first the program was confined to one day, and consisted of a single event, a footrace the length of the stadium. Other events were added as time went on, such as the discus throw, the javelin, the long jump, boxing, wrestling, the pentathlon, and chariot racing. Winners became national heroes and received crowns of laurel leaves. The modern Olympic Games were initiated by a Frenchman, Baron Pierre di Coubertin. They have been held at four-year intervals since then, with the exception of the years of World Wars I and II. In 1924, a program of winter sports was begun.

UNIT 3 ❧ CHAPTER 3

VOCABULARY REVIEW

1. strait 2. Golden Age of Greece 3. phalanx 4. Hellenistic Age 5. emigrate

SKILL BUILDER: USING A CARD CATALOG

1. I 2. II 3. The Mask of Jove; Stringfellow Barr
4. Ancient History; III 5. 930 B 6. It is about the history of Graeco-Roman civilization from the death of Alexander to the death of Constantine. 7. 1966 8. 598
9. 1897

SKILL BUILDER: CRITICAL THINKING AND COMPREHENSION

1. Spatial Relationships
a. 50 b. Golden Age c. 47 d. 11 e. 14
2. Summarizing
The period between 480 B.C. and 399 B.C. was called the "Golden Age" of Greece because it was a period when Greece was free from threats from its neighbors and could devote its wealth and energy to developing its culture.
3. Generalizing
Ancient Greece was weak and in disarray because the city-states were fighting each other.
4. Sequencing
a. Asia Minor b. Egypt c. Mesopotamia d. Babylon
e. India
5. Drawing Conclusions
The Peloponnesian Wars had a negative effect on Greek culture. Instead of being able to spend time on cultural pursuits, the Greeks had to devote themselves to waging wars. Also, many Greek works of art were probably destroyed in the fighting.

ENRICHMENT

1. The main battles of the Graeco-Persian Wars were:
a. Marathon b. Thermopylae c. Bay of Salamis
d. Plataea e. Mycale f. River Eurymedon
The main battles of the Peloponnesian Wars were:
a. Battle of Sybota b. Battle of Delium c. Mantineia
d. Euboea e. Cyzicus f. Battle of Notium g. Battle of the Arginusae Islands
2. Answers will vary, but should site Cleopatra's influence with powerful men in government. Arsinoe was sometimes referred to as the king's wife not queen and, as such, she was not even allowed to keep her own children once the king had married another woman.

SKILL BUILDER/MAPS

1. Sparta **2.** Alexandria **3.** Approximately 1,875 miles **4.** Alexandria

UNIT 3 ❧ CHAPTER 4

VOCABULARY REVIEW

1. e **2.** d **3.** a **4.** c **5.** f **6.** g **7.** b **8.** h

SKILL BUILDER: MAKING A TIME LINE

Check students' time lines for placement. Time line reference dates could be in 10 or 20 year increments. Order of events should be:
• Julius Caesar is born 100 B.C.
• Caesar, Pompey, and Crassus form Rome's First Triumvirate 60 B.C.
• Caesar is elected consul of Rome 59 B.C.
• Julius Caesar invades Britain 55 B.C.
• Senate orders Julius Caesar to disband his army 49 B.C.
• Caesar defeats Pompey in Greece 48 B.C.
• Senate names Caesar dictator for life 44 B.C.

SKILL BUILDER: CRITICAL THINKING AND COMPREHENSION

1. Summarizing
b. The early Romans set up a representative form of government called a republic.
2. Generalizing
Rome fought several wars during the period of the republic that added greatly to the size of its empire.
3. Compare and Contrast
a. Both b. Alexander c. Caesar

ENRICHMENT

1. Answers will vary.
2. Answers will vary.

UNIT 3 ❧ CHAPTER 5

VOCABULARY REVIEW

barbarians: A name given to non-Greeks and non-Romans by the ancient Greeks and Romans. They felt that other peoples were inferior, lacking in refinement and learning.
coup: A sudden and highly successful act.
emperor: Supreme ruler of an empire.
manufactured: Raw materials made into useful goods by hand or machine.
orations: Elaborate speeches given in a fanciful, pompous manner.
Pax Romana: The "Roman Peace," 31 B.C. to A.D. 180, during which the Romans fought few outside enemies.
raw materials: Natural resources, like wool, cotton, minerals, which can be turned into finished products.
stoicism: Indifference to pleasure or pain; unmoved by joy or grief.

SKILL BUILDER: INTERPRETING A DIAGRAM

1. Structure of the Roman Government During the Republic **2.** Senate **3.** Assembly of Centuries **4.** Senate; they proposed laws, appointed governors, determined foreign policy, and had veto power over any act of the popular assembly of consuls. They also served for life.

SKILL BUILDER: CRITICAL THINKING AND COMPREHENSION

1. Cause and Effect
a. Marc Antony and Octavian each wished to rule Rome and all its territories.
b. The people so disliked Nero, they started a story blaming him for starting the fire in Rome. He wanted to put an end to the rumor.
c. Augustus promised to restore Rome to the greatness and glory of earlier times, bringing with it stability and prosperity. Most Romans wanted to see an end to the constant civil wars as well.
2. Generalizing
Roman laws were much like the laws that we have today in the United States.
3. Spatial Relationships
a. northwest b. east c. north d. northeast

ENRICHMENT

1. Roman roads were characterized by straightness, no matter what the obstacles. The earliest road dates from 312 B.C. First, they would excavate trenches about 40 feet apart to mark location. Then the foundation was covered with sand or mortar, which was then covered with four additional stages:
(a) statumen layer of large flat stones
(b) a rudus layer of smaller stones mixed with lime
(c) the nucleus layer, consisting of small gravel and coarse sand mixed with hot lime
(d) the wearing surface, made of flint-like lava stone
Roads had a two-way central lane, cambered to facilitate drainage. It was built to withstand the heaviest traffic. It was flanked by two curbs. These in turn had parallel one-way side lanes. Cross-section pictures of a Roman road can be found in various encyclopedias.
2. Answers will vary.
3. Answers will vary.

A GEOGRAPHIC VIEW OF HISTORY

1. The Roman Empire along the Atlantic Ocean and the parts of the empire located on the Mediterranean Sea had coastal boundaries.
2. Coastal boundaries made it impossible for an enemy to attack these parts of the empire other than by sea. An enemy would have to have a strong navy to attempt an attack on Rome.
3. The southern part of the empire in Africa (Sahara Desert) and the eastern and southeastern part of the empire in Asia (Arabian Desert, Syrian Desert) had desert boundaries.
4. The barren desert could not feed an army large enough to attack the military strength of Rome. The desert prevented potential attackers from getting through.
5. The Danube River and the Rhine River served as boundaries of the Roman Empire.
6. River boundaries gave the Romans time to prepare to meet an attacker. They could see the attacker coming, and in the time it would have taken the enemy to advance across the river, the Romans would have responded.
7. The boundary of the Roman Empire between the Black Sea and the Caspian Sea was the Caucasus Mountains. Another natural boundary was formed by the Tigris and Euphrates Rivers. However, there was a large section to the north of the Black Sea that had no natural boundaries, thus making it harder to defend. Any attacking force in Africa would have to come across the Sahara Desert, which was sparsely inhabited. Also, there was a

much larger population in Asia with which to stage an attack across the Asian border.

UNIT 3 ✿ CHAPTER 6

VOCABULARY REVIEW

1. atrium   2. forum   3. thermae   4. amphitheater
5. gladiator   6. arch   7. prose   8. vault   9. peristylum

SKILL BUILDER: INTERPRETING A TIME LINE

1. T   2. F; 8 years   3. F; 51 years old   4. T   5. F; 150 years

SKILL BUILDER: CRITICAL THINKING AND COMPREHENSION

1. Cause and Effect
a.   Freedom meant joining the ranks of the unemployed. Slaves lived better than did the unemployed.
b.   Public and military roads were constructed from Rome to the provinces.
c.   Rome was the capital and largest city. It had better marketplaces and shops and more beautiful buildings and temples than did any other city of the empire. It had the largest population and highest standard of living of any city in the Western world up to that time.
2. Generalizing
a.   Roman roads were well constructed.
b.   Aristocrats rarely did any manual labor
3. Sequencing
d, c, a, b.

ENRICHMENT

1. Answers should include that she worked to ensure that Tiberius, her son by her first husband, became emperor, and that to do this she caused the deaths of many of his rivals. She was born January 30, 58 B.C. and died in A.D. 29.
2. Answers will vary. The key word in this quote is "nobler." To be noble is to be honorable and aristocratic. Students should determine whether enlarging the Roman Empire—acquiring land, conquering city after city—was a noble "thing."

THE ARTS AND ARTIFACTS

1. chariot racing, gladiator fights
2. The Colosseum has less than half the seating capacity of the Rose Bowl. It would be considered a relatively small stadium by today's standards.

UNIT 3 ✿ CHAPTER 7

VOCABULARY REVIEW

1. mercenaries   2. persecution   3. dioceses   4. inflation

SKILL BUILDER: READING A MAP THAT HAS ARROWS

1. Gaul and Spain   2. Vandals   3. southwest

SKILL BUILDER: CRITICAL THINKING AND COMPREHENSION

1. Generalizing
Answers will vary. Examples: Splitting the empire weakened the West. Splitting the empire caused the two re-

gions to pull apart. The East was better suited militarily and economically than the West to survive.
2. Sequencing
b, e, c, d, f, a.
3. Spatial Relationships
a. southwest   b. north, east, and south   c. northwest   d. north
4. Cause and Effect
Answers will vary. Examples: Germanic tribes migrated south looking for new lands. Germanic tribes crossed the Danube into Roman territory in search of land.

ENRICHMENT

1. Answers will vary. The tribal customs were very similar.
The Germanic tribes relied on cattle herding rather than agriculture as their main source of food.
There was no private ownership of land. It was redistributed to families according to need by the village elders each year.
Iron making technology was known, but it was used primarily for weapons.
There was no central governing authority.
A temporary confederation of the villages was formed only in times of war.
2. Answers will vary.

UNIT 3 ✿ REVIEW

SKILL BUILDER: READING A MAP

1. The Roman Empire.   2. The Persian Empire.
3. Maurya Gupta India.   4. The Roman Empire.
5. Maurya Gupta India.   5. The Mayan Civilization.

SKILL BUILDER: CRITICAL THINKING AND COMPREHENSION

1. Sequencing
a.   Rome becomes a Republic (509 B.C.)
b.   The Greek city-states unite to defeat the Persians (499 B.C.)
c.   Sparta defeats Athens in the Peloponnesian War (404 B.C.)
d.   Alexander rules the Hellenistic World (336 B.C.)
e.   Rome conquers Italy (270 B.C.)
f.   Rome defeats Carthage for the final time (146 B.C.)
g.   Julius Caesar is made dictator for life (44 B.C.)
h.   Augustus is made the first Roman emperor (27 B.C.)
i.   Pax Romana comes to an end (A.D. 167)
j.   Germanic tribes invade the Roman Empire (A.D. 378)
2. Classifying
a.   Plato
b.   Constantine
c.   Aristotle
d.   Virgil
e.   Pericles
3. Making Judgments
Answers will vary. Some possible answers might be:
a.   The Greeks and Romans spread their ideas by conquest. Greek culture was spread by Alexander as he conquered his empire; this remained long after the empire had crumbled. The Romans adopted Greek ideas and developed them, spreading them through further conquests as the empire grew.
b.   Nations fall apart for many reasons. Greece fell apart because internal bickering made it easy prey for invaders. The decline and fall of Rome was more complicated because it happened over a longer period of time. Both nations lacked good leadership. Good leaders can

inspire people, giving them a sense of national purpose. A series of incompetent leaders can lead to the decline of a civilization.

ENRICHMENT

1. Answers will vary. Students might mention that two capitals would create two governments and split the empire. Neither half would be as strong as the whole.
2. Answers will vary.

UNIT 4 ❧ CHAPTER 1

VOCABULARY REVIEW

1. Messiah: h
2. crucifixion: f
3. Resurrection: j
4. persecute: c
5. missionaries: *distractor*
6. hierarchy: d
7. pope: i
8. bishop: b
9. monk: g
10. monastery: e
11. catacombs: a

SKILL BUILDER: USING AN ENCYCLOPEDIA

1. A general encyclopedia is used to find general information on any subject, with many volumes in the set. A special encyclopedia gives information about one subject, and generally the number of volumes in the set is smaller.
2. Spine
3. first—Gary, last—Halibut
4. Volume 3

SKILL BUILDER: CRITICAL THINKING AND COMPREHENSION

I. Introducing Comparing and Contrasting
Answers will vary, but should include some of the following points:
a. The Christian religion believes that Jesus was the Son of God who died in order that the sins of the world be forgiven. Entrance into heaven was only through the intercession of Jesus, while unforgiven sinners would suffer an eternity of pain in hell. Christians believe that God and Jesus know all, and are intimately involved and concerned about their life on earth.
b. Buddhism is a search for truth, ultimately resulting in the attainment of Buddhahood. This process is divided into many stages, and teaches acceptance of things as they are, patience, endeavor, perseverance, insight, and enlightenment. Buddhism teaches that salvation comes from yourself through meditation rather than from a god. Buddhism shares the element of mysticism with Christianity.

2. Sequencing
1. Jesus travels his homeland of Judea teaching about the kingdom of God. 2. Jesus is crucified. 3. Christianity is made an equal with other religions of the Roman Empire. 4. Christianity becomes the official religion of the Roman Empire.

3. Cause and Effect
3-1. c **3-2.** a **3-3.** d **3-4.** b

ENRICHMENT

1. Answers will vary.
2. The main categories in the church hierarchy are:
a. the pope: the spiritual head of the church, the successor of Peter.
b. The College of Cardinals: these clergy elect the pope from among their ranks. They are appointed by the pope. They are further divided into cardinal bishops, cardinal priests and cardinal deacons.
c. The college of bishops: this is the successor to the college of the apostles. Each bishop is a bishop of a place, either a proper area or a jurisdiction. Their duties are to teach Catholic doctrine, to sanctify the church through administering the sacraments, and to govern the area that they head.
d. The priesthood: these clergy are the officers of the bishop. They preach and help the bishop govern. Priests have a hierarchy of their own, including the various monastic orders. Priests can administer the sacraments, but only by proper permission of a bishop. Priests do not govern unless they are pastors. These pastors supervise a parish. Curates assist the pastor, but not as administrators. Other priests assist the pastor in special areas, such as teaching, scholarship, and other activities.

UNIT 4 ❧ CHAPTER 2

VOCABULARY REVIEW

a. missi dominici b. longships c. counts d. baptism

SKILL BUILDER: READING A MAP

1. Charles's **2.** Charles's **3.** Louis's **4.** Germany, Switzerland, Austria **5.** Lothair's

SKILL BUILDER: CRITICAL THINKING AND COMPREHENSION

1. **Sequencing** f. d. b. e. c. a.
2. **Compare and Contrast**

	BEFORE CHARLEMAGNE	DURING CHARLEMAGNE'S REIGN
Education	• Warrior training was valued over classic education	• Education was encouraged • Schools were set up • Old documents were copied
Government	• Europe was a mixture of competing petty states	• Charlemagne organized his empire with centralized authority
Christianity	• The Christian church had little support during the years before Charlemagne's rule	• Charlemagne increased the power of the church and became its protector

ENRICHMENT

1. Answers will vary.
2. Long ships ranged from 45 to 75 feet in length, built with overlapping planks. Both front and rear were raised, with the prow decorated with a dragonhead. Amidships there was a mast and square sail and room for oars and rowers. In the stern was a single side rudder on the starboard side. Long ships have been found dating from 300 B.C., but these had hides covering a wood frame. The classic Norse long ship was built in the 800s. Some of these were actually buried with their owners, and can still be seen today.

UNIT 4 ❧ CHAPTER 3

VOCABULARY REVIEW

1. mosaics 2. icons 3. law code 4. profits

SKILL BUILDER: INTERPRETING A PHOTOGRAPH

1. Empress Theodora's position in the center of the mosaic and her ornate crown shows her importance.
2. Their dress is lavish and looks very expensive. Therefore, they must have been wealthy women.
3. Theodora is giving the priest a gift. She must have given a great deal of imperial wealth to the church.

SKILL BUILDER: CRITICAL THINKING AND COMPREHENSION

1. Sequencing
c.   Constantine I moves the capital of the Roman Empire to Byzantine.
f.   Justinian I marries Theodora.
a.   Justinian becomes emperor of the Byzantine Empire.
d.   Justinian I dies.
b.   The Byzantine Empire loses much of its lands.
e.   Christianity is split between an eastern church and a western church.

2. Spatial Relationships
The Byzantine Empire was located at the midpoint between Asia and Europe. It was central to all the Mediterranean trade routes. Moving goods by water was much faster and cheaper than transporting them by land. Therefore, anyone controlling access to these routes was destined to become rich and powerful, since there simply was no other convenient way to go.

3. Cause and Effect
3-1. a. C b. E 3-2. a. E b. C 3-3. a. E b. C 3-4. a. C b. E 3-5. a. C b. E

4. Compare and Contrast
During Justinian's reign, the Hagia Sophia was built and attempts were made to bring together the eastern and western parts of the Roman Empire. The old Roman laws were reformed in the Justinian Code of law. After Justinian's death, the Byzantine Empire was at war most of the time. Most of the lands in the empire that had been won by Justinian were conquered. Greece, Asia Minor, and small sections of Italy were the only parts of the Byzantine Empire left by A.D. 800.

ENRICHMENT

1. Answers will vary. 2. Answers will vary.

UNIT 4 ❧ CHAPTER 4

VOCABULARY REVIEW

1. c 2. i 3. d 4. f 5. j 6. e 7. b 8. a 9. g 10. h 11. k

SKILL BUILDER: READING A TIME LINE

1. 1137 2. 15 3. Eleanor was imprisoned. 4. 82 years

SKILL BUILDER: CRITICAL THINKING AND COMPREHENSION

1. Cause and Effect
1-1: c. Feudalism was created.

1-2: a. The power of the nobles in France declined.
1-3: b. Otto I was named Holy Roman emperor.
1-4: d. Germany did not become a unified country.

2. Introduction to Drawing Conclusions
2-1. Warriors in the Middle Ages protected themselves by wearing metal armor.
2-2. Women of the Middle Ages wore layers of clothing because houses and castles often were cold and damp.
2-3. Castles helped protect lords from attack by their enemies.

ENRICHMENT

1. Boys taken on by a noble for training as knights almost always had to be of noble birth. Being a page was the first step in this process. Pages were taught to read and write, to play chess and other games, music, and the rules of courtesy and chivalry. Squires originally were shieldbearers for the knights. They also were trained in how to handle the various weapons and in how to manage large and small groups of men. When they were judged worthy by their master, they became knights. Many chose not to exercise their option to advance to knighthood due to the high expense involved. A knight was the lowest rank of the nobility, and usually had to provide something, such as military service, to a lord above him in return for his fief.
2. Answers will vary.

UNIT 4 ❧ CHAPTER 5

VOCABULARY REVIEW

1. **moat:** a deep wide trench around the walls of a castle, usually filled with water.
2. **guilds:** The organizations of businessmen or skilled workers.
3. **credit:** The trust that a person will pay back the money he or she borrows.
4. **corporation:** A business or company whose identity remains the same regardless of changes in the ownership or work force.
5. **chivalry:** The rules or code of behavior for knights.
6. **troubadours:** Poet-musicians who lived in the eleventh, twelfth and thirteenth centuries. They wrote poems of love and chivalry. Traveling throughout southern France and northern Italy they performed their poems set to music.
7. **freemen:** Persons enjoying civil or political liberties.
8. **middle class:** Group of people such as professional people and skilled crafts workers, who are neither rich nor poor.
9. **serfs:** Farm peasants who owed their loyalty to a noble during the Middle Ages.

SKILL BUILDER: COMPLETING A TABLE

	REASONS FOR CHANGE	DESCRIPTION OF CHANGE
Middle Class	Growth of towns and trade	Power and wealth measured by money
Guilds	Increased trade	Set trade standards; proctected members
Credit	Need to increase profits	Enabled merchants to buy businesses

	REASONS FOR CHANGE	DESCRIPTION OF CHANGE
Corporations	Increase profits in banking, moneylending and trade	Several merchants together could own or control what one alone could not
Education	Guilds needed educated people	Guilds and the church started schools

SKILL BUILDER: CRITICAL THINKING AND COMPREHENSION

1. Spatial Relationships
The trade fairs brought people into contact with each other, much as they do today. This resulted in the transfer and sharing not only of goods and manufacturing processes, but of ideas and culture as well.

2. Cause and Effect
a. Cause: Establish rules and standards for doing business
b. Effect: Troubadours, trouveres, and minnesingers were held in high esteem in the courts they traveled to
c. Cause: People wanted to increase trade with other towns, regions, and countries.
d. Cause: Glass was rare and expensive
e. Effect: New towns sprang up where it was most convenient to trade, such as places with harbors, or where trade routes crossed.

3. Compare and Contrast

PEASANT	LORD
Lived in a one-room mud or wood hut with a thatched roof and a dirt floor	Lived in a stone castle or mansion
Traveled by foot	Traveled by horseback or cart
Most of their time was spent farming	Most of their time was spent fighting or getting ready to fight

4. Drawing Conclusions
4-1. Answers will vary, but should reflect that those who had money bought and used an extensive variety of beauty aids.
4-2. Sanitation was a real problem during the Middle Ages. This problem created the perfect breeding ground for the various plagues and diseases that swept through the population periodically. Life expectancy was relatively short by modern-day standards.

ENRICHMENT

1. Answers will vary.
2. Answers will vary.
3. The apprentice was accepted by a master for training at an early age, such as seven or eight. Masters were not allowed to take more apprentices than they could effectively train. Traditionally apprentices slept in the shop of the master. Eventually they either had to pass an examination or create a "masterpiece" to acquire the status of master. Sometimes they did not become masters immediately after their examinations, so they became journeymen. Journeymen were paid according to the days they worked rather than by the job.

A GEOGRAPHIC VIEW OF HISTORY

1. red triangles, 7 2. Strait of Gibraltar, English Channel, Skaggerak, Kattegat, the Gulf of Finland 3. Answers will vary. They both control access to inland seas. Between them they represent outlets for Russia to the rest of the medieval world.

UNIT 4 🐚 CHAPTER

VOCABULARY REVIEW

1. a: clergy **2.** k: sacraments **3.** j: parish **4.** f: friar **5.** l: tithe **6.** d: ecclesiastical **7.** g: heresy **8.** e: ex-communicated **9.** i: investiture **10.** b: Concordat of Worms **11.** c: crusades **12.** h: infidel

SKILL BUILDER: READING A MAP

1. Most routes passed through the Mediterranean Sea. The exception was the land route to Antioch through Constantinople.
2. The route from England passed through the Atlantic Ocean as well as the Mediterranean.
3. The route from France passed through the Holy Roman Empire and Venice to Constantinople and from there across Asia Minor.
4. Answers will vary.

SKILL BUILDER: CRITICAL THINKING AND COMPREHENSION

I. Cause and Effect
1-1. b: People believed that their souls could be saved only through the church.
1-2. a: The church owned a great deal of land.
1-3. b: The Seljuk Turks had taken over Palestine and were threatening the Byzantine Empire.
2. Compare and Contrast
Answers will vary, but all should reflect the fact that monks live apart from the people whereas friars live among them.

ENRICHMENT

1. Answers will vary. Suggest that students read more about this story before they begin writing their scene.
2. Answers will vary.

THE ARTS AND ARTIFACTS

1. Romanesque buildings looked like fortresses. They had domed roofs and rounded arches and they were very gloomy inside. Gothic-style buildings were tall and seemed to soar into the heavens. Flying buttresses supported the thinner church walls and larger windows were used. This made the interiors very light and bright.
2. The importance of Christianity to the people of the middle ages was reflected in the architecture of Gothic churches. Flying buttresses allowed architects to build churches that were light and airy. Large stained-glass windows showed religious scenes.

UNIT 4 🐚 CHAPTER 7

VOCABULARY REVIEW

1. papacy **2.** schism **3.** bubonic plague **4.** Black Death **5.** cardinals **6.** simony **7.** optics

SKILL BUILDER: MAKING A TIME LINE

Check student's time lines for correct placement of the events in this order:
- 1301 Conflict begins between King Philip IV and Pope Boniface VIII.
- 1309 The papacy moves from Rome to Avignon.
- 1377 Pope Gregory XI moves the papacy back to Rome.
- 1378 The schism begins with the election of two popes.
- 1417 The schism ends.

SKILL BUILDER: CRITICAL THINKING AND COMPREHENSION

1. Hypothesizing
Answers will vary, but should include that as more Europeans made contact with the East over many years, discoveries such as gunpowder began to appear in western Europe.

2. Cause and Effect
Answers will vary, but should include that the social relations between serfs and their lords were changed, and serfs could bargain for better conditions because of the shortage of laborers after the plague.

3. Compare and Contrast
Answers will vary.

4. Classifying
Answers will vary, but should include that the chart shows the weakness of the church's leadership.

ENRICHMENT

1. The Peasants Revolt of 1381 had many causes, but the most immediate one was when the government tried to collect a poll tax from the peasants to finance the Hundred Years' War in France. Resentment had built up to a point where the peasants revolted when the king's tax collectors appeared to collect the poll tax. Eventually the peasants did march on London, where the king met with them. The rebel leader, Wat Tyler, was killed in a skirmish with the king's guards. The king promised the peasants what it took to pacify them, and they dispersed toward their homes. Eventually the king hunted down the ringleaders of the revolt and had them executed. None of the promises the king made were kept. However, the government never again tried to collect a poll tax. In addition, the power of the peasants had been demonstrated, and had to be taken into account in subsequent government policies.
2. Answers will vary, according to which medieval scientist is selected. Students should be encouraged to try a biographical encyclopedia as an alternative to *Britannica* or *World Book*.
3. Answers will vary. Students should be encouraged to do further research on the decline of feudalism prior to beginning their murals.

UNIT 4 ❧ REVIEW

SKILL BUILDER: CRITICAL THINKING AND COMPREHENSION

1. Main Idea
1-1. b: The church played a leading role in every aspect of life.
1-2. c: By the end of the Middle Ages, the middle class was an important part of society.

2. Classifying
Church monastery excommunication investiture sacrament
Feudal System
manor fief vassal
Life in Medieval Towns
guild university

3. Cause and Effect
3-1. Trade revives in Europe.
f. Towns grow in size and number.
3-2. The Black Death strikes Europe.
c. Many serfs escape to freedom.
3-3. Clovis is baptized.
a. The Franks accept Christianity.
3-4. The pope moves from Rome to Avignon.
d. The prestige of the Church suffers.
3-5. William of Normandy wins the Battle of Hastings.
e. Feudalism is introduced to England.
3-6. Viking raids strike Europe.
b. Collapse of Charlemagne's empire is hastened.

ENRICHMENT
1. Answers will vary.   2. Answers will vary.

UNIT 5 ❧ CHAPTER 1

VOCABULARY REVIEW

1. federation: A group of city-states that give up individual sovereignty to a central authority but retain certain limited power.
2. boyars: Members of the Russian aristocracy until abolished by Peter the Great.
3. steppe: Large treeless plain that has cold winters and hot summers, and receives from 10 to 20 inches of rain a year; called a prairie in the United States.
4. allegiance: Devotion or loyalty to one's group or country.
5. absolute power: Complete control.
6. dvoryane: Russian land owners at the top of the class system created by Ivan the Terrible.
7. banished: Forced to leave a country; expelled.
8. kremlin: A stockade wall. The first one was built in Moscow in 1147 to protect the settlement from invaders.

SKILL BUILDER: INTERPRETING A TIME LINE

1. a 2. c 3. a 4. a 5. a

SKILL BUILDER: CRITICAL THINKING AND COMPREHENSION

1. Cause and Effect 1-1. c 1-2. b 1-3. a
2. Compare and Contrast

SIMILARITIES	DIFFERENCES
• Both were cruel rulers	• Ivan the Great established a strict code of law for the people of all classes; Ivan the Terrible created a new class system and took rights away from the peasants.

SIMILARITIES	DIFFERENCES
• Neither improved conditions in Russia during their rule	• Ivan the Great expanded Russia into Novgorod; Ivan the Terrible expanded the eastern frontier.
• Both held the title of czar	• Ivan the Great defeated the Mongols; Ivan the Terrible formed a secret police and drove the boyars from their land.

3. Drawing Conclusions
b. The Mongols caused the Russians to become isolated from Byzantine and western influences.

4. Predicting
Kiev would become a very important economic and political center for Russia as long as north/south trade routes were active.
a. Kiev soon became the most important trading town in the developing Russian state.
b. Kievan Russia was a federation, or loosely organized political group, of about 200 towns.

ENRICHMENT

1. Answers will vary.
2. The most direct route for the North people would have been travel by way of the West Divina River to beyond Polotsk, and then go overland until they reached the Dnieper River. The Dnieper River would take them to Kiev, and then down to the Black Sea to Constantinople. The early Moscow princes would have taken the Don River to the Sea of Azov, and then to the Black Sea and Constantinople.

UNIT 5 ❧ CHAPTER 2

VOCABULARY REVIEW

Muslims: A believer in, or follower of Islam.
pilgrimage: A journey or trip to a holy place.
convert: To change from one belief, faith, or religion to another.
submit: To give in or yield to the power or will of another.
prophet: One gifted with more than ordinary spiritual and moral insight, usually divinely inspired.
Koran: The holy book of Islam.
mosque: Muslim house of worship.
minaret: A tower attached to a mosque from which the call to prayer is made.
caliph: A title for the religious and civil head of a Muslim state and successor of Muhammad as civil and spiritual head of Islam.

SKILL BUILDER: OUTLINING

Answers will vary, but might include some of the possibilities listed below. The life of Muhammad
  I. Grew up in Mecca
    A. Spent early life as a camel driver
    B. Married Khadija at 25
  II. Religious and Social Concerns
    A. Worried about the poor
    B. There were too many gods
  III. Develops Religious Leadership
    A. Visions and dreams at age 40
    B. Preaching to large crowds in Mecca

  IV. Escapes from and Returns to Mecca
    A. Fled to Medina to escape murder plot
    B. Returned to Mecca and defeated his enemies

SKILL BUILDER: CRITICAL THINKING AND COMPREHENSION

1. Cause and Effect
Cause **1.** e **2.** b **3.** d **4.** c **5.** a **6.** f
2. Drawing Conclusions
Answers will vary, but might include that the poor feel unequal and oppressed in society. It would be appealing for them to think that being poor only reflected an inequality of money and possessions rather than spiritual worth and moral goodness.
3. Predicting
Answers will vary according to sex, but might include some of the following:
a. No alcohol or tobacco
b. Men may take up to four wives
c. Women must dress modestly
d. All must pray five times a day
e. Penalties for crimes would be more severe
f. Education would include religious as well as secular subjects
4. Compare and Contrast
Answers will vary, but might include some of the following:
Pillar 1: Must declare publicly that there is only one god, Allah, and that Muhammed is Allah's prophet. (Public baptism and declaring an acceptance of Jesus Christ.)
Pillar 2: Muslims must pray five times a day. (Christians and Jews pray before meals and before bed.)
Pillar 3: Muslims must give alms to the poor. (There is a strong tradition in Judaism and Christianity of helping the less fortunate, such as the homeless.)
Pillar 4: A Muslim must fast from dawn to sundown each day of the holy month of Ramadan. (Jews cannot eat pork, and have strict dietary laws. Catholics must eat fish on Fridays.)
Pillar 5: Muslims must make a journey to Mecca once during their life. (Many Christians and Jews make pilgrimages to the Holy Land during the various religious holidays and festivals.)

ENRICHMENT

1. Answers should include: a. minaret, or a tower from which the faithful were called to pray b. minbar, or pulpit for preaching c. zullah, or covered colonnade d. qiblah, or side of the covered courtyard that faced Mecca e. mihrab, or a highly decorated niche of varying size **2.** Answers will vary.

A GEOGRAPHIC VIEW OF HISTORY

1. Less **2.** Egypt, Sudan, Ethiopia, Chad, Libya, Algeria, Morocco, Mauritania, Mali, Nigeria, Cameroon, Ghana, Guinea, Ivory Coast, Central African Republic, Somalia, Tunisia **3.** Cordoba **4.** a. Asia, Africa, the Middle East b. Indonesia

UNIT 5 ❧ CHAPTER 3

VOCABULARY REVIEW

1. sultan **2.** Anatolia **3.** visionary **4.** Turkic

SKILL BUILDER: USING AN INDEX

(Bach) p. 264; (Roger Bacon) 3 pages
1. Pages 236–237 **2.** Seljuks, Turks **3.** Constantinople, Byzantine Empire, or Ottoman Empire

SKILL BUILDER: CRITICAL THINKING AND COMPREHENSION

1. Cause and Effect
a. The crusades b. Leaders fought amongst themselves
c. The Mongol armies of Genghis Khan
2. Drawing Conclusions
a. The capture would symbolize a religious victory of Islam over Christianity.
3. Predicting
The crusade did not succeed.
a. In 1354 Ottoman troops led by Murad I crossed the Dardanelles into eastern Europe.
b. Over the next hundred years, the Ottomans conquered the Balkan kingdoms one by one, including Greece.
4. Compare and Contrast
Answers will vary, but should include some of the following:
a. Suleiman expanded trade and brought about many reforms that made life better for his people. Selim cared only for war and expanding the empire.
b. Suleiman respected the rights of his people. He compensated merchants for goods that had been seized unlawfully by his father.

ENRICHMENT

1.

	BYZANTINE EMPIRE	OTTOMAN EMPIRE
Territories	• Anatolia, Greece, the Balkans, Italy, the Middle East, northern Africa, parts of Spain	• Anatolia, Syria, Mesopotamia, Palestine, Egypt, Tripoli, Tunisia, Algeria, Greece, the Balkans, Hungary, Crimea
Capital City	• Constantinople	• Istanbul
Important Rulers	• Constantine I, Justinian, Heraclius	• Selim I, Suleiman the Magnificent, Murad II

2. Suleiman lived from 1494–95 to September 5, 1566. He undertook bold military campaigns and also oversaw what came to be regarded as the Golden Age of the Ottoman Empire. Advances were made in the fields of law, literature, art, and architecture. He became sultan in 1520 upon the death of his father, Selim I. He built up the naval forces until the Ottoman Empire was the dominant seapower in the Mediterranean area. He also surrounded himself with poets, writers, and artists. He was able to oversee the transition of the Ottoman Empire into a structure that was able to govern as well as conquer.
3. Constantinople had been isolated by land since the Battle of Kossovo. Since the city was considered invulnerable to attack from the sea because of a huge chain stretched across the harbor entrance, the defenses of the city were concentrated on the walls. Murad II got around this by dragging 70 ships overland to the harbor, thus bypassing the chain. Turkish troops eventually did manage to breach the city walls in several places, killing the emperor Constantine XI in the process. There had been extensive negotiations regarding the reunion of the eastern and western churches as a price for the west coming to the aid of Constantinople. You might explore whether this would have made any difference in the outcome.

UNIT 5 ❧ CHAPTER 4

VOCABULATY REVIEW

1. Sudan: a **2.** civil servant: g **3.** mansa: c **4.** Berbers: e **5.** Swahili: d **6.** architect: b **7.** terra-cotta: f

SKILL BUILDER: COMPARING MAPS

1. Vegetation of West Africa; Early kingdoms of West Africa **2.** Kumbi **3.** Timbuktu and Gao **4.** Semiarid steepe; It was a relatively good area for people to live in. It was a good compromise between the dense jungle and the arid desert. **5.** Savanna grasslands and woodlands **6.** Niger River

SKILL BUILDER: CRITICAL THINKING AND COMPREHENSION

1. Compare and Contrast
Answers will vary slightly dependent on East African city chosen. Chart headings will also vary.

	TIMBUKTU	KILWA
Location	inland, in West Africa (Mali)	on east coast
Special Features	university and schools	stone buildings
Religion	Islam	Islam

2. Drawing Conclusions
Possible conclusion: Mali was a large and wealthy empire.
3. Predicting
Possible changes: each language would take some words from the other; a new language would grow up, combining the two.
4. Fact versus Opinion
a. Fact b. Fact c. Fact d. Opinion e. Opinion

ENRICHMENT

1. Answers will vary.
2. Timbuktu is located in the present-day country of Mali. It is important as an administrative center. The population of Timbuktu declined rapidly after an invasion from Morocco in 1591.

UNIT 5 ❧ CHAPTER 5

VOCABULARY REVIEW

1. memoirs **2.** sultan **3.** untouchables **4.** Mogul

SKILL BUILDER: INTERPRETING A TIME LINE

1. 20 years **2.** Shah Jahan is born 1592; Shah Jahan dies in prison 1666 **3.** 1632; 1653 **4.** He was imprisoned by his son, Aurangzeb **5.** Between birth of Shah Jahan (1592) and death of Mumtaz Mahal (1626)

SKILL BUILDER: CRITICAL THINKING AND COMPREHENSION

1. Fact versus Opinion
Facts include:
There is no ice or cold water.
There are no colleges.
There is no running water in the residences.

Opinions include:

Hindustan is a country of few charms.
There are no good horses.
There are no first-rate fruits.

2. Compare and Contrast
Answers will vary according to the building chosen. Areas of comparison would include architectural style, building materials, religious influences, decorations, and purpose of the building.

3. Drawing Conclusions
India prospered as a result of Akbar treating everyone equally and tolerating religions other than Islam.

4. Predicting
Many were probably stolen. To test the prediction, one could do research about the Taj Mahal in an encyclopedia, travel book, or other source.

ENRICHMENT

1. Answers will vary, but should reflect dissatisfaction over this discrimination.

2. The Taj Mahal was started in 1632 and took 22 years to complete. It consists of a rectangle measuring 634 by 334 yards (580 by 304 meters) aligned north and south. The complex is divided into three areas: a central garden, an entrance gateway on the south side, and the mausoleum itself on the north. The complex was conceived as a whole, in keeping with Mughal building practices; there were no provisions for additions. Its cost is estimated to be 40 million rupees, and it took a workforce of more than 20,000 to complete it. More detailed descriptions can be found in the *Encyclopedia Britannica* and the *Encyclopedia of World Art.* A diagram and cross-section of the complex can be found in *The History of Architecture.*

3. Pakistan broke off from India because most of its people were Muslims. Bangladesh was originally a part of Pakistan, but won its independence in the mid-1970s after a long and bloody war. Several wars have been fought between India and Pakistan, and tensions still remain high. India, at present, is by far the stronger of the two countries. Bangladesh is one of the poorest countries in the world, plagued with natural disasters, hunger, and poverty.

4. Sikhs desire autonomy from India. They feel that they are discriminated against by Hindus and Muslims alike.

THE ARTS AND ARTIFACTS

1. He had the magnificent Taj Mahal built as a tomb. (There may be several additional answers.)

2. Customs vary, but many people honor their dead by burying them in graveyards that are carefully maintained. Some have the remains of their dead cremated and placed in beautiful urns. Headstones, and plaques on monuments and statues often tell of important deeds or memories of the person who died. Some people plant trees or flowers to honor their dead. Memorial Day is a national holiday for honoring soldiers who have died. Buildings, streets, and other community sites are often named after someone who has died. Students should share their customs with the class.

UNIT 5 🍂 CHAPTER 6

VOCABULARY REVIEW

1. vernacular **2.** alliances **3.** daimyos **4.** kabuki
5. haiku **6.** translated

SKILL BUILDER: INTERPRETING A TABLE

1. Whoever went to live with the other one's family probably had somewhat less power or rights in the relationship.
2. Women had some, if not equal, rights with men.
3. They had few rights and were at the mercy of their husbands.
4. Before Tokugawa: see items 2, 3, & 4 on chart.

SKILL BUILDER: CRITICAL THINKING AND COMPREHENSION

1. Compare and Contrast
Mongols were open to foreign trade; they built roads and encouraged trade. The Mings favored trade for a time; then they stopped it.

2. Drawing Conclusions
Possible conclusions: He made China strong and unified. He took actions to protect against new foreign influence.

3. Predicting
They would probably oppose it again, as they did before. The Chinese thought of outsiders as inferior barbarians. Chinese culture flourished as a result of isolationism.

4. Fact versus Opinion
Answers will vary.

ENRICHMENT

1. This complex consisted of hundreds of buildings, including the palaces of the emperor and his retainers. The Forbidden City was planned and built according to traditional Chinese beliefs of the square or rectangle symbolizing the earth. The entire city of Beijing is laid out along a north-south axis. All buildings face south, for symbolic, as well as climatic reasons. The walls run a total of 2.5 miles, and are 35 feet (11 meters) high. To get further information, students could try the *National Geographic* magazine or other books on Chinese architecture.

2. Answers will vary.

3. Wood-block pictures were by and for the common people. Monochrome, or one-color prints, appeared in Japan around 1650. They dealt mainly with works of fiction. These evolved into single-sheet prints of women or kabuki stars that were done either in black lines (sumizuri-e) or beni-e, which combined the black lines with other colors put in by hand.

UNIT 5 🍂 CHAPTER 7

VOCABULARY REVIEW

1. steles **2.** hereditary **3.** tribute **4.** chinampas
5. quipu **6.** Anesthetics

SKILL BUILDER: CREATING A TABLE

	MAYA	AZTECS	INCAS
Gods	worshiped many gods; gods of corn, earth, rain, sun, etc.	worshiped many gods; main god—Huitzilopochtli —god of the sun and war; practiced human sacrifice	worshiped many gods, but sun god was most important; believed ruler was a descendant of the Sun God

	MAYA	AZTECS	INCAS
Cities	built pyramids topped with temples for religious ceremonies; buildings were made of stone; used stone shafts called steles (Tikal, Chichen Itza)	stone; used piles to build on soft swamp land; there were zoos, orchards, and open air theaters	stone buildings with no cement; road system; bridges; gold work, temples of shining white stone (Cuzco, Machu Picchu)
Farming Methods	farming villages outside center city; planted corn, sweet potatoes, beans, onions, squash, etc.	planted crops on floating gardens, called chinampas, which were rafts covered with roots, weeds, and mud. Aztecs planted flowers everywhere, and also had orchards.	used animals to do work; built terraces up steep hillsides for potatoes and corn; used irrigation ditches

SKILL BUILDER: CRITICAL THINKING AND COMPREHENSION

1. Drawing Conclusions
b. The Aztecs developed an advanced civilization.
2. Predicting
a. The Spanish and Incas fought a war. Reason: The Spanish came to conquer, so they would not be likely to live under Inca rule. The Incas had a working empire to which the people were loyal, so they would not choose to be part of someone else's empire. Therefore, the most likely outcome was that they would fight a war.
3. Fact versus Opinion
a. F b. O c. F d. F e. O
4. Main Idea
a. The Incas worked for the empire because the emperor took good care of them.
5. Sequencing   a, e, b, c, d

ENRICHMENT

1. Suggest that students find a picture of a quipu before they begin making one, in order to make theirs as authentic as possible.
2. Crossword puzzles will vary.

UNIT 5 ɘ REVIEW

SKILL BUILDER: READING A MAP

1. Asia, Africa, and Europe. 2. The Byzantine Empire.
3. Japan is a nation of islands. 4. The Holy Roman Empire. 5. They made their conquests by land.

SKILL BUILDER: CRITICAL THINKING AND COMPREHENSION

1. Drawing Conclusions
Answers will vary. A thriving trade in gold and salt crossed the Sahara between sub-Saharan Africa and North Africa.

2. Compare and Contrast
a. In Islam all men are equal before Allah. Any Muslim can lead other Muslims in prayer.
b. The main trading partners of the East Africans were the kingdoms along the coast of the Red Sea, in India, and in Egypt.
c. They all were invaded by the Mongols.
d. The policy was isolationism.
e. They all established great centers of learning by supporting scholars and artists, which in turn attracted students.
f. They built floating gardens made of rafts covered with roots, weeds, and mud called chinampas.
3. Point of View
a. Hindustan is a nation of few charms: Babur, the Mogul emperor.
b. I must divide Songhai into provinces in order to improve the government: Askia the Great.
c. I must end our contact with the West and expel all Portuguese and Spanish from our island nation: Iemitsu, the shogun of Japan.

ENRICHMENT

Answers will vary.

UNIT 6 ɘ CHAPTER 1

VOCABULARY REVIEW

1. scholars 2. Renaissance 3. classical 4. humanists 5. realism 6. patrons 7. perspective 8. poet laureate 9. tyrant

SKILL BUILDERS: OUTLINING

1. paragraph 16
2. b: The rebirth in the Renaissance was a rebirth of learning.
3. I. The spread of the Renaissance
    A. Contributions of northern Europe
       1. Painters
         a. Albrecht Durer
         b. Pieter Brueghel
       2. Invention of printing
       3. English writers
         a. Thomas More
         b. William Shakespeare

SKILL BUILDER: CRITICAL THINKING AND COMPREHENSION

1. Drawing Conclusions
b. Artists began to study Greek and Roman statues.
2. Predicting
b. European rulers will establish colonies in newly discovered lands.
3. Fact versus Opinion
a. Fact b. Opinion c. Opinion d. Fact e. Opinion
f. Opinion g. Fact
4. Point of View b, c, d

ENRICHMENT

1. Answers will vary.
2. Answers will vary.

UNIT 6 ɘ CHAPTER 2

VOCABULARY REVIEW

1. Protestants: e 2. Reformation: g 3. predestination: d 4. diet: f 5. theses: a 6. indulgences: b 7. doctrine: h 8. Counter-Reformation: c

SKILL BUILDER: INTERPRETING PRIMARY SOURCES

1. a: According to the quote, "The gospel...demands only faith in Christ."
2. It would fit better in a report on church and government in the Reformation.

SKILL BUILDER: CRITICAL THINKING AND COMPREHENSION

1. Drawing Conclusions
Answers will vary, but should include the idea that the peasants would probably be angry at Luther and would feel that he had betrayed them.
2. Predicting
Answers will vary, but one prediction might be that the Counter-Reformation would have served to polarize artists and writers. Those who remained loyal to the church would probably have created works concerning the strengths of the church, and beliefs and devotional subjects that the Protestant Reformation was attacking. Those sympathetic to the Protestant Reformation would use their art for the opposite effect.
3. Fact versus Opinion
a. Opinion b. Fact c. Opinion d. Fact
4. Point of View
4-1. a 4-2. Answers will vary.

ENRICHMENT

1. Answers will vary.
2. Answers will vary.

UNIT 6 ❧ CHAPTER 3

VOCABULARY REVIEW

1. parliament: g **2.** armada: h **3.** Magna Carta: f
4. absolute monarch: m **5.** monarchs: a **6.** civil war: i
7. Moors: b **8.** Restoration: k **9.** Inquisition: d
10. heretics: c **11.** commonwealth: j **12.** limited monarch: l **13.** barons: e **14.** commune: n

SKILL BUILDER: INTERPRETING TIME LINES

Check students' time lines for placement of events in this order:
1469 Isabella and Ferdinand marry and begin unification of Spain.
1512 Ferdinand takes over the kingdom of Navarre.
1558 Elizabeth I becomes queen of England.
1588 England defeats the Spanish Armada.
1642 Civil war breaks out in England.

SKILL BUILDER: CRITICAL THINKING AND COMPREHENSION

1. Drawing Conclusions Set 1: c Set 2: d
2 Predicting
Answers should indicate that the people might begin to demand their rights and civil wars and revolts might break out.
3. Fact and Opinion
a. Fact b. Opinion c. Fact d. Opinion
4. Points of View
a. Spain should be united as a Catholic country.
c. An inquisition should be set up to rid Spain of Jews and Muslims.

ENRICHMENT

1. Answers will vary. Students might want to research symbols and trademarks to get some ideas.
2. Answers will vary.

A GEOGRAPHIC VIEW OF HISTORY

1. Portugal, Leon, Castile, Navarre, Aragon
2. Cadiz, Seville, Cordoba, Granada, Murcia, Gibraltar, Valencia
3. Granada
4. Majorca, Mediterranean Sea
5. The Christian reconquest of the Iberian Peninsula gave Portugal and Spain greater access to the Atlantic Ocean and the Mediterranean Sea.

UNIT 6 ❧ CHAPTER 4

VOCABULARY REVIEW

1. caravel: c **2.** Indies: a **3.** explorations: d **4.** Inca: b
5. circumnavigate: f **6.** viceroy: e **7.** scurvy: g

SKILL BUILDER: READING A MAP

1. Europe and the lands bordering the Mediterranean
2. Signified by red lines and arrows. Columbus, De Gama, Frobisher, Cartier, Cabral, Magellan
3. Most of North and South America, most of Asia, Africa, Australia, and Antarctica
4. western coast of Africa; eastern coast of South America
5. The southern United States, Central America, and the northern and western coasts of South America
6. Eastern Canada and the Mississippi River
7. Spain

SKILL BUILDER: CRITICAL THINKING AND COMPREHENSION

1. Predicting
a. Answers will vary, but might include the search for wealth, the search for a passage through the Americas to Asia, and the desire to start new lives away from the political and religious persecution of Europe.
b. Answers will vary, according to which nationality is being considered. The Spanish and Portuguese treated them as subhuman savages, while stealing their wealth. The English and French were slightly better; for a while the Indians were considered "noble savages."
2. Fact versus Opinion
a. Opinion b. Fact c. Opinion d. Fact e. Fact f. Fact
3. Point of View b
4. Making Judgments
Answers will vary, but might include the following:
a. It added greatly to scientific knowledge.
b. It opened up the North and South American continents to development in the twentieth century.
c. It widened the horizons of European thinking.
d. The establishment of colonies would lead to industrial expansion and advancement in Europe.

ENRICHMENT

1. Answers will vary.
2. Answers will vary, according to the nations selected.

T149

THE ARTS AND ARTIFACTS

1. Cities like Chichén Itzá were used only for religious ceremonies. Priests and other officials lived in the cities. Other people only visited on important holidays.
Buildings were carved with pictures of gods, animals, and people. Many buildings had pictures of important religious events on the walls. These carvings and paintings are some of the only records we have of Mayan culture.
2. Since most of the scenes were of religious events, the people portrayed were probably priests, officials, or worshippers.

UNIT 6 ❧ CHAPTER 5

VOCABULARY REVIEW

1. petty monarchy **2.** elector **3.** concordat

SKILL BUILDER: INTERPRETING A TABLE

1. Answers will vary, but might include the following: without a strong central government, local rulers would get used to doing things their own way; laws and regulations would be hard to enforce because the emperor had insufficient authority.
2. The military power had decreased.
3. Issues that would make government difficult might include differences in language, customs, and ideas of law and order among the various ethnic groups.
4. No colonies belonged to the empires.
5. The power of the empires are weak, and probably will get weaker in the future.

SKILL BUILDER: CRITICAL THINKING AND COMPREHENSION

1. Predicting
a. International laws would be made to govern the conduct of armies in war.
2. Fact or Opinion
a. Opinion b. Fact c. Fact d. Fact
3. Point of View
c. Care should be taken during war to avoid the killing of innocent people.
4. Making Judgments
b. Life in the Holy Roman Empire was similar to life elsewhere in Europe.

ENRICHMENT

1. Answers will vary, but should include something about the destruction, disease, and starvation that this conflict brought about.
2. Answers will vary, but might include references to the Holy Roman emperor as the loser and the Protestant princes and nobles as the victors.

UNIT 6 ❧ CHAPTER 6

VOCABULARY REVIEW

1. enlightened despot **2.** Junkers **3.** czar **4.** Huguenots **5.** elector

SKILL BUILDER: READING A BIOGRAPHICAL TIME LINE

1. Frederick William **2.** yes **3.** no **4.** Peter the Great **5.** no

SKILL BUILDER: CRITICAL THINKING AND COMPREHENSION

1. Hypothesizing
Answers will vary, because the next king might not care that much about war. He might choose to invest the money in making life better for his people. The more obvious side of this would be that the next king would choose to use these funds to enlarge his power through various military adventures.
2. Fact versus Opinion
a. Opinion b. Fact c. Opinion d. Fact e. Fact
f. Opinion
3. Point of View
a. noble b. noble c. peasant d. noble e. peasant
4. Making Judgments
Answers will vary. Military expenditures have always been a terrible drain on countries, both in terms of money and in manpower. Given the state of the world as it was at that time, building up the military first was the best way to foster growth in Prussia.

ENRICHMENT

1. Answers will vary.
2. The name of Hohenzollern was derived from its ancestral seat of Zolorin, the modern-day Burg Hohenzollern, located about 15 miles from Tübingen. The line originatled with Burchard I, count of Zollern, who died in 1061, and continued in power until the end of World War I in 1918. The genius of Frederick William, the Great Elector, was in taking a war-ravaged principality, that was occupied by foreign troops after the Thirty Years War, and turning it into a sovereign power in its own right. William was also able to add a lot of strategically valuable territory to his original domain by changing sides in several conflicts when it profited him politically and militarily. William passed on a state to his son, Frederick I, that was dramatically different from what he inherited. Fortunately for Brandenburg-Prussia, the kings who succeeded William were also very able rulers, who were able to build on his achievements. Prussia would never have occupied the place in history that it did without the accomplishments of the Hohenzollern family.

UNIT 6 ❧ REVIEW

SKILL BUILDER: READING A MAP

1. b: England, Spain, and Portugal
2. a: They controlled one large area
3. a: Russian, Chinese, and Mogul empires
4. b: The Ottoman Empire

SKILL BUILDER: CRITICAL THINKING AND COMPREHENSION

1. Point of View
a. Leonardo da Vinci b. Isabella of Castile c. Peter the Great d. Martin Luther
2. Fact versus Opinion
a. Fact b. Opinion c. Opinion d. Fact
3. Predicting
b. The slaves will rebel.

ENRICHMENT

1. Answers will vary. **2.** Answers will vary.

UNIT 7 🦪 CHAPTER 1

VOCABULARY REVIEW

1. calculus: b 2. vacuum: d 3. scientist: e 4. deductive method: g 5. inductive method: c 6. gravity: a
7. astronomy: f

SKILL BUILDER: USING A DICTIONARY

1. planet: b 2. nature: a 3. telescope: a 4. orbit: b
5. universe: b

SKILL BUILDER: CRITICAL THINKING AND COMPREHENSION

1. Fact versus Opinion
a. Fact b. Opinion c. Opinion d. Fact
2. Point of View
a. D b. D c. C d. N
3. Making Judgments
3-1. It was important because it forced people to see not only their world, but their universe differently. His work was basic to the fields of astronomy and physics, and provided a foundation upon which later scientists and astronomers were able to build.
3-2. c. Francis Bacon developed the inductive method to study science. This is basic to the other three events occurring.
4. Hypothesizing
c. Newton supposed that an apple fell straight down to the ground because it was being pulled by the earth's power.

ENRICHMENT

1. Answers will vary.
2. Answers will vary.

UNIT 7 🦪 CHAPTER 2

VOCABULARY REVIEW

Age of Reason: The period in history when people questioned old beliefs based on magic or superstition and began to depend upon their ability to figure out causes of events.
philosophes: They believed that science and reason could improve the lives of people. They also believed in the preservation of all knowledge.
encyclopedia: A work that contains information on all branches of knowledge.
the Englightenment: A period in Europe beginning in the late 1600s when ideas from the Scientific Revolution spread to other areas of thought.
social contract: The belief that government is based on an agreement made by the people.
The Enlightenment, the Age of Reason, philosophies, social contract, Encyclopedia

SKILL BUILDER: MAKING A TABLE

WRITER	COUNTRY	IMPORTANT IDEAS
Hobbes	England	1. People by nature are cruel and interested only in themselves. 2. People needed a strong government with an absolute monarch to protect them from one another.
Locke	England	1. Every person has natural rights to life, liberty, and property. 2. People have the right to rise up and replace a government that does not serve their needs.
Rousseau	France	1. The purpose of life is to bring greater happiness to people through progress in science and art. 2. Human beings are born good, but are spoiled by society. (Another answer could be the idea of the social contract.)
Voltaire	France	1. The purpose of life is to bring greater happiness to people through progress in science and art. 2. He argued for reform of French society along the lines of all men being equal.

SKILL BUILDER: CRITICAL THINKING AND COMPREHENSION

1. Main Idea
1.1 Paragraph 2: d 1.2 Paragraph 4: c
2. Classifying
Books: *The Social Contract, Philosophical Letters, Encyclopedia*
English Philosophers: Thomas Hobbes, John Locke
French Philosophes: Denis Diderot, Jean-Jacques Rousseau, Voltaire
3. Summarizing
The philosophes, or thinkers of the Enlightenment, believed that science and reason could improve the lives of people. Voltaire spent two years in England, and brought back many of Locke's ideas to France. Rousseau and Voltaire agreed in their ideas of *The Social Contract.* Rousseau felt that people were more than just reasoning machines. Humanity was born in a state of innocence, but spoiled by exposure to society. Diderot compiled the *Encyclopedia,* which was a collection of Enlightenment ideas by all the thinkers of the time. The Catholic church was greatly alarmed by this; Diderot found later that his publisher had removed some of the more controversial material.
4. Making Judgments
The statement is not valid. The nobles and other people of privilege viewed these ideas with alarm, because they threatened their positions. Voltaire, among others, spent time in jail because of his views. Diderot's encyclopedia in effect was censored by his own publisher.

ENRICHMENT

1. Answers will vary according to which person is chosen.
2. Answers will vary.

THE ARTS AND ARTIFACTS

1. symphonies, piano and other instrumental pieces, concertos, masses, operas, chamber music, art songs
2. Joseph II, emperor of Austria
3. Mozart wanted to be treated and paid like the artist he was rather than as someone's servant. Mozart also desired to write operas and songs in German rather than the mandatory Italian.

UNIT 7 ❧ CHAPTER 3

VOCABULARY REVIEW

Old Regime: An earlier period of rule.

Tennis Court Oath: The declaration that the Third Estate would serve as the National Assembly and that it would write a constitution for France. The meeting took place on the royal tennis court.

constitutional monarchy: A government where the king supports the constitution, thus confining the king's power to its system of principles.

radicals: People that favor quick or revolutionary changes in government.

guillotine: A machine, popular in France, used to behead a person by means of a heavy blade.

bourgeoisie: The social class between the very wealthy and the poor; middle class.

Bastille: A fortress jail in France whose fall in 1789 marks the beginning of the French Revolution.

SKILL BUILDER: INTERPRETING A CARTOON

1. The man in the blindfold and chains represents the Third Estate, or the common people of France.

2. The figures represent the king, the clergy, and the nobles. The way they are dressed gives a clue as to who they represent.

3. The king, the clergy, and the nobles were oppressing the common people of France by making them suffer under the burden of the privileged upper classes.

4. Answers will vary, but might include that the clergy and nobles were exempt from many taxes that the lower classes had to pay; and the king supported the clergy and nobles against the lower classes in the dispute over voting in the Estates-General.

5. Answers will vary, but should include something about oppression of the common people.

6. Answers will vary, but might include that many ordinary people did not know how to read. The message in the cartoon is much more direct and easier to understand than a long article.

SKILL BUILDER: CRITICAL THINKING AND COMPREHENSION

1. Main Idea
1-1. M   1-2. M   1-3. D   1-4. M   1-5. M   1-6. M

2. Classifying
Answers will vary. Possible answers include:

Act of the First Continental Congress
The delegates pledged to stop trade with Britain until the colonies were represented in Parliament.

Act of the Second Continent Congress
Chose Thomas Jefferson to write the Declaration of Independence, and Washington to lead the Continental Army.

Act of the National Assembly
Passed new laws to end special privileges of nobles and clergy.

Act of the National Convention
Ended the monarchy and made France a republic.

3. Summarizing
Answers will vary, but should include some of the following details:
Dissatisfaction had been building for many years prior to the colonies issuing their Declaration of Independence from Britain on July 4, 1776. Initial fighting took place in Lexington and soon spread to Boston. George Washington was picked to lead the Continental armies. After a difficult beginning, Washington started to win victories, most notable of which were Saratoga and Yorktown. On September 3, 1783 Britain recognized the independence of the United States. It should also be noted that the United States received some timely help from France and the Netherlands.

4. Generalizing
Answers will vary, but might include the following sentences from the chapter:
a. The colonists, however, felt that these taxes were unfair because the colonies were not represented in Parliament. In the ten years following the British victory of 1763, new laws and taxes were passed that were irritating to the colonists.
b. Robespierre ordered his forces to seek out anyone who supported the king or spoke out against Committee policy. More than 17,000 people were guillotined, while thousands of others died in prisons or in massacres.

ENRICHMENT

1. Answers will vary.

2. Jacques-Louis David was born August 30, 1748 and died December 29, 1825. He was one of the most famous French artists of his day. He supported the French Revolution, and was briefly its official painter, painting all of the main leaders. Later he was appointed as a painter to Napoleon. Although his pictures are known for their historical themes, he was also an excellent portraitist and teacher. When Napoleon was defeated, David was exiled to Brussels where he died.

3. Answers will vary.

GEOGRAPHIC VIEW OF HISTORY

1. Ohio, Tennessee

2. New Orleans

3. Answers will vary, but could include some of the following: the United States would be roughly one-third of its present size. New Orleans would belong to France, which would give the French control over trade on the Mississippi. The ports along the eastern coast would be even more important than they are today, since most exports from the interior of the country would have to pass through them.

UNIT 7 ❧ CHAPTER 4

VOCABULARY REVIEW

1. consulate: f **2.** coup d'etat: g **3.** directory: b
4. Napoleonic Code: a **5.** nationalism: c **6.** plebiscite: d **7.** allies: e

SKILL BUILDER: READING A MAP

1. London **2.** Kingdom of Norway and Sweden, Kingdom of Denmark, and Kingdom of Prussia, Kingdom of Russia **3.** south or southeast **4.** Mediterranean Sea
5. Spain, Portugal, Austria, Prussia

SKILL BUILDER: CRITICAL THINKING AND COMPREHENSION

1. Sequencing   c, e, a, d, b
2. Spatial Relationships
a. He controlled much territory in both eastern and western Europe.
b. The empire was much larger.
3. Cause and Effect
a. Napoleon set up secondary schools in France.
b. Freedom for French citizens was limited.
c. The nations of Europe allied themselves against France.

4. Compare and Contrast

Answers will vary, but should include that Napoleon's idea of waging war was to attack with a large army and defeat the armed forces of the other country. Alexander refused to fight large military battles. His troops fell back into Russia, burning crops and destroying villages so that Napoleon's army would have no food or shelter from the terrible Russian winter.

ENRICHMENT

1. Answers will vary. **2.** Marie-Josephe-Rose Tascher de La Pagerie, or Josephine, as she came to be known, was born June 23, 1763, and died May 29, 1814. She was the eldest daughter of an impoverished aristocrat, and spent the first 15 years of her life on Martinique. In 1779 she married a rich army officer and bore two children by him. Unfortunately her husband was ashamed of her lack of sophistication, and would not present her at the French court. She obtained a separation and eventually returned to Martinique, but was forced to return to Paris due to a slave uprising in 1790. She was endangered when her husband fell out of favor with the Jacobins; he was later beheaded. She had acquired much sophistication by this time, and managed to attract the attention of Napoleon Bonaparte, marrying him after he had been appointed head of the Italian expedition. She was completely indifferent to him, refusing to answer his love letters. After Napoleon became emperor in 1804, she persuaded him to marry her with full religious rites. Eventually Napoleon had the marriage annulled on a technicality, but he continued to provide for her until his fall from power. Upon the abdication of Napoleon, she persuaded Czar Alexander I to protect her, but died soon afterward. **3.** Answers will vary.

UNIT 7 ꙮ CHAPTER 5

VOCABULARY REVIEW

1. creoles **2.** viceroyalties **3.** peninsulares **4.** mestizos **5.** mulattoes

SKILL BUILDER: TIME LINE

1. 30 years **2.** A.D. 1789 **3.** the French Revolution began **4.** A.D. 1791 **5.** to stop the revolt **6.** A.D. 1804 **7.** 11 years **8.** two years **9.** Dessalines

SKILL BUILDER: CRITICAL THINKING AND COMPREHENSION

1. Sequencing a, b, d, c
2. Spatial Relationships

NATION	VICEROYALTY	YEAR OF IN-DEPENDENCE	LIBER-ATOR
Mexico	New Spain	1821	Iturbide
Guatemala	New Spain	1821	Iturbide
El Salvador	New Spain	1821	Iturbide
Costa Rica	New Spain	1821	Iturbide
Venezuela	New Granada	1830; Separated from Colombia	Bolivar and Miranda
Colombia	New Granada	1819	Bolivar and Miranda

3. Compare and Contrast

Brazil attained its independence without a revolution. The Portuguese did not have the military manpower to contest it. The Spanish colonies, by contrast, struggled for many bloody years for their independence.

4. Cause and Effect

Cause: When Napoleon replaced the king of Spain in 1810, creoles began to demand a greater voice in the colonial government.

Effect: Spain was forced to recognize the independence of Mexico.

ENRICHMENT

1. Panama, Belize

Panama: Panama declared its independence from Spain in 1821, but after a few months elected to become part of Columbia. In 1902 Panama revolted over concerns that the proposed canal would be constructed across Nicaragua instead. The United States sent a warship that prevented Columbian troops from putting down the revolt, and was one of the first nations to recognize Panama. This is a good example of "gunboat diplomacy."

Belize: Belize was formerly named British Honduras. It was formerly under the jurisdiction of the governor of Jamaica, but was made a separate colony in 1862. The revolutions of the early 1800s bypassed Belize, perhaps because of its relative isolation and also because it was governed by Britain rather than Spain. It was declared independent from Britain on September 21, 1981.

2. Answers will vary.

UNIT 7 ꙮ REVIEW

SKILL BUILDER: READING A MAP

1. a: Russian Empire **2.** b: Slaves were traded. **3.** c: North America and South America **4.** c: The Spanish colonies

SKILL BUILDER: CRITICAL THINKING AND COMPREHENSION

1. Main Idea
a. D b. D c. M d. D

2. Classifying

Scientists Galileo Galilei, Johannes Kepler, Issac Newton

Political Leaders King Louis XVI, Toussaint L'Overture, Robespierre

Philosophers Thomas Hobbes Voltaire

3. Sequencing
d. The British surrender to revolutionary troops at Yorktown.
a. Paris citizens storm the Bastille.
b. Napoleon invades Russia.
c. Constitutional government is started in Brazil.

4. Compare and Contrast
Answers will vary.

ENRICHMENT

1. Answers will vary.
2. Answers will vary.

UNIT 8 ꙮ CHAPTER 1

VOCABULARY REVIEW

1. balance of power **2.** liberalism **3.** conservatives

SKILL BUILDER: INTRODUCTORY PARAGRAPHS

a. 2 **b.** 11, 12 **c.** 11 **d.** 11 **e.** 11

SKILL BUILDER: CRITICAL THINKING AND COMPREHENSION

1. Sequencing 15 to 16 years
2. Spatial Relationships
a. England b. Prussia, Austria, and Russia c. Belgium
3. Compare and Contast
a. decrease b. the Netherlands c. Austria, Prussia, and Russia d. yes, Malta
4. Cause and Effect
Causes Conservatives did not want changes Prevent the spread of nationalism Metternich System
Effects European monarchies were restored Quadruple Alliance was formed Revolutions occurred

ENRICHMENT

1. Answers will vary.
2. The essential idea to keep in mind is the division of the allies into liberal and conservative factions.
3. Portugal, Spain, France, United Kingdom of Great Britian and Ireland, Kingdom of the United Netherlands, Denmark, Kingdom of Sweden and Norway, German Confederation, Prussia, Kingdom of Poland, Austrian Empire, Switzerland, Kingdom of Sardinia, Russia, Ottoman Empire, Kingdom of the Two Sicilies; Russia received Finland and Poland; the Kingdom of the United Netherlands was created from the Austrian Netherlands and the Batavian Republic; Norway was taken away from Denmark and given to Sweden to compensate it for the loss of Finland; Britain retained Ceylon, the Cape of Good Hope, Malta, and a protectorate over the Ionian Islands.

UNIT 8 🍃 CHAPTER 2

VOCABULARY REVIEW

1. Victorian **2.** pocket borough **3.** reform **4.** rotten borough **5.** borough

SKILL BUILDER: READING A MAP

1. Wales **2.** 1707 **3.** Edinburgh, London, Belfast, Dublin **4.** Scotland, Northern Ireland, England, Wales **5.** just over 300 miles

SKILL BUILDER: CRITICAL THINKING AND COMPREHENSION

1. Drawing Conclusions
1-1. b 1-2. a 1-3. b 1-4. b
2. Predicting
a. Less. Reforms strengthened parliament.
b. Yes. Union leadership could control or influence elections by telling members how to vote. The Labour party provides an example of how labor grew to play a major role in English politics.
c. Answers may vary. Answers will vary on why the government is stronger or weaker. Some may argue that a greater diversity of ideas in government is a good thing. Others may feel that in the long run this has a paralyzing effect on decisions that have to be made.

ENRICHMENT

1. Answers will vary. Possible arguments for abolishment might be that the monarchy is expensive and anach-

ronistic. The House of Lords certainly does not represent the will of the people, but rather, gives an aristocratic minority veto power over that will.
2. Answers will vary. 3. Answers will vary.

UNIT 8 🍃 CHAPTER 3

VOCABULARY REVIEW

1. tariffs **2.** Second Republic **3.** delegates **4.** scandals **5.** anti-Semites **6.** Second Empire

SKILL BUILDER: USING A TABLE

1. 4,469,000 workers; 27.6% **2.** 1896 **3.** 1876
4. The number of workers increased by more than a million, while the percentage of workers decreased by a little over 6%. The population as a whole was growing, which meant that more people than ever before were engaged in agriculture; but as a percentage of the working population, the numbers working in agriculture were declining.
5. Services
6. Less than 45%; the percentage of workers involved in agriculture declined steadily between 1856 and 1896. One would expect the decline to continue.
7. More than 25.5%; the percentage of workers involved in service jobs increased steadily between 1856 and 1896. One would expect the increase to continue.

SKILL BUILDER: CRITICAL THINKING AND COMPREHENSION

1. Drawing Conclusions
a. Rights can be granted and taken away as dictated by the government in power. Citizens must always be watchful of their rights and fight for them when necessary, lest a government or group steal them away.
b. Women had no political rights.
2. Predicting
a. Ministers would be chosen from various parties that many times did not have much in common in terms of goals, methods, and priorities. What they did have in common was a desire for power. Ministerial positions would be allotted to create a balance of power, making for a weak government.
b. They would have overthrown it.

ENRICHMENT

1. Answers will vary, but might include descriptions of barricades, civilians and troops clashing, or possible buildings that were damaged.
2. The cartoon should reflect that high tariffs make both foreign and domestically manufactured goods more expensive. Tariffs also lead to inefficient production methods within the country because of a lack of economic competition.
3. Answers will vary. 4. Answers will vary.

UNIT 8 🍃 CHAPTER 4

VOCABULARY REVIEW

absolute; censors; minority; groups; russify; pogrom; zemstvos; duma

SKILL BUILDER: OUTLINING

Childhood; shows an early liking for literature; forced into exile; watched closely by secret police; Government Work and the Czar's Court; forced to fight a duel

SKILL BUILDER: CRITICAL THINKING AND COMPREHENSION

1. Drawing Conclusions
a. Their use of censorship was proof of this. People's freedom of speech and press were crushed so that no one would get any ideas about overthrowing the czars. When people were given freedom, they responded with protests for more freedom. Since such protest threatened the czars' position, they took away the freedoms they had already given to the people.
b. So they could be more easily controlled. People who could identify closely with their cultural and national traditions were thought to be dangerous to the unity of the Russian Empire. The czars wanted people of the various ethnic groups to think of themselves as Russians first, very much as we expect the various ethnic groups in our country to think of themselves as Americans first.
c. Czar Nicholas II was willing to grant the people representative government as long as the representatives agreed with his policies. As soon as they suggested reforms that went against the wishes of the czar, he dissolved the duma. The czar kept on doing this until the representatives were more in agreement with him. Since any liberal reform was a threat to the czar's power, democracy would never come to Russia under the czars.

2. Predicting
Answers will vary, but students might predict that the future leaders of Russia would come from minority groups, intellectuals, the lower classes, or children of noble families.

ENRICHMENT

1. Answers will vary, but students should mention censorship and reform.
2. Pictures should show a sharp contrast between rich and poor people in Russia and should underscore the injustices present in the country.
3. Answers will vary.
4. Russian occupation of Siberia dates from a Cossack expedition in 1581 that overthrew the khanate of Sibir. During the late 16th and 17th centuries fur trappers, traders, and explorers roamed throughout this vast land. It was used as a place of exile chiefly because of its isolation from the rest of Russia. The climate made life extremely hard. Just to have to live there was thought to be punishment enough. Many criminals and political prisoners were sent there as settlers, much as Britain sent many of its criminals to settle in Australia during the 1800s. The Trans-Siberian Railroad opened the area to large-scale settlement and to large-scale confinement. Concentration camp exile was increasingly common with the advent of the revolution in 1917, with conditions that were barbaric in their severity. Students should be encouraged to use library resources to find further information.

THE ARTS AND ARTIFACTS

1. The Ballets Russes was popular in Paris because of the amazing abilities and notoriety of dancers such as Nijinsky. The colorful costumes and exceptional music composed by some of the great masters of the day also added to its appeal.
2. Ballet performances integrate many forms of art and design. Parisians might have learned about other aspects of Russian culture from the set designs, costumes, music, and ballet themes or stories. The Russian Ballet might also have taught Europeans that Russians put great value on excellence and discipline especially in the arts.

UNIT 8 ✥ CHAPTER 5

VOCABULARY REVIEW

1. national anthem: b **2.** romanticism: d **3.** ethnic group: c **4.** cultural revival: a **5.** opera: e

SKILL BUILDER: UNDERSTANDING A CARTOON

1. by an explosion
2. The magnet shows how nationalism pulled all the German states together to form a nation.
3. Nationalism brought states together while pulling empires apart.

SKILL BUILDER: CRITICAL THINKING AND COMPREHENSION

1. Drawing Conclusions
a. The French Revolution introduced the ideas of liberalism and freedom to Europe. Napoleon inspired feelings of nationalism among various ethnic groups as he conquered Europe.
b. Students should conclude that romanticism inspires nationalism through appreciation for and identity with a national culture.
c. Answers will vary. Nationalism is good as long as it is not taken to extremes. Nationalism has inspired countries to incredible acts of endurance and courage against oppression. However, nationalism also inspired the Nazis; their record on human rights abuses is well-known.

2. Predicting
a. The German states and the Italian states each had a language and cultural tradition to bind them together. Eastern Europe has many distinct ethnic groups, each feeling that it should have independence from the others. Students should predict that this area will have continued nationalist uprisings.
b. It became part of the national heritage because it inspired and strengthened the struggle for independence.
c. Nationalism creates tension, not better understanding, in relations between countries. Countries are more prone to view matters solely from their point of view when they are convinced they are inherently superior to others.

3. Compare and Contrast
Answers will vary. They were alike in that they both looked to earlier periods for inspiration. They were dissimilar in that the Italian Renaissance was sparked by feelings of humanism rather than nationalism.

ENRICHMENT

1. Answers will vary. **2.** Answers will vary. **3.** Answers will vary.
4. Romantic artists chose subject matter that involved and appealed to emotions. Their works frequently dealt with nature and the historical past. These traits were also found in the music and literature of the period.
5. Answers will vary.

UNIT 8 ✥ CHAPTER 6

VOCABULARY REVIEW

1. Zollverein: German word for Customs Union, which allowed states to trade freely with one another without having to pay taxes on traded goods.
2. depression: A period of low economic activity.

T155

3. **political repression:** A condition in which people are not allowed the freedom to say or write what they feel about the government.
4. **Realpolitik:** The tough-minded hardnosed politics of the real world.
5. **reparation:** The compensation that a nation defeated in war pays a victorious nation for damages or losses suffered during the war.
6. **Junkers:** Members of the Prussian land-owning aristocracy.
7. **Reich:** Germany or the German government.
8. **Gymnasium:** A high school that prepared male students for the universities.

SKILL BUILDER: COMPLETING A CHART

Chart
1. DATE: 1806
2. RESULTS: German Confederation is formed
3. STEPS: Many German states join the Zollverein
4. STEPS: A severe depression hits Germany; nationalist leaders see need for a united government of German states
5. RESULTS: Prussia receives Schleswig, Austria receives Holstein
6. STEPS: Prussia's superior army defeats Austria in the Seven Weeks' War
7. RESULTS: Southern German states join forces with Prussia; strong feelings of German nationalism are stirred
8. DATE: 1871
Questions
1. the German Confederation 2. the Zollverein 3. the Franco-Prussian War

SKILL BUILDER: CRITICAL THINKING AND COMPREHENSION

1. Fact versus Opinion
a. opinion b. fact: true c. fact: false d. opinion e. fact: true
2. Point of View
Since the members of the assembly had written a constitution, it would seem that they would not be supporters of the divine right principle. Therefore, the members of the assembly would have been insulted that the king rejected their offer. By describing the offer as a "crown from the gutter," the king equated the assembly with the gutter.
3. Making Judgments
Answers will vary.
4. Hypothesizing
Germany would not have become a nation at that time. Prussia would not have been strong enough to lead the other states to unity. It might also be hypothesized that World Wars I and II would never have occurred.
5. Classifying
a. false: It was completely unified after the Franco-Prussian War.
b. false: The king of Prussia was asked to lead the German states.
c. false: The Holy Roman Empire was abolished by Napoleon I.

ENRICHMENT

1. Answers will vary.
2. Refer students to maps in Unit 7, Chapter 5, and Unit 8, Chapters 1 and 6.
3. Answers will vary.

UNIT 8 • CHAPTER 7

VOCABULARY REVIEW

1. Risorgimento 2. Carbonari 3. unification 4. toleration 5. ghettos

SKILL BUILDER: INTERPRETING A TIME LINE

The time line should have the dates listed in ascending order, from earliest to latest, listed from left to right.

SKILL BUILDER: CRITICAL THINKING AND COMPREHENSION

Fact versus Opinion
a. Opinion b. fact c. fact d. opinion e. opinion
2. Point of View
Cavour wanted to bring Rome into the new Italian nation and make it the capital because of its glorious past.
3. Making Judgments
Answers will vary; answers may illustrate the importance of freedom of religion.
4. Hypothesizing
Answers will vary.

ENRICHMENT

1. The forces of Sardinia triumphed in the north of Italy, but no one thought of the revolution as being over while southern Italy remained in the hands of foreign rulers. Sicily was a natural place to start, because of an extreme amount of political unrest. In April 1860, an insurrection broke out in Palermo. This was quickly crushed, but it spread to other cities. Garibaldi and his 1,000 redshirt volunteers sailed from Quarto, near Genoa, and landed in Marsala on May 11, 1860. They had very few arms and little preparation, but owing to the military genius of Garibaldi and the political ferment of the general populace, they were able to conquer Sicily in three months. Nationalism obviously played a large part in making this possible. Students should be encouraged to research this in more detail with books on Italian history and biographies of Garibaldi.
2. Answers will vary.

UNIT 8 • CHAPTER 8

VOCABULARY REVIEW

1. regency: c 2. Slav: e 3. Ausgleich: a 4. grandeur: d 5. Ringstrasse: b

SKILL BUILDER: MAKING A TIMELINE

1. Eliminate these dates: 1789 French Revolution; 1848 Zachary Taylor is elected President of the United States
2. Answers will vary

SKILL BUILDER: CRITICAL THINKING AND COMPREHENSION

1. Fact Versus Opinion
a. Fact b. Opinion c. Fact d. Fact e. Opinion f. Fact g. Opinion h. Fact i. Opinion j. Fact
2. Point of View
In making this statement he was trying to undermine the pride the empire's ethnic groups felt for their cultures and ways. To the emperor, all people were the same; they were under his control.

3. Making Judgments

Answers will vary. Opinions that could be examined might include something about tradition and inertia—people are often frightened of radical change unless their current condition is intolerable. Another opinion might be that the army and police kept the empire together, playing one ethnic group against another. In this way the various groups could not unite against the Austrian monarchy but rather fought among themselves.

4. Hypothesizing

Eventually the Austrian Empire would be troubled with rebellions of ethnic groups whose concerns and desires had not been properly addressed by the agreement.

ENRICHMENT

1. Answers will vary.
2. Germans, 23%; Magyars, 20%; Czechs and Slovaks, 17%; Poles, 10%; others, 30%.
3. Answers will vary but should reflect the basic difference between the two men: Szecheny advocated reforms from within the system, whereas Kossuth advocated change through violent overthrow of the system.

A GEOGRAPHIC VIEW OF HISTORY

1. Germany, Austria, Slovakia, Hungary, Croatia, Yugoslavia, Ukraine, Moldova, Romania
2. Austria, Slovakia, Hungary, Yugoslavia, Romania
3. Romania; unfriendly; Romania
4. Political turmoil in the countries around the river discouraged traders from using it.

UNIT 8 · CHAPTER 9

VOCABULARY REVIEW

1. **pashas:** Men of high rank or office.
2. **fez:** A brimless flat-crowned hat that usually has a tassel and is made of red felt.
3. **Tanzimat:** A period in Ottoman history in which the government and society were reorganized.
4. **military dictatorship:** A government ruled by a soldier, usually of high rank.

SKILL BUILDER: MAKING A CHART

BALKAN NATION	DATE OF INDEPENDENCE	HOW INDEPENDENCE WAS WON
Greece	1929	Revolt from Ottoman Empire
Serbia	1878	Congress of Berlin
Montenegro	1878	Congress of Berlin
Romania	1878	Congress of Berlin
Bulgaria	1908	declaration of independence

SKILL BUILDER: CRITICAL THINKING AND COMPREHENSION

1. Fact versus Opinion

a. Fact   b. Opinion   c. Fact   d. Opinion   e. Opinion
f. Fact   g. Fact   h. Opinion

2. Drawing Conclusions

Lord Byron felt that Greece was the cradle of bravery, the arts, and liberty and must be preserved and defended. He had great affection for Greece.

3. Predicting

The czar thought the empire was about to fall apart. By "necessary arrangements" he meant that the nations of Europe needed to make some decisions about what to do with the territory of the empire before it was lost to other nations or empires.

4. Hypothesizing

a. Answers will vary. On the negative side, students could point out that the feelings of nationalism among the various ethnic groups in the Balkans would have produced revolts eventually. On the positive side, students might point out that dissatisfaction among the various groups within the empire might have been contained if the reforms had been carried out sooner, because the government was stronger and had more money.
b. Possibly they would have united into one nation, as Italy and Germany did, and then declared their independence from the Ottoman Empire.

ENRICHMENT

1. The Dardanelles were the only outlet to the Mediterranean Sea available to the Russians.
2. Answers will vary.
3. In the poem Byron discusses his deep feelings for Greece, its people, and their independence.
4. Students should do research to expand upon the information in the chapter. Answers should include something about restoring the former glory of the empire through reform and modernization.

UNIT 8 · REVIEW

SKILL BUILDER: READING A MAP

1. Crete was controlled by the Ottoman Empire in 1878.
2. Switzerland, Bosnia, and Serbia were all landlocked nations in 1878.
3. Four
4. It enabled them to dominate the eastern Mediterranean and to protect the Suez Canal.
5. Their Baltic ports were frozen for long periods of each year. Control of the Dardanelles would provide them with warm-water ports and access to the Mediterranean.

SKILL BUILDER: CRITICAL THINKING AND COMPREHENSION

1. Fact versus Opinion

1-1. a: The nineteenth century was a time of great progress.
1-2. c: Britain had the best government in Europe after 1867.
1-3. d: The Second Empire of Napoleon III lasted 18 years.

2. Cause and Effect

2-1. d: The Second Empire of Napoleon III collapsed.
2-2. e: The kingdom of Italy came into being.
2-3. a: Greece gained its independence.
2-4. c: Almost all British men had the right to vote.
2-5. c: There were no major European wars for many years after 1815.
2-6. b: The Crimean War was fought.

ENRICHMENT

1. Answers will vary.
2. Answers will vary.
3. Answers will vary.

UNIT 9 ❧ CHAPTER 1

VOCABULARY REVIEW

1. Industrial Revolution: c 2. steam engine: a 3. cotton gin: h 4. factories: e 5. crop rotation: d 6. cottage industry: f 7. capital: g 8. mortgage: b

SKILL BUILDER: READING A TABLE

1. Power source 2. Eli Whitney: 1793 3. Three 4. Flying shuttle 5. Sewing machine 6. Cotton gin; flying shuttle; sewing machine; spinning jenny; steamboat; steam engine; water frame

SKILL BUILDER: CRITICAL THINKING AND COMPREHENSION

1. Sequencing c, b, e, a, d
2. Compare and Contrast
a. Farming was done without labor-saving machinery. Grain was harvested using a scythe and then separated, or threshed, by hand. Plows were made of wood and were drawn by horses. Seeds were planted by hand, many times by just scattering them over the field.
b. More and more of the jobs that had been done by hand were taken over by machines, thus enabling the farmer to farm more land in less time, using fewer people. More scientific farming methods increased the yield per acre and improved the quality of the food.
3. Predicting
Answers will vary. Undoubtedly the world would be much different. Answers could include that the pace of life would be slower owing to less communication. Areas would tend to be more isolated from each other. Many things that we take for granted, such as automobiles, computers, and other labor-saving devices, would probably not exist. More jobs would be done by hand, such as spinning cloth for clothes. Leisure time would probably be curtailed because more time would be needed to accomplish basic tasks such as food preparation. Many other answers are possible.
4. Summarizing
a. These were basic to the development of the Industrial Revolution. Textile machinery speeded up the production of textiles and also increased the demand for raw materials such as cotton and wool. These inventions also brought about a huge change in people's lives as they moved from agriculture into factory jobs.
b. Improve methods of farming meant that farmers could produce more food per acre with less labor and fewer people. These displaced people were then absorbed into the factories. Increased food production also brought an increase in the general population.
c. This also was basic, for without capital to invest the Industrial Revolution would have been over before it began. People found new ways to get money to build factories, which then generated more money. When there

is a profit to be made, it is amazing how inventive the human race can be.

ENRICHMENT

1. Answers will vary.
2. Answers will vary.

SKILL BUILDERS/MAPS

1. seven
2. six
3. Glasgow, Newcastle, Liverpool, Manchester, Bradford, Nottingham, Birmingham, Cardiff
4. Wales: Cardiff Scotland: Glasgow

UNIT 9 ❧ CHAPTER 2

VOCABULARY REVIEW

1. industrialization
2. investors
3. indigo
4. casts

SKILL BUILDER: USING A DICTIONARY

mill, materials

SKILL BUILDERS: CRITICAL THINKING AND COMPREHENSION

1. Summarizing
a. Industrialization of weaving occurred at about the same time in Britain and Belgium.
b. An important early step in the industrialization of Germany was the birth of the Krupp steel plant in the Ruhr Valley in about 1810.
c. Timber, cotton, rice, and indigo were natural resources of Great Britain's American colonies that were valuable to British industry.
2. Cause and Effect
2-1. The Flemish had been weavers of fine woolens for hundreds of years: d
2-2. The demand for raw materials grew rapidly: a
2-3. Raw materials could be transported quickly from one place to another: e
2-4. France lost lands with important natural resources to Germany and Belgium: c
2-5. William Cockerill set up textile machinery in Belgium: b
3. Predicting
a. World trade will continue to grow.
c. After regaining their independence, most nonindustrial nations will work hard to become industrialized.
4. Point of View
William Cockerill: b Francis Lowell: c Samuel Slater: a

ENRICHMENT

1. Alsace-Lorraine was coveted for its coal and iron ore deposits. The factories that grew up next to these deposits also added to the value.
2. Answers will vary.
Possible positive points for colonization:
a. modernization of health care
b. education
c. discovery and development of natural resources
d. being brought into the world mainstream of economic development
3. Answers will vary.

A GEOGRAPHIC VIEW OF HISTORY

1. The country that produces the most goods and services is the United States. This country is in the North American Region.
2. The name of the 12-member organization is the European Community (EC).
3. Today's nonindustrial countries need to become future NICs so that they can raise the standard of living for their people.

UNIT 9 ❧ CHAPTER 3

VOCABULARY REVIEW

1. communication revolution **2.** steamboat **3.** wireless telegraph **4.** locomotive **5.** telegraph

SKILL BUILDER: READING A TIME LINE

1. steam engine **2.** steam engine and the water frame
3. 20 years
4. Samuel Slater builds America's first water loom 1789
George Stephenson invents the steam locomotive 1814
5. The development of the textile industry depended on machine parts for its looms and steam engines. In addition, the rails, locomotives, and steamships needed to transport both raw materials and finished goods all required iron and steel products on a scale that had not been known up to that time.

SKILL BUILDER: CRITICAL THINKING AND COMPREHENSION

1. Main Idea 1-1. a **1-2.** a
2. Cause and Effect
2-1. The Industrial Revolution brought about improvements in travel: c
2-2. The steam engine was invented: a
2-3. Electrical signals could be sent through the air: d
2-4. Messages could be sent thousands of miles without wires: b
3. Fact versus Opinion
a. Fact b. Opinion c. Opinion d. Fact e. Opinion

ENRICHMENT

1. Answers will vary according to which machine is chosen.
2. Canals were built because transport by wagons was slow and costly. Canals have a long history, dating back to the Assyrians in 700 B.C. The Egyptians, Greeks, and Romans all constructed elaborate canal systems. The U.S. had only 100 miles of canals at the beginning of the 1800s but had constructed 4,000 miles by the end of the century. The Erie Canal between Albany on the Hudson River and Buffalo on Lake Erie was 363 miles long, with 82 locks. This canal succeeded in opening up the land west of the Allegheny Mountains. Many of the European and American canals declined in importance with the development of the railroads. Canals that continue to be important to this day are the Suez and Panama Canals and the St. Lawrence Seaway.

Construction of canals is done with giant excavators and earth movers. During the Industrial Revolution horse-drawn earth movers were used. Along the banks of the canal were walkways for horses and mules that pulled the boats through. Locks must be installed if there is a difference in elevation to be negotiated. Canals are lined with various materials such as concrete, sheet polythene, or fly ash to prevent water losses by absorption into the ground or levees.

UNIT 9 ❧ CHAPTER 4

VOCABULARY REVIEW

1. immigrants **2.** socialism **3.** proletariat **4.** utopian socialists **5.** bourgeoisie **6.** suffrage **7.** urbanism **8.** communism **9.** labor unions

SKILL BUILDER: USING A PRIMARY SOURCE

1. He feels that factory workers are better off than farm workers.
2. The improvements are due to the increase of national wealth that the manufacturing system has produced.
3. They live longer because they are better fed, better lodged, better clothed, and better attended in sickness.

SKILL BUILDER: CRITICAL THINKING AND COMPREHENSION

1. Making Generalizations
Group A: Several factors contributed to the growth of cities in the Industrial Revolution.
Group B: The quality of life in the cities during the Industrial Revolution was not good.
2. Summarizing
Advances in education, science, and technology improved the lives of many people in the later 1800s. Factories needed better-educated people for more demanding jobs. The higher standard of living brought demands for political and social reforms. Two of the most important of these were the right to form unions and the child labor laws.
3. Fact versus Opinion
a. fact b. opinion c. fact d. opinion e. opinion
4. Making Judgments
Answers will vary.

ENRICHMENT

1. Answers will vary. The Occupational Health and Safety Administration (OSHA) should also be contacted about providing a speaker.
2. Answers will vary. Students might research the zoning laws and plans of their towns before starting this project, to gain a deeper understanding of what is involved in land-use planning.

THE ARTS AND ARTIFACTS

1. from the painting, *Impression, Rising Sun* by the French artist Claude Monet
2. Answers will vary. Possible answers might include that many portrait painters would have been thrown out of work. Artists might have felt freed from the need to paint literal copies of scenes in order to concentrate on impressions of them. Photography, with its various lenses, could also make artists more aware of distorted shapes and moods that would not be noticed under ordinary circumstances.

UNIT 9 ❧ CHAPTER 5

VOCABULARY REVIEW

1. bacteria **2.** theory of evolution **3.** pasteurized **4.** natural selection **5.** incandescent **6.** theory of relativity **7.** yellow fever **8.** radioactive

SKILL BUILDER: MAKING A TIME LINE

The time line should have the dates listed in ascending order, earliest to latest. Time lines could be either horizontal or vertical. The teacher might explore with the students other types of time lines.

SKILL BUILDER: CRITICAL THINKING AND COMPREHENSION

1. Sequencing
g. Faraday builds the first electric generator.
c. Darwin's theory of evolution is published in his book *The Origin of Species*.
f. Lister discovers how to kill germs that cause infections.
e. Latimer becomes an expert electrical engineer.
d. The Curies win the Nobel Prize.
b. Marie Curie receives the Nobel Prize in chemistry.
a. The Panama Canal opens.
2. Drawing Conclusions
b. Through careful scientific research, dangerous bacteria can be controlled.
3. Point of View
a. Charles Darwin b. Alexander Fleming c. Louis Pasteur d. Lewis Latimer e. Thomas Edison f. Marie Curie
4. Hypothesizing
a. Answers will vary. One answer might be that since heat kills bacteria, and bacteria in milk are responsible for tuberculosis, it follows that heating the milk will prevent tuberculosis for people who drink milk.
b. Answers will vary. One might be that since workers digging in areas of mosquito-infested swampland have the highest incidence of yellow fever, it follows that destroying the breeding grounds of the mosquitoes will lead to a lowered incidence of yellow fever.

ENRICHMENT

1. The volt is the unit of the electromotive force that drives current. It was named to honor Alesandro Volta for his invention of the first electric battery in 1800.
2. Social Darwinism was a perversion of Darwin's theory of natural selection. People who subscribed to this felt that if they were rich, it was only because they were superior to the poor and disadvantaged. To help anyone then would be to disturb the balance of nature. Answers may vary on the other points of the question because they are opinions rather than facts.

UNIT 9 ❧ REVIEW

SKILL BUILDER: READING A GRAPH

1. b: increased by 41 million **2.** b: almost doubled
3. c: increased by 130 million **4.** c: more than three times **5.** c: almost doubled

SKILL BUILDER: CRITICAL THINKING AND COMPREHENSION

1. Making Judgments
1-1. a: Steam engines could be build almost anywhere.
2. Sequencing
a. Samuel Morse invents the telegraph.
Alexander Graham Bell invents the telephone.
Thomas Edison invents the light bulb.
b. Samuel Slater builds a textile mill in America.
Eli Whitney invents the cotton gin.
The Krupp family builds steel mills in the Ruhr Valley.
The Trade Union Act is passed in England.

T160

---

c. Karl Marx writes *The Communist Manifesto*.
Charles Darwin writes *On the Origin of Species*.
Albert Einstein publishes his theory of relativity.

ENRICHMENT

Answers will vary.

UNIT 10 ❧ CHAPTER 1

VOCABULARY REVIEW

1. imperialism: d **2.** colony: c **3.** protectorate: a
4. sphere of influence: e **5.** Boers: f **6.** Zulus: b

SKILL BUILDER: WRITING FOOTNOTES AND BIBLIOGRAPHIES

a. p. 47 b. p. 46 of *Weekday* magazine, December 19, l984 c. 1965
d. Footnote: the author's name is given in normal order; the city of publication, publisher's name, and date of publication are in parentheses. Bibliography entry: Author's last name is first; no parentheses around city of publication, publisher's name, and date and publication.

SKILL BUILDER: CRITICAL THINKING AND COMPREHENSION

1. Classifying
a. David Livingstone: 2 b. Germany: 3 c. Henry Stanley: 5 d. France: 1 e. Britain: 6 f. Italy: 4
2. Cause and Effect
a. Industrial nations looked for new sources of raw materials and new markets.
b. The Boers set out on the Great Trek north.
c. Many African traditions and cultures were destroyed.
3. Fact versus Opinion
a. A, B, E b. C,D, F c. Opinion C and supporting fact B; opinion F and supporting fact E d. D

ENRICHMENT

1. The Zambezi River is 2,200 miles (3,540 kilometers) long. It begins at Kalene Hill, Zambia, and flows southeast to the Indian Ocean, crossing the territories or frontiers of Angola, Zambia, Botswana, Zimbabwe, and Mozambique. Victoria Falls and Kariba Dam are situated along its course.
2. Answers will vary according to the country chosen.

A GEOGRAPHIC VIEW OF HISTORY

1. tropical rainy and tropical with a dry season; diamonds and copper
2. peanuts, coffee, cocoa, and palm oil; peanuts
3. desert and semiarid; cotton, wine; irrigation
4. along the coast of West Africa, the highlands of East Africa, and Madagascar; mountainous and hilly areas, and tropical rainy areas.

UNIT 10 ❧ CHAPTER 2

VOCABULARY REVIEW

1. Boxers: A group of Chinese belonging to a secret society who tried to drive foreigners out of China and abolish Christianity in the late 19th century.
2. Open Door policy: a policy announced by the United States in 1899 to keep trade with China open to all nations.

SKILL BUILDER: INTERPRETING LINE GRAPHS

1. 1400 to 1900
2. 150 million; 350 million
3. China's population grew tremendously.
4. possible answers: peace; increase in the food supply; new medicines to fight diseases

SKILL BUILDER: CRITICAL THINKING AND COMPREHENSION

1. Summarizing
c. Although the Manchus put down the rebellion, they lost ground to the Europeans, who attacked during the uprising.
2. Generalizing
Large parts of China were part of foreign nations' spheres of influence by the early 1900s.
3. Contrasting and Comparing
a. Both wanted to trade with China.
b. The Taiping Rebellion was an internal peasant uprising crushed by the Ching government. The Boxers, who directed their rebellion against foreigners, were defeated by an international force.
4. Point of View
a. The imperialists were unfair to force China to trade drugs for goods.

ENRICHMENT

1. Answers will vary.
2. Sun Yat-sen (Sun U-Xian) was born November 12, 1866, in Hsiang-shan, Guangdong Province, and died November 12, 1925, in Beijing. When he was young, he lived in Hawaii and became acquainted with Christianity and Western ideas. He later studied medicine in Hong Kong and Canton. In 1894 he founded the Revive China Society, which later evolved into one of the many secret revolutionary groups of the period. He tried and failed in a rebellion in 1895 and spent the next 16 years in exile in the U.S. He returned to China after the revolution that toppled the Manchu Dynasty and was elected president of a provisional government. He resigned from this after two months because many felt he was too radical to appeal to the masses. Not until 1923 did he finally gain control of the country with the help of the Soviets. During his last two years he reorganized the Kuomintang along the lines of the Soviet Communist party. Both the Chinese Communists and the Kuomintang revere him as the founder of modern China.

UNIT 10 ▪ CHAPTER 3

VOCABULARY REVIEW

1. Meiji: "Enlightened government," the name chosen by the 15-year-old emperor of Japan (1868). He ruled for 45 years. Japan became a modern industrial state under his leadership.
2. prime minister: The chief officer, or leader of a government, as in Great Britain.
3. constitution: A system of principles, usually a document, by which a nation or an organized group of people is governed.
4. zaibatsu: The wealthy business families in 19th century Japan.
5. ukiyo-e: Inexpensive or affordable wood block drawings.

SKILL BUILDER: INTERPRETING LINE GRAPHS

1. 200,000 square miles
2a. approximately 157,000 square miles
b. approximately 14,000 square miles
3. approximately 470,000 square miles
4. approximately 555,000 square miles

SKILL BUILDER: CRITICAL THINKING AND COMPREHENSION

1. Main Idea
The Meiji officials believed that their first task was to reshape Japanese society.
The Meiji government's plan to modernize Japan brought many changes. Details: Answers will vary. Possible answers include: end of feudalism; building industry and railroads; setting up a new education system.
2. Sequencing
b. Commodore Matthew Perry arrives in Japan to open it to trade with other nations, 1853.
d. Japan ends shogun rule and begins the Meiji government, 1868.
e. Prince Ito travels to Western nations to study their governments, 1882.
c. Japan gets a new Meiji constitution, 1889.
f. Japan gains the island of Formosa from China, 1895.
a. Japan defeats Russia and gains Port Arthur, Manchuria, and part of Sakhalin, 1905.
3. Drawing Conclusions
c. The heads of government in China and Japan in the late 19th century disagreed about the need to adopt Western ideas.
4. Making Judgments
Answers will vary. Japan's adoption of Western ways contributed greatly to its becoming an imperialist power. Western ideas emphasized modern industry and technology that demanded more and more raw materials. Japanese leaders felt that by conquering other countries they could assure supplies of these raw materials.

ENRICHMENT

1. Answers will vary. Answers might include public buildings, parks, recreational activities, or natural features that are strongly associated with the community, such as waterfalls or mountains.
2. Answers will vary.

THE ARTS AND ARTIFACTS

1. The Japanese had a special love for the beauty of nature. This method was cheaper, enabling more people to afford them.
2. They showed the streets of Tokyo, its bridges, and its rivers. They also showed people and children enjoying special occasions in Tokyo.
3. His drawings depicted everyday life in Tokyo during this period.

UNIT 10 ▪ CHAPTER 4

VOCABULARY REVIEW

1. rajah: d 2. suttee: a 3. sepoy: f 4. mutiny: c
5. resident commissioner: e 6. reforms: b

SKILL BUILDER: INTERPRETING A TIME LINE

1. No; Roy died in 1833 and Gandhi was born in 1869.
2. Indian National Congress

3. Most of the career of Mohandas Gandhi, who lived from 1869 to 1948, took place after the reign of Queen Victoria, who died in 1901.

4. 1857–1858; no; the Muslim League was not formed until 1906.

SKILL BUILDER: CRITICAL THINKING AND COMPREHENSION

1. Main Idea b, c, d

2. Spatial Relationships

a. Afghanistan and Nepal

b. Most of India (three-fifths) was ruled directly.

c. The French had a higher number of possessions in India than the Portuguese.

d. The distance from east to west was about 2,500 miles (4,000 kilometers).

3. Cause and Effect

a. Some of these customs, such as suttee, were abolished by the British.

b. Indian farmers stopped growing food crops, and severe food shortages resulted.

c. An educated middle class was created; this class later lead the country to independence

d. The British allowed Indians to elect members of local governments.

4. Hypothesizing

Answers should vary, owing to the nature of the section. Possible answers might include:

a. India would still be fragmented into small principalities.

b. India would have contended with the British East India Company for independence.

c. Other Indian intellectuals would have accomplished Roy's work at a later date.

ENRICHMENT

1. The immediate cause of the Sepoy Mutiny was the issuing of cartridges for the new Enfield rifles. These cartridges were coated with a mixture of beef and pork grease that made it easier to insert them in the rifles. However, the end of each cartridge had to be bitten off before it could be inserted. Cows were sacred to the Hindus, and pork was forbidden to Muslims. Although the cartridges were immediately recalled once the mistake was noticed, Indian soldiers did not believe the explanation and refused to accept the substitutes. These Indian soldiers were then arrested and thrown into irons. The revolt started when their comrades rescued them, shot their officers, and proceeded to Delhi, which had no British garrison at the time.

2. Answers will vary.

UNIT 10 ❧ CHAPTER 5

VOCABULARY REVIEW

Malay Peninsula   Filipinos   coaling stations

SKILL BUILDER: READING A MAP

1. the Dutch   **2.** the British   **3.** Siam (now called Thailand)   **4.** the Germans

SKILL BUILDER: CRITICAL THINKING AND COMPREHENSION

1. Summarizing

b. The Dutch colonized the East Indies in order to increase trade for the benefit of the mother country.

2. Generalizing

b. Britain was interested in colonies in Southeast Asia

mainly as sources of raw materials and places for trading posts.

Explanations may vary. Britain did not really care much about converting people it considered inferior to Christianity. The British did build roads, schools, dams, and railroads in the countries they occupied, basically because this served their business interests.

3. Compare and Contrast

Wording will vary. Possible answer: Britain and France differed in how directly they ruled their colonies. Britain tried to influence Indian customs through its educational system and method of direct rule. France did not interfere in Indochinese affairs directly. Instead, it allowed educated Indochinese to govern their own country on behalf of France.

4. Fact versus Opinion

a. Fact; could be checked in any encyclopedia entry on the history of the Dutch East Indies

b. Opinion; stated in the quotation from President McKinley

c. Fact; nations wanted islands for coaling stations and naval bases; this could be checked in an encyclopedia

ENRICHMENT

1. Sir James Brooke inherited a considerable fortune when his father died in 1835. In 1838 he sailed his armed yacht, *Royalist*, to the East Indies, planning a settlement in the area of Borneo. He found the Raja Muda Hassim of Borneo engaged in a war with several tribes in the province of Sarawak. Brooke helped Hassim crush the revolt, for which he was named raja of Sarawak, starting a dynasty that ruled until 1941.

2. The Aborigines of Australia numbered about 300,000 when the first Europeans set foot on the continent. With rare exceptions, these natives had no form of cultivation and no domesticated animals, except for dogs and dingoes. Food gathering in the bush was their principal activity, along with religious ceremonies. Religion was considered essential for survival. Aborigines of the north built bark shelters or stilted huts, or lived in caves when the monsoons came. During good weather they preferred to sleep outside. Social structures, such as government, were strictly local in nature, with little direct communication among the tribes scattered across the continent. The Aborigines continue to fight for equality and compensation for their land to this day. Rock groups such as Midnight Oil have written many songs in support of their cause.

The Maori got their name from their use of an extinct bird called the Moa. The original group of Polynesians probably reached New Zealand about A.D. 800. A second wave in A.D. 1350 started the "Classic" period of Maori culture. Social organization depended on the relationship to members of the "great fleet" that arrived in the 14th century. Local subtribes are the primary landholding groups. British colonization in 1840 led to the Maori Wars over the sale of their traditional lands. These lands were either confiscated or purchased after the British victory. The Maori have succeeded in getting the New Zealand government to help them, but to date they have not attained economic parity with those of European descent.

UNIT 10 ❧ CHAPTER 6

VOCABULARY REVIEW

caudillo: "Strong man"; a Latin American dictator, usually a military figure who, although harsh, is greatly loved by the people for bringing order and stability.

Monroe Doctrine: The U.S. policy opposing European colonies in the Western Hemisphere.
economic imperialism: A country controlling the economic systems of other countries.
Platt Amendment: Gave the U.S. the right to intervene in Cuba to protect American lives and property.
Roosevelt Corollary: U.S. policy of intervening in Latin America to make nations there pay their debts without interference from other nations.
scarcity: Not plentiful or abundant.

SKILL BUILDER: MAKING AN OUTLINE

I. Problems facing Latin American nations after independence
  A. Unprepared for self-goverment—caudillos
  B. Economic imperialism
  C. Social instability
II. How foreign investors gained control of Latin American economies
  A. Latin American nations needed money for expansion
  B. Heavy demand for Latin American natural resources
  C. Heavy loans to governments who were unable or unwilling to repay them
III. Failure to repay loans
  A. Causes
    1. Foreign ownership of natural resources and businesses
    2. Social instability
  B. Repercussions
    1. Foreign investors
    2. Foreign troops are sent to collect the debts

SKILL BUILDER: CRITICAL THINKING AND COMPREHENSION

1. Classifying
a. Events leading to the Monroe Doctrine
b. United States Develops an Empire
2. Sequencing
c. Cuba rebelled against Spanish rule.
e. American investors who owned businesses in Cuba grew concerned about their investments.
a. The *Maine* exploded in Havana harbor.
b. The United States declared war against Spain.
d. The Platt Amendment was written.
3. Drawing Conclusions
a. American investors pushed the United States government to protect their investments in Cuba.
b. The United States strongly promoted the building of a canal across Central America.
4. Point of View
a. Roosevelt
b. Monroe
c. sad, reluctant, that aggression must be a last resort; "force," "reluctantly"

ENRICHMENT

1. Answers should include things such as: The American newspapers were already strong in their support of the Cuban revolution. Newspapers across the nation were outraged by the event and used it to prod the American government into war with Spain. The real cause of the sinking of the *Maine* was never determined, but "Remember the *Maine*" became a widely used slogan for the Spanish-American War.
2. Answers will vary.
3. Answers will vary.

UNIT 10 ❧ CHAPTER 7

VOCABULARY REVIEW

Triple Alliance Triple Entente neutral mobilized Allied Powers Central Powers Western Front Eastern Front stalemate armistice

SKILL BUILDER: INTERPRETING A TIME LINE

The Beginning of World War I
1914: June 28, Archduke Francis Ferdinand and wife assassinated.
July 23, Austria-Hungary makes demands Serbia refuses to meet.
July 28, Austria-Hungary declares war on Serbia.
August 4, Britain declares war on Germany.
September 1–7, German troops advance to within 40 miles of Paris.
1. The assassinations of Archduke Francis Ferdinand of Austria and his wife
2. Austria-Hungary declared war on Serbia on July 28, 1914.
3. French and British troops stopped the Germans at the Marne River near Paris in the first week of September 1914.

SKILL BUILDER: CRITICAL THINKING AND COMPREHENSION

1. Classifying
Alliances as a Cause of World War I:
Germany, Austria-Hungary, and Italy formed the Triple Alliance.
Russia and France signed a mutual aid agreement in 1894.
Britain had an agreement to protect Belgium.
Nationalism as a Cause of World War I:
Balkan peoples wanted their own nations.
Germany and Italy became unified nations in the 1800s.
Serbian Slavs wanted a Slavic nation in the Balkans.
2. Spatial Relationships
a. 25 years
b. Prior to the start of World War I, both alliances had been in existence for longer periods than the length of the War.
c. Answers will vary. Some students may feel that four years of fighting is a long war, considering the high death toll. Others may compare it to longer wars in history, such as the Hundred Years War.
3. Predictions
Predictions should be judged according to logical development of historical facts. Have students review their predictions after they have read Chapter 8 in this unit.
4. Making Judgments
Answers will vary owing to the subjective nature of the section. Possible answers might include the following:
a. It is possible, but not probable, that World War I could have been prevented if an international organization had been in existence. The League of Nations, created as a result of World War I, was virtually powerless to prevent World War II.
b. World War I is an excellent example of how one small nation can draw the whole world into war. Many other tensions besides nationalism caused the war and kept it going. Both sides expected quick victories, making one think they had no idea of what they were getting into. It could be argued convincingly that one of the many tensions of that time would eventually have drawn the alliances into war with each other.

ENRICHMENT

1. Answers will vary.
2. It is suggested that this project be assigned to a small group of students who would make a report to the class.
3. Answers will vary. Some of the main battles to be considered are the battles of the Marne, Belleau Wood, Verdun, Chateau-Thierry, Jutland, Tannenberg, Gallipoli, Ypres, the Somme, and Amiens.

UNIT 10 ❧ CHAPTER 8

VOCABULARY REVIEW

1. League of Nations 2. mandates 3. Fourteen Points
4. Treaty of Versailles 5. "war guilt" clause 6. self--determination 7. reparations

SKILL BUILDER: INTERPRETING CARTOONS

1. The figure on the left represents the United States.
2. The figure on the right represents Germany and Austria-Hungary.
3. Figure on right is meek and subjugated. Figure on left is strong, determined, and confident.
4. The cartoonist seems to be for reparations. He shows the United States as a frontier law enforcement officer and the Central Powers as thieves who have stolen countries from their rightful owners.

SKILL BUILDER: CRITICAL THINKING AND COMPREHENSION

1. Summarizing
Answers will vary. Sample answer: The general effect of the treaty was to punish Germany for starting the war. First, Germany lost some of its territory to France, Belgium, Denmark, and Poland. Second, Germany lost control of its colonies in Africa, Asia, and the Pacific to the League of Nations, which took them over as mandates. Third, the German army and navy were greatly reduced. Fourth, and most humiliating of all, Germany was forced to accept blame for the war and was billed $33 billion for damages.
2. Cause and Effect
a. The Treaty of Versailles specified that some national groups were to have their own homelands.
b. The German people felt that their leaders had betrayed them by signing a treaty that humiliated Germany.
c. President Wilson would not compromise with Congress on deleting the League of Nations provision from the Treaty of Versailles.
d. Russia dropped out of the war early in 1918 and signed a separate peace treaty with Germany.
3. Fact versus Opinion
a. Opinion: Germany, Austria-Hungary, Bulgaria, and the Ottoman Empire were not invited to the peace conference.
b. Opinion: Wilson proposed that there be general disarmament, not just disarmament of the losers, and that disputes over colonies be settled peacefully.
c. Fact: Wilson might have been able to win acceptance of the treaty in Congress if he had not insisted on this point.
d. Opinion: Germany began its revenge by getting rid of some of its own leaders who signed the treaty.
4. Hypothesizing
a. If all nations had cut back their armaments, Germany might have felt less penalized by the treaty.
b. If the fate of Germany's colonies had been decided without favor to any side, Germany would have had less cause for resentment.

c. Limiting reparations to direct damages would have lowered the amount of money Germany had to pay, although the bill would still have been an oppressive burden.

ENRICHMENT

1. Answers will vary.
2. Answers will vary.

UNIT 10 ❧ REVIEW

SKILL BUILDER: READING A MAP

1. Germany and Austria-Hungary were known as the Central Powers.
2. German East Africa, Namibia, and Kamerun supported the Central Powers.
3. The Ottoman Empire supported the Central Powers.
4. Mexico remained neutral.
5. The Allied Powers and their supporters had the largest total land area.

SKILL BUILDER: CRITICAL THINKING AND COMPREHENSION

1. Sequencing
b. British settlers seize land in Australia and New Zealand (1788)
i. French troops invade Algiers (1830)
d. American warships arrive in Japan (1854)
h. British government assumes rule of India (1858)
e. Germany, Austria-Hungary, and Italy form the Triple Alliance (1882)
f. Berlin Conference divides Africa among European powers (1884)
a. Sun Yat-sen leads a revolt against Manchu rule in China (1911)
c. Archduke Ferdinand is assassinated (1914)
j. Russian Revolution takes place; United States enters World War I (1917)
g. German officials refuse to sign the "war guilt" clause (1919)
2. Predicting
2-1. c: Russia will mobilize; Germany will declare war on Serbia.
2-2. b: Japan and the United States will eventually fight over control of the Pacific.

ENRICHMENT

(1) This map should show the German route of attack through Belgium and the province of Lorraine.
(2) The German attack of 1914 reached within 40 miles of Paris. Maps should show that by 1916 it had been pushed back only slightly. On the Eastern Front, maps should show that the initial attack of 1914 had gotten close to Minsk, and changed only slightly in two years of warfare.
(3) Maps should show that the Western Front was pushed back into Belgium when the U.S. joined the fighting.

UNIT 11 ❧ CHAPTER 1
VOCABULARY REVIEW

1. disarmament: e 2. domestic goods: b 3. League of Nations: *distractor* 4. fascism: f 5. prosperity: d
6. protective tariffs: c 7. Great Depression: a 8. self-determination: g

SKILL BUILDER: USING A GRAPH

1. b 2. a 3. c 4. b 5. b

SKILL BUILDER: CRITICAL THINKING AND COMPREHENSION

1. Main Idea
In the 1920s, Europe suffered from inflation, unemployment, and the damages of war.
2. Generalizing
b. The European economy suffered from unemployment and the damage of war.
3. Contrast and Compare
Answers will vary. Possible responses include:
Similarities
1. Industrial production and world trade fell sharply in the U.S. and Europe.
2. American and European banks failed.
Differences
1. In the 1920s the U.S. enjoyed great prosperity. However, European nations were suffering from inflation and unemployment.
2. After World War I the Europeans had to rebuild their nations. The U.S. had no war damages within its own borders.

ENRICHMENT

1. Answers will vary.
2. Answers will vary.
3. Answers should include the fact that the League of Nations was established after World War I. The League was established to try and prevent another world war by preserving the postwar peace agreements.

UNIT 11 &. CHAPTER 2

VOCABULARY REVIEW

1. kulaks **2.** soviets **3.** collectives **4.** Bolsheviks **5.** Great Purge **6.** White Russians **7.** Five-Year Plan **8.** New Economic Policy

SKILL BUILDER: DIAGRAMS

1. Supreme Soviet **2.** Local Soviets **3.** General Secretary **4.** All-Union Party Congress **5.** Politburo

SKILL BUILDER: CRITICAL THINKING AND COMPREHENSION

1. Classifying
a. Karl Marx: change did not come as a result of ideas, but rather, was a result of the successes or failures of the economy. All of history could be viewed in terms of class struggle, the "haves" against the "have-nots."
b. Lenin: This is a statement he might have issued during the revolution in 1917, for these three things were in short supply because of Russia's involvement in World War I.
2. Sequencing
d. Lenin becomes leader of the Communist government
a. Russia ends the war with Germany
b. The first Five-Year Plan begins
c. Stalin carries out the Great Purge
3. Drawing Conclusions
Students should conclude that people were very much opposed to the government and did what they could to fight back. However, Stalin was one of the greatest and most brutal tyrants in history. He did not shrink from killing millions of citizens who opposed his plans.
4. Hypothesizing
Answers will vary due to the nature of the section. One possible answer would be that Russia's economy today would be more like those of other socialized countries,

such as France. Important industries, banks, and other sectors of the economy would still be owned by the state, but private ownership of some businesses would be permitted. Farmers might be permitted some degree of private enterprise. Possibly they could lease their land from the state in return for a portion of the crops. The surplus could be sold on the private market. In many respects this is the direction that the Soviet Union is taking under the policies of Gorbachev.

ENRICHMENT

1. Art of this period was heroic in nature. There was no concept of art for art's sake; art was to advance the ideals of the revolution. Figures in these works look stiff and posed and for the most part have no individual identity; figures are meant to be symbols of struggle. This art is not characterized by subtlety. Slogans are simplistic, but they serve to direct the attention of the masses to a common purpose; this kind of art is the equivalent of a slogan.
2. This Enrichment question is large and complex in scope. It is suggested, therefore, that the teacher divide this report into several areas and then assign a group of students to research and report on each.

UNIT 11 &. CHAPTER 3

VOCABULARY REVIEW

1. Fascist party: A political group representing the ideas of fascism.
2. Rome-Berlin Axis: Agreement of cooperation between fascist Italy and fascist Germany.
3. Left: A liberal as distinguished from a conservative (Right) position.
4. Right: A conservative as distinguished from a liberal (Left) position.

SKILL BUILDER: OUTLINING

Missing answers:
B. Farmers and workers were quite poor.
1. The sympathies of the army were with the property-owning class.
2. The struggle ended in violence and bloodshed.
1. The military government could not solve Spain's problems either.
2. A republic was proclaimed.

SKILL BUILDER: CRITICAL THINKING AND COMPREHENSION

1. Summarizing
a. Up until this time Italy had been praised by people such as Winston Churchill for helping to keep Hitler under control. Italy was also one of the Allied countries during World War I; by doing this, Italy changed sides.
b. This illustrates the loss of freedom of speech and freedom of the press under the Fascist dictatorship.
c. The Republican government tried to separate church and state, but this was going against a deeply ingrained tradition in Spain.
d. Economic conditions were so bad in these countries after World War I that many people were glad to give up their freedoms in return for prosperity and security.
2. Predicting
2-1. a. The victors will take revenge upon them as war criminals.
2-1. b. If they are isolated, the offenders might be put on trial. Usually atrocities are either covered up or explained away as the natural consequence of war.

2-2. The people would rise up and replace the government.

3. Spatial Relationships
a. The Communist armies triumphed over the White Russian armies in 1921.
b. Lenin was instituting his New Economic Policy in 1922 to help Russia recover from the effects of the civil war.
c. Much of the same was happening in Russia.

4. Making Judgments
a. disagree: The black Shirts were members of the National Fascist party in Italy.
b. disagree: A Fascist party was first organized in Italy.
c. disagree: The Italians invaded the African country of Ethiopia.
d. disagree: Unlike many other western European countries, Spain was an undeveloped agricultural society.
e. disagree: The state religion of Spain was Roman Catholicism.
f. agree

ENRICHMENT

1. These situations could very definitely be interpreted as supporting Marxist ideas. Marx felt that all of history was a struggle between the classes. The proletariat would finally rise up against the ruling classes and overthrow them, leading to a classless society. This would seem to be exactly what was happening here.
2. Germany and Italy supported the Fascist forces of General Franco; Russia supported the Republican forces. Germany used this war to test out new equipment and strategies. They also used it to give their soldiers combat experience; Allied soldiers during this period had none. Many of the techniques that Germany used to devastating effect in World War II, such as the blitzkrieg, were first developed and tested in the Spanish Civil War. Germany and Italy were also hoping that Spain would join them militarily in World War II. It would have been a far different war if, for instance, Spain had been able to dislodge the British from Gibraltar.

UNIT 11 ❧ CHAPTER 4

VOCABULARY REVIEW

1. chancellor: c **2.** Fuhrer: f **3.** Reich: b **4.** propaganda: a **5.** ghetto: g **6.** aggression: e **7.** appeasement: d

SKILL BUILDER: USING PRIMARY SOURCES

1. b: serve in the army **2.** b: more noble and virtuous **3.** a: armed forces **4.** b: build up Germany militarily

SKILL BUILDER: CRITICAL THINKING AND COMPREHENSION

1. Main Idea
a. Paragraph 9 b. Paragraph 16 c. Paragraph 3 d. Paragraph 7 e. Paragraph 10

2. Generalizing
Answers will vary. Propaganda is the presentation of one-sided information as fact. Truth becomes irrelevant many times to the need to uphold an ideology or other ideas, such as that the government can do no wrong. Goebbels said that if a lie is repeated enough times, it becomes fact.

3. Cause and Effect
3-1. a. effect b. cause
3-2. a. effect b. cause
3-3. a. cause b. effect

4. Fact versus Opinion
Answers will vary but might include some of the following:
a. **Mein Kampf**
Fact: It was written while Hitler was in jail for trying to overthrow the German government.
Opinion: This book is the work of a dangerous man.
b. **Nazi party**
Fact: This was a shortened name for the National Socialist party.
Opinion: All its members were brutal thugs.
c. **Storm Troopers**
Fact: Hitler used them to disrupt political gatherings of other political parties.
Opinion: They were doing what they thought to be their duty to Germany.
d. **Nuremberg Laws**
a. Fact: These laws took away the citizenship rights of Jews.
b. Opinion: These laws were unfair to the Jews.

ENRICHMENT

1. You may want to divide students into groups to report on different periods in Hitler's life. You may also want to have some students research Churchill's life and have a class discussion comparing these two leaders.
2. Answers will vary.

UNIT 11 ❧ CHAPTER 5

VOCABULARY REVIEW

1. Greater East Asia Co-Prosperity Sphere: Another name for the Japanese Empire in the 1930s.
2. condemned: To be pronounced guilty; convicted.
3. Rome-Berlin-Tokyo Axis: Agreement of cooperation between fascist Italy and fascist Germany.

SKILL BUILDER: READING A TIME LINE

1. It seems to have led to a rise in fascism. The Great Depression began in 1929, in the years following Hitler gains power and Japan is taken over by the military.
2. Japanese invasion of Manchuria.
3. 11 years. **4.** 3 years **5.** Japan
6. Germany invading Poland.
7. Germany invades Poland.
8. 6 years. **9.** 6 years

SKILL BUILDER: CRITICAL THINKING AND COMPREHENSION

1. Classifying
Japan
a. Began modernizing in the late 1800s.
b. Invaded and conquered Manchuria.
c. Resigned from the League of Nations after the Manchurian invasion.
d. Needed to import food to feed its people.
United States
e. Placed an embargo on Japan.
China
f. Was torn by fighting between Nationalists and Communists during the 1930s.

2. Sequencing

c. Japanese men age 25 and older gain the right to vote.
a. Manchuria is attacked by the Japanese.
d. Prime Minister Inukai is assassinated by terrorists.
b. Japanese invade Indochina.
e. Japan attacks Pearl harbor.

3. Contrasting and Comparing

Answers may vary but should conform to historical facts.
a. militaristic; divided
b. Europe; the United States

4. Point of View

4-1. d   4-2. a   4-3. b   4-4. c

ENRICHMENT

1. Answers will vary.
2. Answers will vary.

A GEOGRAPHIC VIEW OF HISTORY

1. Hokaido, Honshu, Shikoku, and Kyushu.
2. Honshu
3. Hiroshima-Kure, Osaka-Kobe, and Kyoto.
4. Kawasaki, Tokyo-Yokohama, Nagoya, Kyoto, Osaka-Kobe.
5. Its geographic location, the climate that keeps its ports ice free year-round, and its cities along the coast.
6. Nearly all raw materials have to be imported. Also, only 20 percent of its land is suitable for farming or settlement, making it a very densely populated nation.
7. The climate is more hospitable. Also, this is a heavily industrialized part of Japan; people move there looking for jobs.

UNIT 11 ⋙ CHAPTER 6

VOCABULARY REVIEW

1. **civil disobedience:** Gandhi's philosophy that urged people to disobey unjust laws and refuse legal responsibilities.
2. **Zionism:** The movement to set up a Jewish national or religious community in Palestine.
3. **Mahatma:** Indian word for Great Soul.
4. **satyagraha:** Hindi word for truth force. This is a philosophy introduced by Mahatma Gandhi based on principles of courage and truth. Satyagraha provides a method for direct social action through nonviolent resistance.

Fill in the blanks
Mahatma   satyagraha   civil disobedience   Zionism

SKILL BUILDER: READING A MAP

a. Europe, Asia, and Africa
b. Syria, Israel, Jordan, Lebanon, Iraq, Greece, Kuwait, Albania, Bulgaria, Rumania
c. Caspian, Mediterranean, Black, and Red seas
d. west

SKILL BUILDER: CRITICAL THINKING AND COMPREHENSION

1. Summarizing
1-1. e   1-2. b   1-3. a   1-4. d

2. Drawing Conclusions
a. He concluded that he had to devote his life to the independence movement in India.
b. They concluded that they would be able to establish an independent homeland in Palestine.
c. They concluded that they were capable of ruling themselves.

3. Making Judgments

a. Answers may vary. The Arabs felt betrayed and threatened by the Balfour Declaration. In years to come Jews would use it as part of the legal basis for the creation of Israel in 1948.
b. Answers will vary. Students might mention that the Ottoman Empire included many ethnic groups and nationalities that wanted their independence. Before deciding right or wrong, students might also research what efforts the Ottoman government made to accommodate or repress these desires among its peoples.

4. Spatial Relationships

a. east   b. the Black Sea; an outlet to the Mediterranean Sea   c. Black and Mediterranean seas   d. an inland city

ENRICHMENT

1. Answers will vary.
2. Answers will vary.

THE ARTS AND ARTIFACTS

1. They were taught by their mothers, grandmothers, and other women of the village.
2. They were used as gift wrappings on religious occasions, as decorations on the marriage proposal letter, and also in rooms where a wedding was to take place.
3. Their brushes were made of bamboo tipped with cotton.

UNIT 11 ⋙ CHAPTER 7

VOCABULARY REVIEW

1. **pact:** An agreement or treaty, especially one between nations.
2. **blitzkrieg:** Lightning war, or swift movement of armed forces against the enemy.
3. **campaign:** A series of military operations designating phases of a war.
4. **Lend-Lease program:** Wartime U.S. program that sent the Allies food, medicines, and other material.
5. **strategy:** A plan of action.

SKILL BUILDER: MAKING A TIME LINE

Events should be displayed from left to right in the following order:
b. Germany invades Poland, September 1.
e. Britain and France declare war on Germany, September 3.
d. Soviet Union invades Poland, September 17.
c. Poland surrenders, September 27.
a. Soviet forces invade Finland, November 30.

SKILL BUILDER: CRITICAL THINKING AND COMPREHENSION

1. Cause and Effect
1-1. e   1-2. c   1-3. f   1-4. b   1-5. d

2. Generalizing
2-1. e   2-2. d   2-3. c   2-4. b

3. Predicting
Answers may vary; the following are offered as suggestions:
a. Yes. Germany would have developed the atomic bomb before the United States and used it to end the war.
b. Yes. The Germans were not in agreement with the Japanese concerning the bombing of Pearl Harbor. However, Hitler thought it was the destiny of Germany to rule the world. He might not have attacked the U.S. immediately, because distance across the Atlantic would have

been too great. All this would have changed, though, once the Germans developed the atomic bomb, operational jet aircraft, and longer-range missiles.

c. No. They would have fought to the bitter end as the Germans did. Devotion to duty, honor, and the emperor were deeply ingrained in their national culture. Death was preferable to capture.

d. The Germans would then have been free to turn all their resources to defeating Britain. This would have had disastrous consequences for the U.S. when it entered the war, for we would not have had a staging area from which to conduct attacks on Germany.

4. Hypothesizing

Answers should vary due to the nature of the section. The following are offered as possible points of discussion:

a. Isolationism was very strong in the U.S. at this time. A case could be made for either side of this argument. Roosevelt knew, however, that the U.S. would have to be involved sooner or later. It is probable that he would have used some pretext to enter the war eventually. The Lend-Lease program was the first step in breaking our neutrality, and this process would have continued.

b. Germany would have sued for peace much earlier rather than be totally destroyed.

ENRICHMENT

1. Answers will vary.
2. Answers will vary according to the battle chosen.

SKILL BUILDER/MAPS

1. Longitude: 140° east
latitude: 40° north
2. east or southeast
3. the Marshall, Marianna, Caroline, and Philippine islands
4. They fought for them because of their strategic value. Military bases could be established on them that enabled whoever possessed them to project military power hundreds of miles away.

UNIT 11 ❧ REVIEW

SKILL BUILDER: READING A MAP

1. The Allied Powers and the Axis Powers.
2. Japan, Germany, and Italy. They conquered: Finland, France, Belgium, the Netherlands, Austria, Hungary, Czechoslovakia, Romania, Bulgaria, Denmark, Norway, Greece, Libya, Ethiopia, China, Dutch East Indies, the Philippines, Thailand.
3. China, India. China favored the Allies because they were fighting against the Japanese. India favored the Allies because it was a colony of Britain; it also hoped to gain its independence in return.
4. Spain, Switzerland, Portugal.
5. The Allied nations and Europe

SKILL BUILDER: CRITICAL THINKING AND COMPREHENSION

1. Cause and Effect
1-1. a: Cause   b: Effect
1-2. a: Effect   b: Cause
2. Fact versus Opinion
a. Fact   b. Fact   c. Opinion   d. Opinion
3. Hypothesizing
Answers will vary. Possible answers include:
a. Many new weapons were used for the first time in World War II.
b. The Jewish people had been persecuted for more than 2000 years.

c. High unemployment and inflation create social instability.
d. The United States was the first nation to develop and use the atomic bomb.

ENRICHMENT

1. Answers will vary.
2. Answers will vary.

UNIT 12 ❧ CHAPTER 1

VOCABULARY REVIEW

1. a **2.** c **3.** d **4.** b

SKILL BUILDER: USING PRIMARY SOURCES

1. true 2. false: ignorance of each other's ways and lives 3. false: World War II 4. true 5. false: It is in the minds of people that the defenses of peace must be constructed.

SKILL BUILDER: CRITICAL THINKING AND COMPREHENSION

3. Classifying

	GERMANY	JAPAN
Occupying nations(s)	United States, Soviet Union, Great Britain, and France	United States
Postwar government(s)	Democratic and Communits	Constitutional monarchy
When occupiers left	1949	1952

2. Sequencing
b. Bombing and battles destroyed many European and Japanese cities.
d. The United Nations was formed
a. In order to disarm Germany, Soviet troops seized German factory equipment and machinery and shipped them to the Soviet Union.
c. The European Coal and Steel Community was formed to help Western European countries increase their production of steel.
e. The European Economic Community was formed.
3. Compare and Contrast
Answers may vary but should reflect the following information:
a. All the Allies agreed that the Nazi leaders should be made to answer for their conduct during the war.
b. Britain, France, and the United States wanted to rebuild Germany. These countries felt that it could lead to another war if Germany were left in ruins. The Soviet Union felt that the Germans should be punished and made to pay for the cost of the war. For this reason, they carried factories and machinery from Germany to the Soviet Union.

ENRICHMENT

1. Answers will vary.
2. Answers will vary.
3. Answers will vary.

THE ARTS AND ARTIFACTS

1. This monument salutes the courage of the Marines and honors those who were killed in World War II.
2. Answers will vary. Statues often celebrate the glories of war and conquest. The new monument in Iwo Jima

seeks to emphasize peace and the hope that wars such as World War II never be permitted to occur again.

UNIT 12 ❧ CHAPTER 2

VOCABULARY REVIEW

1. super powers: The strongest militarily and most influential nations on earth.
2. capitalism: An economic system under which people are free to own and develop their own property in order to make a profit.
3. satellite nations: Countries which are economically and politically controlled by a foreign government.
4. ideology: A systematic body of concepts.

SKILL BUILDER: READING A CIRCLE GRAPH

1. Steel Production in the Soviet Union By Region, 1963
2. 4 **3.** Central Region **4.** Southern Region

SKILL BUILDER: CRITICAL THINKING AND COMPREHENSION

1. Main Idea
c. Stalin wanted the Soviet Union to have as many bombs as the United States in case of a conflict between the two nations.
2. Spatial Relationships
a. The Soviet Union.
b. The Soviet Union shared its borders with many more nations than does the United States. This means that there was a greater chance of friction between the Soviet Union and its neighbors.
c. Alaska
d. The Soviet Union. The United States is closer to the equator than the Soviet Union, thus giving it a warmer climate.
3. Drawing Conclusions
The loss of so many young men left industries without a strong male labor force. The Soviets had to use more women and younger people to staff their industries. By the end of World War II, the Soviet economy was near collapse. Rebuilding the economy was the first national priority. This is one of the reasons that the Soviets seized German machinery and moved it to the Soviet Union.
4. Point of View
Answers will vary.

ENRICHMENT

1. Answers will vary.
2. Answers will vary.

A GEOGRAPHIC VIEW OF HISTORY

1. Canada, Denmark (Greenland), Iceland, Norway.
2. Because western Europe shares land borders with the Warsaw Pact nations.
3. They could invade Yugoslavia or Albania. They could get to the Persian Gulf by invading Iran or Iraq.

UNIT 12 ❧ CHAPTER 3

VOCABULARY REVIEW

1. Truman Doctrine: A policy that evolved from a statement made by President Harry Truman. In it, the U.S. promised to aid all nations threatened by communism.

2. Cold War: War of words between Soviet Union and the United States after World War II.
3. foreign policy: A country's plan or pattern of relations with other countries.
4. containment: To be checked, not allowed to spread.
5. Berlin Airlift: In response to the Soviet blockade of all roads and rail lines to Berlin, American and British planes began to fly food, fuel, clothing, and supplies into West Berlin.
6. confrontation: To oppose face-to-face a challenge.
7. dismantle: To take apart or tear down.
8. Marshall Plan: Nonpolitical U.S. plan that gave $17 billion in aid to war-torn countries to strengthen their economies.

SKILL BUILDER: READING A MAP

1. Berlin: A Divided City
2. On the border between East and West Berlin. The wall was built to stop the emigration of people to the West.
3. France, the United States, and Britain. East Berlin was occupied by the Soviet Union.
4. They represent military checkpoints.
5. Berlin was surrounded by East Germany.
6. No **7.** Outside

SKILL BUILDER: CRITICAL THINKING AND COMPREHENSION

1. Summarizing
Answers will vary but should mention the U.S.'s developing the policy of containment in response to Soviet attempts to spread communism.
2. Cause and Effect
2-1. c: President Truman offered to help small countries threatened by communism.
2-2. a: Khrushchev refused to attend a summit meeting with President Eisenhower.
2-3. b: Under Soviet pressure, the East Germans constructed the Berlin Wall.
3. Making Judgments
Answers will vary. In terms of international law, the Soviet Union was entirely justified in shooting down the spy plane. The U.S. certainly would not have tolerated it if the situation had been reversed.
4. Point of View
Answers will vary. Khrushchev felt justified in putting missiles in Cuba since the U.S. had installed missiles in Turkey. Even more importantly, he had concluded that Kennedy was a weak and inexperienced President. Khrushchev felt that Kennedy would back down in a test of nerves. If Kennedy had not drawn the line in Cuba, it would inevitably have invited additional Soviet challenges in other parts of the world.

ENRICHMENT

1. Answers will vary.
2. Answers will vary. Things that might be mentioned would be the anxiety of a communist takeover, lack of food, shelter, and electricity, and the constant flights going to and from Berlin around the clock.

UNIT 12 ❧ CHAPTER 4

VOCABULARY REVIEW

1. welfare state **2.** summit meetings **3.** peaceful co-existence **4.** détente

SKILL BUILDER: CREATING A TIME LINE

Events should be entered in chronological order, progressing from left to right.
1947 communist rebels try to take over Greek government; United States begins Truman Doctrine.
1948 Berlin Airlift begins.
1952 European Coal and Steel Community forms.
1956 Khrushchev becomes Soviet leader.
1956 riots occur in Poland and Hungary.
1957 European Common Market forms.
1960 United States spy plane is shot down in the Soviet Union.
1962 Cuban Missile Crisis.

SKILL BUILDER: CRITICAL THINKING AND COMPREHENSION

1. Generalizing
After World War II, the Soviet Union took control of almost every aspect of life in eastern Europe.

2. Compare and Contrast
The problems of business and industrial development were similar in that both regions were recovering from extensive war damage. Western Europe benefited from the Marshall Plan, while Eastern Europe stagnated under rigid central planning. Many people in the eastern European countries fled to the West, further depleting the industrial workforce. This was one of the main reasons for the erection of the Berlin Wall. Trade between countries was also a problem for both. Western Europe responded by creating the European Common Market, eliminating most trade barriers between its members. The economies of the nations of eastern Europe were dependent on the economy of the Soviet Union. These satellite nations provided markets for Soviet goods, but they never developed a good system of working together. Even if they had, their economies were so depressed, and their technology so backward, that one could not really help the other. Most of these countries went through periods of unrest during which Soviet troops were sent to intervene. This only added to the sense of demoralization of the populace. The countries of western Europe were the opposite side of the coin. With massive aid from the United States and economic systems that combined elements of socialism and capitalism, these nations quickly recovered and became stronger economically than before the war.

3. Fact versus Opinion
a. Opinion b. Fact c. Opinion d. Opinion

4. Hypothesizing
Answers will vary owing to the nature of the section. The economies of these nations could only have benefited from this free trade. However, they would never have surpassed the countries of western Europe economically, owing to the lack of the profit incentives of capitalism. From these come inventiveness, motivation, and a sense of involvement that communism cannot match.

ENRICHMENT
1. Answers will vary.
2. Answers will vary.
3. Answers will vary.

UNIT 12 ❧ CHAPTER 5

VOCABULARY REVIEW
1. **truce:** A halt in fighting during a war.
2. **bureaucracy:** A body of appointed or hired government officials.

3. **classless society:** The ultimate goal of communist principles in which all class differences will disappear and complete equality will exist.
4. **diplomatic relations:** Countries that are able to handle affairs between themselves without arousing hostilities.
5. **Third World:** The developing nations of Latin America, Africa, and Asia.

SKILL BUILDER: USING PRIMARY SOURCES

1. a poisonous snake 2. None; she was completely isolated. 3. Yes; if she was beaten or abused, at least she could return to her shed at night. During this imprisonment, there was nothing to look forward to. 4. She was not allowed to have paper or a pen. 5. She could sit facing the wall or pace about between the walls.

SKILL BUILDER: CRITICAL THINKING AND COMPREHENSION

1. Classifying
Answers will vary but should reflect elements of the following:
1-1. Civil War in China: A Power Struggle Between the Nationalists and the Communists
Chinese Nationalists and Communists fought in the 1920s and 1930s. After World War II, the Chinese Communists defeated the Nationalists.
1-2. Korea Is Divided
After World War II, the Soviet Union sent troops to North Korea and the United States sent troops to South Korea. Two Koreas emerged.

2. Sequencing
a. China became a republic in 1912.
c. Dr. Sun Yat-sen and his followers started the Nationalist party.
b. Chiang Kai-shek became the Nationalist leader.
d. The Chinese civil war was halted when the Japanese invaded China.
e. In 1949 the Nationalists fled to the island of Taiwan.

3. Drawing Conclusions
b. The United Nations took the lead in sending troops to Korea in 1950.

4. Point of View
c. The author does not know how the Chinese peasant feels about his life now but thinks that the peasant's life has improved a little.

ENRICHMENT
1. Answers will vary.
2. Answers will vary.

UNIT 12 ❧ REVIEW

SKILL BUILDER: READING A MAP
1. c: Mongolia and the Soviet Union. 2. b: The Philippines, Taiwan, and Japan. 3. c:India, China, and the Soviet Union. 4. b: Taiwan and Bhutan. 5. a: South Korea and China. 6. b: Taiwan, Japan, and the Philippines.

SKILL BUILDER: CRITICAL THINKING AND COMPREHENSION

1. Point of View
a. Mao Zedong b. Charles de Gaulle c. Harry S. Truman d. John F. Kennedy

2. Fact versus Opinion
a. Opinion b. Fact c. Opinion d. Opinion

ENRICHMENT

1. Answers will vary.
2. Answers will vary.

UNIT 13 ❧ CHAPTER 1

VOCABULARY REVIEW

1. assassinated 2. terrorism 3. autonomy 4. martial law 5. nationalized

SKILL BUILDER: OUTLINING

I. B. The government tried to unite the two groups.
II. B. Prime Minister Bandaranaike promotes the idea that one language and one culture are necessary to unite the nation.
III. Sri Lanka in the 1970s
III. A. The people vote to change the name of their country to the Republic of Sri Lanka.
III. C. Jayewardene refuses to give in to TULF demands.
IV. B. Sri Lanka and India sign an agreement giving the Tamil areas of Sri Lanka greater autonomy and calling for an end to the fighting.

SKILL BUILDER: CRITICAL THINKING AND COMPREHENSION

1. **Summarizing**
Pakistan was created in 1947 when India was partitioned. Pakistan consisted of two states almost 1,000 miles apart. East Pakistanis felt they were not being treated equally with West Pakistanis. Unrest and rioting led to civil war in 1971, and eventually East Pakistan became the independent nation of Bangladesh. Political unrest has continued to trouble Pakistan. Benazir Bhutto, the first woman prime minister of Pakistan, lost power to a rival party in 1990.
2. **Cause and Effect**
a. Cause: India enters the civil war in Pakistan.
Effect: West Pakistan is defeated and East Pakistan becomes the new country of Bangladesh.
b. Cause: Communist China invades India in 1962.
Effect: India develops nuclear weapons.
c. Cause: In 1983 groups of Tamils turn to terrorism to achieve independence in Sri Lanka.
Effect: The army retaliates by killing Tamils suspected of helping the terrorists.
3. **Hypothesizing**
Answers will vary. Students might hypothesize that religious and ethnic differences have caused conflict and prevented these countries from moving forward.
4. **Fact versus Opinion**
a. Fact b. Fact c. Opinion d. Opinion e. Fact f. Opinion

ENRICHMENT

1. Answers will vary.
2. Answers will vary.

UNIT 13 ❧ CHAPTER 2

VOCABULARY REVIEW

1. c: a group that forms to limit competition 2. e: ban
3. d: a person held by one party in a conflict as a pledge that promises will be kept or terms met by another party

4. a: hostility toward Jews 5. b: less extreme
Fill in the blanks
anti-Semitism pogroms moderate cartel embargo hostage

SKILL BUILDER: INTERPRETING A TIME LINE

1. 3 years 2. 31 years 3. 1946 4. Saudi Arabia

SKILL BUILDER: CRITICAL THINKING AND COMPREHENSION

1. **Main Idea**
1-1. a: Israel 1-2. c: Golda Meir
2. **Cause and Effect**
a. Arab nationalism grew stronger after World War I.
b. Israel engaged in the Six-Day War with Arab nations.
c. OPEC nations agreed to limit the amount of oil they would sell.
3. **Generalizing**
3-1. a: nationalism 3-2. a: adopting western customs
4. **Point of View**
Answers will vary.

ENRICHMENT

1. Maps show how the borders of Israel expanded through the Six-Day War. Current maps should show that Israel has returned the Sinai Peninsula to Egypt and expanded its holdings on the Golan Heights.
2. Answers will vary.

A GEOGRAPHIC VIEW OF HISTORY

1. Iran, Iraq, Saudi Arabia, the United Arab Emirates, and Oman. All except Oman are OPEC members.
2. Most of the oil fields are in or around the Persian Gulf.
3. It contains valuable oil fields in addition to providing the main route of transport for tankers delivering oil around the world.
4. Oil is vital to the world economy. Any event that might disrupt or affect oil production is newsworthy.

UNIT 13 ❧ CHAPTER 3

VOCABULARY REVIEW

1. **speculators:** People who take business risks in hope of gain or profit.
2. **coalition:** A temporary alliance of persons, parties, or countries for joint action.
3. **Vietcong:** The national front for liberation of Vietnam; they waged guerrilla warfare and expressed the communist philosophy in their politics. Politically they were known as the Provisional Regional Government of South Vietnam.
4. **guerrilla warfare:** Small bands of fighters, not part of a regular army, who ambush or strike without warning, whose methods of warfare are unconventional.
5. **Vietnamization:** Policy by U.S. president Richard Nixon that the job of fighting would be handed over to the South Vietnamese Army. The United States would continue to provide air support, but American troops would be gradually withdrawn.

SKILL BUILDER: READING A MAP

1. It shows the region illustrated on the larger map in relation to the rest of the world.
2. It shows the different kinds of lines used to indicate the borders of French Indochina in 1954 and the national boundaries today.

3. Laos, North Vietnam, South Vietnam, and Cambodia.
4. China and North Vietnam
5. Initials that stand for the Demilitarized Zone, established by the 1954 truce.

SKILL BUILDER: CRITICAL THINKING AND COMPREHENSION

1. Classifying
a. P b. V c. V d. P
2. Sequencing
b. Manila lay in ruins. c. Marcos declared martial law.
a. Benigno Aquino was assassinated at the airport in Manila. d. Marcos and his followers lost the election, but the Philippines legislature proclaimed him the winner. e. Corazon Aquino became president.
3. Drawing Conclusions
a. The Vietnamese were as opposed to Japanese domination as to French domination.
c. Ho Chi Minh wanted Vietnam to have a coalition government after it gained its independence.
e. The government of Suharto has helped improve Indonesia's economy and its relations with the West.
4. Making Judgments
a. False b. True c. False d. True e. True

ENRICHMENT

1. Answers will vary according to the leader chosen.
2. Answers will vary.

UNIT 13 ❧ CHAPTER 4

VOCABULARY REVIEW

1. segregation 2. apartheid 3. sabotage 4. boycotts
5. sanctions 6. famine

SKILL BUILDERS: USING A CHART

1. Egypt 2. Zambia
3. Life expectancy is highest in the countries that have the highest literacy rates. People who can read and write are able to take better care of themselves. This may be because they can stay better informed regarding advances in general health care. It could also be attributed to their being able to enter better-paying professions because of their education.
4. Ethiopia
The factors of famine and civil war certainly contribute to the lower life expectancy rates.

SKILL BUILDER: CRITICAL THINKING AND COMPREHENSION

1. Summarizing
1-1. b: By releasing Nelson Mandela from jail, the South African government showed it was willing to change some of its policies.
1-2. a: Hopes for African nationalism were high following World War II.
2. Spatial Relationships
Yes. South Africa is at the strategic point where the Atlantic and Indian oceans meet. A high volume of shipping traffic passes through this area every year, including oil tankers from the Persian Gulf. Most of these tankers are too big to use the Suez Canal.
Namibia and Botswana increase South African control over this strategic region of Africa. These countries also serve as buffers to separate South Africa from the rest of the continent. The South African government does not want to see regimes come to power in these countries

that would threaten the position of the white minority in South Africa.
3. Predicting
a. Blacks are forced to live in "independent" homelands that contain some of the poorest land in South Africa.
b. Blacks have little political representation and few rights.
c. Blacks need passes to work in South Africa outside the bantustan.
Answers will vary. History has shown that people turn to violence in frustration if their concerns and rights cannot be addressed through normal political processes. Whether it happens now or ten years from now, change to a more representative government in South Africa is inevitable.
4. Hypothesizing
a. The economy has prospered because of money earned from exports of coffee and cocoa. The country has done this with a mixture of publicly and privately owned businesses.
Answers will vary. The economy of the Ivory Coast should invigorate the economies of the countries around it in a spillover effect. However, much of this would depend on factors such as the stability of the government and how much freedom it granted its people.
b. Answers will vary. A possible answer might be a rediscovery of national pride in their cultures and traditions among the various peoples of Africa.

ENRICHMENT

1. Answers will vary.
2. Answers will vary according to which country is chosen.

THE ARTS AND ARTIFACTS

1. Senghor felt that African culture could infuse European cultures with a certain passion and spirituality.
2. Answers will vary. Possible answers might include "The Star-Spangled Banner," "America The Beautiful," "We Shall Overcome," and "This Land Is Your Land."

UNIT 13 ❧ CHAPTER 5

VOCABULARY REVIEW

1. recession: c 2. censor: a 3. contras: b 4. abertura: d

SKILL BUILDER: INTERPRETING A TIME LINE

1. 7 years 2. Cuba and Grenada 3. Kubitschek
4. Two years 5. Castro; 30 years

SKILL BUILDER: CRITICAL THINKING AND COMPREHENSION

1. Classifying
a. Cuba, Nicaragua
b. Brazil, Argentina, Mexico
c. Democratically elected leaders of Latin America
d. How Cuba turned to Communism
2. Generalizing
a. Invalid b. Valid c. Valid
3. Making Judgments
a. Criticism of the government was outlawed.
b. Castro tried to overthrow the Batista regime.
c. He raised salaries, gave land to the poor, and cut the cost of services.

4. Fact versus Opinion
a. Fact **b.** Opinion **c.** Fact **d.** Fact

ENRICHMENT

1. Answers will vary. **2.** Answers will vary.

UNIT 13 ☙ REVIEW

SKILL BUILDER: READING A MAP

1. Baghdad
2. Egypt, Saudi Arabia, Israel, Yemen
3. Because of its location to the north of Israel.
4. Iran, Iraq, Kuwait, Saudi Arabia, Bahrain, Qatar, Abu Dhabi
5. The Strait of Hormuz; because all shipping leaving the Persian Gulf must travel through this narrow passage.

SKILL BUILDER: CRITICAL THINKING AND COMPREHENSION

1. Classifying
Africa: Ethiopia, Zimbabwe **Asia:** Cambodia, the Philippines **Latin America:** Brazil, Mexico, Cuba, Argentina
2. Making Judgments
a. False b. False c. True d. False e. False
3. Fact versus Opinion
a. F b. F c. O d. F e. F
4. Generalizing
Answers will vary. A possible answer might be:
The new Indian constitution of 1950 loosened the grip of the caste system, bringing profound changes to India.

ENRICHMENT

1. Answers will vary.
2. Answers will vary.

UNIT 14 ☙ CHAPTER 1

VOCABULARY REVIEW

1. free trade **2.** currency **3.** standard of living

SKILL BUILDER: READING A PRIMARY SOURCE

1. It is taking place in Europe.
2. In the United States of America.
3. The author favors the creation of a United States of Europe.

SKILL BUILDER: CRITICAL THINKING AND COMPREHENSION

1. Classifying
France
a. François Mitterrand was elected president in 1981.
e. It produced more farm products than any other Western European country.
Germany
b. It was divided into two parts and occupied by foreign troops from 1945 to 1990.
d. It developed a strong new economy in such a short time that it was called Europe's "economic miracle."
Great Britain
c. Margaret Thatcher served as prime minister from 1979 to 1990.
f. The Conservative party sold many government-owned industries to private groups.

2. Generalizing
Answers will vary.
2-1. A general feeling developed in Western Europe that everyone should work together for the common good.
2-2. The European Community is a major force in the world economy.
2-3. The German people embraced the idea of a unified Germany.
3. Drawing Conclusions
3-1. Germany will continue to grow as an economic power.
3-2. The countries of Western Europe stand as an "economic miracle."
3-3. Margaret Thatcher enjoys wide support in Great Britain.
4. Point of View
a. (F) b. (T) c. (T)

ENRICHMENT

1. Answers will vary. **2.** Answers will vary.

A GEOGRAPHIC VIEW OF HISTORY

1. Belgium, France, West Germany, Italy, the Netherlands, and Luxembourg
2. United Kingdom, Ireland, Spain, Denmark, Portugal, and Greece
3. Member nations remain self-governing; the Parliament has little power except to set policy guidelines. Each nation still maintains its own currency and foreign capital.

UNIT 14 ☙ CHAPTER 2

VOCABULARY REVIEW

1. quotas **2.** Politburo **3.** perestroika **4.** Solidarity
5. bureaucracy **6.** Union Treaty

SKILL BUILDER: READING A MAP

1. Mongolia, East Germany, Poland, Romania, Bulgaria, and Czechoslovakia
2. Russia
3. Russia, Azerbaijan, Turkmenistan, Kazakhstan
4. Armenia, Azerbaijan, Turkmenistan
5. Siberia

SKILL BUILDER: CRITICAL THINKING AND COMPREHENSION

1. Main Idea
1-1. a. The Soviet Union faced serious economic problems in the 1960s and 1970s.
1-2. b. Mikhail Gorbachev provided new leadership in the Soviet Union.
1-3. b: Gorbachev and reform-minded economists disagreed about how to solve the Soviet Union's economic problems.
1-4. b: Ethnic and religious disputes have exploded into violence in the newly independent republics.
2. Sequencing
c. Soviet troops move into Afghanistan. d. Soviets pressure Poland to act against Solidarity trade union. a. Soviet troops pull out of Afghanistan. e. Satellite nations abandon communism. b. Gorbachev and Bush sign START pact.

3. Compare and Contrast

Before Gorbachev, Soviet farming suffered from central planning; the farmers were not involved with most of the basic decisions. Farm workers and leaders did not work together effectively. In addition, there was no incentive for individuals to work harder; all farm laborers were paid the same, and all the crops went to the state. Under Gorbachev, that had all changed. He tried to limit central planning and reward productive workers and leaders with a series of incentives. Moreover, workers were able to keep anything they produced over their quota and sell it on the private market for extra income.

4. Making Judgments

a. Answers will vary. Giving into demands for greater rights presents the problem of distributing power equally among the groups. In addition, the central government would have to be careful to maintain enough power and authority to rule in an effective way. However, completely resisting demands for equality might lead to violent rebellion, causing bloodshed and chaos.

ENRICHMENT

1. Answers will vary.
2. Answers will vary.

UNIT 14 ❧ CHAPTER 3

VOCABULARY REVIEW

1. profit motive 2. Four Modernizations 3. communes 4. joint ventures

SKILL BUILDER: READING A PRIMARY SOURCE

1. 36 percent 2. science 3. The advancement of women's liberation depends on more women entering the work force and attaining leadership roles in fields such as science.

SKILL BUILDER: CRITICAL THINKING AND COMPREHENSION

1. Main Idea

1-1 c: Deng developed a plan for rebuilding China's economy.
1-2 b: The Chinese government introduced many important changes in industry that greatly increased production.

2. Cause and Effect

Answers will vary. Some possible answers are given below.
a. Deng's reforms allowed Chinese farmers to keep any crops they produced over the quota to sell on the open market. The government also encouraged family planning to control the size of China's population.
b. This improved the life of many farmers and increased production.
c. China's industrialization grew and the Chinese learned how capitalists run businesses.

3. Comparing and Contrast

China Under Deng Xiaoping
Farming: Farmers are allowed to grow crops beyond quota and keep money earned from selling these crops.
Industry: Workers are paid bonuses for producing extra products beyond factory quotas; workers who do a poor job can be fired.
Science and Technology: China has made advances in its space program and in developing nuclear weapons.
Political Life: Although the Chinese adopted a more capitalistic economy, the government has remained unchanged.

4. Fact versus Opinion

a. Fact b. Fact c. Opinion d. Fact

ENRICHMENT

1. Answers will vary.
2. Answers will vary.

UNIT 14 ❧ CHAPTER 4

VOCABULARY REVIEW

keiretsu: Several large groups of companies.
trade deficit: An inadequate amount of goods exchanged between nations.
Sentences will vary.

SKILL BUILDER: MAKING A TABLE

JAPAN

Students attend school 240 days each year.

Limits are set on imports.

Must import resources from other countries.

SKILL BUILDER: CRITICAL THINKING AND COMPREHENSION

1. Generalizing

a. Paragraph 5 b. Paragraph 15 c. Paragraph 10 d. Paragraph 17

2. Cause and Effect

1-1. c: More Japanese workers with scientific and technical training will be needed.
1-2. a: The prime minister, who is elected by the Diet, represents the people.
1-3. b: The United States had a large trade deficit with Japan.
1-4. b: Japan decided to switch to more profitable high-technology products.

3. Predicting

Answers will vary; responses should be judged on logical development. Some possible answers might be:
a. Agree. The trade deficit is so large that it will take many years to work out a formula for reducing it. The U.S. government has tried in recent years to get the Japanese to open up their markets to American products, with limited success. Efforts within the U.S. Congress to pass protectionist legislation have been gaining support, but the fear is that these would start an all-out trade war with Japan. It should also be remembered that Japan finances a good part of our government's deficit. For this reason and others, the problem of the trade deficit has no quick solutions.
b. Agree. The Japanese spend huge sums on research and development, far more than the U.S. For this reason, it is logical to conclude that the Japanese will be successful.

4. Hypothesizing

Answers will vary. Some possible answers might be:
a. Japan is in the unique position of having a huge surplus of money to invest in developing these countries.
b. A trade war would develop, with dire consequences for the world economy. Japan could flex its economic muscle in other ways as well, such as not being so willing to finance our federal deficit.

ENRICHMENT

1. Answers will vary. **2.** Answers will vary. **3.** Answers will vary. **4.** Answers will vary.

Unit 14 ❧ Chapter 5

VOCABULARY REVIEW

recession: A downturn in business activity.
Persian Gulf War: The 1991 war in which U.S. and UN forces drove Iraq out of Kuwait.
social programs: Government programs that help needy groups of people to improve their lives.

SKILL BUILDER: READING A LINE GRAPH

1. 1982–1992 **2.** half a million **3.** 1986 **4.** 1985 **5.** three years **6.** 1990

SKILL BUILDER: CRITICAL THINKING AND COMPREHENSION

1. Classifying
American government
c. Jesse Jackson was a candidate for the Democratic party's nomination in 1984 and 1988.
f. Sandra Day O'Connor was chosen by President Reagan as the first woman ever to serve on the Supreme Court.
American foreign policy
a. With UN approval, the United States took a leading role in the Persian Gulf War of 1991.
d. In 1983, American troops were sent to the Caribbean island of Grenada.
American economy
b. By the 1990s, more than 50 percent of all American workers were women.
e. Most farming in America was run by large companies and small farm families were not able to compete.
2. Spatial Relationships
a. F b. C c. C
3. Drawing Conclusions
Answers will vary.
3-1. American companies found their market shares declining.
3-2. More women are taking leading roles in American government.
4. Hypothesizing
Answers will vary. Some possible answers might be:
a. Many people have been forced to flee from their native countries because of economic and political factors. America is looked on as a land of opportunity. The low-paying jobs immigrants often perform in this country are still better than what they had before.
b. The United States role in the Western Hemisphere in the 1980s was very successful in putting an end to extremist governments. The United States supplied weapons to the rebels in Afghanistan and Angola and the contras in Nicaragua, and invaded Grenada. Communism has also been forced to include elements of capitalism in Poland, Hungary, Russia, and China.
c. The U.S. government decided to cut taxes in order to spur economic growth, thus bringing in more taxes in the long run. At the same time, military spending was drastically increased. Tax revenues did not increase as expected, leaving the government with an ever-increasing deficit.
d. Although the number of jobs Americans held in the 1990s had increased, their jobs were less secure. U.S.

industries were competing against foreign industries, many of which were more modern than U.S. factories. Because U.S. goods were often more expensive, American companies found their market shares declining.

ENRICHMENT

1. Answers will vary.
2. Answers will vary.
Possible items under "Important Achievements" would be:
a. a long period of economic prosperity.
b. reducing the threat of nuclear war.
c. progress in civil rights and equal opportunity.
Possible items under "Problems to Be Solved" would be:
a. the federal budget deficit.
b. the trade deficit.
c. cleaning up the environment.
d. continued progress in civil rights and equal opportunity.
e. continued progress in arms reduction.
f. upgrading educational programs so that we remain competitive in the world market.
g. revitalizing space exploration.

UNIT 14 ❧ CHAPTER 6

VOCABULARY REVIEW

1. pesticides **2.** solar energy **3.** acid rain **4.** lasers **5.** nuclear fusion

SKILL BUILDER: READING A MAP

1. Average Life Expectancy **2.** Life expectancy is longer in industrialized nations. **3.** North America, Europe, and Australia **4.** Africa **5.** Asia

SKILL BUILDER: CRITICAL THINKING AND COMPREHENSION

1. Summarizing
Answers will vary. They should include sources such as nuclear power, solar power, wind, wave, and water power, and fossil fuels such as coal and oil.
2. Cause and Effect
2-1. b: Oil has polluted Prince William Sound.
2-2. c: Acid rain is destroying forests.
2-3. a: New forms of energy must be found.
3. Predicting
Answers will vary. Some possible answers might be:
a. Life on the earth as we know it today will become impossible. Pollution affects everything we do, from breathing to eating. Once the problem is identified and a solution started, it takes many years before tangible results can be measured.
b. Yes. The United States has the luxury of forgoing nuclear power plants, because of large deposits of coal. Other countries are not so fortunate. Third World countries, for instance, look upon nuclear power as a good way to cut their bills for oil imports. France and the Soviet Union have put major efforts into expanding their nuclear generating capacity.
4. Making Judgments
Answers will vary. Possible answers might include:
a. People who live in industrialized nations tend to have a higher standard of living and a greater life expectancy. Disadvantages would include greater stress, resulting in a higher possibility of suicide. People who live in industrialized nations are also closer to pollution problems

and the health hazards they pose.
b. The most pressing issue for the 21st century is finding ways to reduce the possibility of nuclear war. This is not limited to the United States and Russia; Third World countries can acquire the technology as well. The world's worst nightmare should be that of a lunatic such as Adolf Hitler getting his finger on a nuclear trigger. The danger is that we make some progress on this issue and then become complacent.

ENRICHMENT

1. Answers will vary.
2. Answers will vary. Students should be encouraged to review the entire text in the course of preparing their responses to this question.

THE ARTS AND ARTIFACTS

1. Pei put the needed improvements underground, with only one new structure above the surface of the court-yard. In this way he did not disturb the beauty of the original palace.
2. Answers will vary.

UNIT 14 ❧ REVIEW

SKILL BUILDER: READING A GRAPH

1. 1950–2000 2. Approximately 2.5 billion; approximately 6 billion 3. 1960 4. It more than doubled; by approximately 750 million 5. 50 years

SKILL BUILDER: CRITICAL THINKING AND COMPREHENSION

1. Generalizing
Answers will vary.
1-1. Communism was in decline and democracy on the rise in the former Soviet Union and Eastern Europe.
1-2. As the remaining superpower, the United States assumed more responsibility in matters that affected world peace.

2. Sequencing
2-1. b: Margaret Thatcher became the first woman prime minister of Great Britain.
2-2. b: Japan's economy became the second largest in the world.
2-3. b: Helmet Schmidt became chancellor of West Germany.

3. Predicting
Answers will vary. Some possible answers might be:
a. The former Soviet Union could evolve from a country where everything was centrally controlled to a country where authority is shared between the central government and local governments.
b. Japan will continue to have a high level of education among its people.
c. African Americans and Hispanic Americans will become more integrated into the mainstream U.S. economy.

4. Making Judgments
Answers will vary. Some possible answers might be:
a. Yes. The spinoffs from developing the technology to explore space have been enormous in the past. Research and development creates jobs and keeps the United States competitive in the world. Unfortunately there will probably always be needy people, but there are many other ways of addressing this problem than throwing money at them.
b. China has begun economic reforms that have raised the nation's standard of living and given people new opportunities. The U.S. policy toward China is based on this and its record of human rights' abuses. Under the circumstances, there is no reason for the U.S. to help build up China's communist government unless it gets something in return, such as changes in the government resulting in more freedom for the Chinese people. The downfall of communism in Eastern Europe and the former Soviet Union may also have an effect on the future of China's government. This may provide a lever to bring change.

ENRICHMENT

1. Answers will vary. 2. Answers will vary.